Contents

JEFFERSON
A Revealing Biography

JEFFERSON
A Revealing Biography

By
Page Smith

Published by American Heritage Publishing Co., Inc., New York
Book Trade Distribution by McGraw-Hill Book Company

Staff for this Book

EDITOR
Alvin M. Josephy, Jr.

ART DIRECTOR
Mervyn Edward Clay

PICTURE EDITOR
Devorah K. Cohen

COPY EDITOR
Helen C. Dunn

PICTURE TEXT
Anne Moffat

The Rembrandt Peale portrait of Jefferson on the TITLE PAGE was painted in 1805, when the Virginian was sixty-two. ABOVE is Jefferson's theodolite, a surveying instrument used to measure angles.

Library of Congress Cataloging in Publication Data

Smith, Page.
  Jefferson : a revealing biography.

  1. Jefferson, Thomas, Pres. U.S., 1743–1826.
E332.S63   973.4'6'0924[B]   76-3593 Nov 17, 1976
ISBN 0–07–058461–3

Additional copyright notices appear on page 313

1. Growing Up

Thomas Jefferson was born April 13, 1743, the third child and first son of Peter Jefferson and Jane Randolph. His father was a classic Virginia frontiersman famous for his strength, a textbook example of the largely self-made man, a surveyor, militia officer, church warden, judge of the Chancery Court, justice of the peace, and, finally, representative to the Virginia House of Burgesses from Albemarle County. His mother was a member of one of the wealthiest and most powerful families in Virginia. Peter Jefferson established himself and his family on a plantation, which he named Shadwell, at the edge of the Blue Ridge Mountains on the Rivanna River.

The Jefferson family were hardly settled on their frontier estate when a close friend of Peter Jefferson's, William Randolph, a cousin of his wife's, died at the age of thirty-three and left his four children in Jefferson's care. Under the provisions of William Randolph's will, Peter Jefferson was to move to the Randolph estate at Tuckahoe, a handsome country house that still stands fifty miles to the east. With this remarkable request Peter Jefferson complied. Abandoning Shadwell, he spent the next seven years at Tuckahoe supervising the management of the plantation and the education of the two sets of children.

In 1752, when young Thomas Jefferson was nine years old, his father and mother returned to Shadwell, leaving the lad behind in the care of a tutor, an Anglican minister named Wil-

liam Douglas. During the stay at Tuckahoe, Jane Randolph had
given birth to three more children, Martha, born in 1746, and
two sons, Peter Field, who died soon after his birth, and a still-
born boy. After the return to Shadwell, another daughter, Lucy,
was born in 1752 and finally twins, Anna Scott and Randolph.

From his ninth year until his father's death, five years later,
Thomas Jefferson remained under Douglas's tutelage. Apparently the boy found his master an indifferent teacher and a poor
scholar. He seems to have developed no special affection for
him. But it appears clear from comments in later life that Jefferson felt a deep admiration for his father. We can only guess at
the effect on him of being abandoned by his father and left in
the charge of a man for whom he had little respect or affection.
Young Tom undoubtedly made frequent trips to Shadwell, but
he would have been a most unusual boy if he had not felt pangs
of homesickness. Even though his later references to his father
are respectful and admiring, there is about them an unmistak-
able reserve. Perhaps even more striking is that he never during
a long lifetime spoke with any warmth of feeling about his
mother. Indeed he hardly spoke or wrote of her at all. In terms
of what we might understand today to be a normal boyhood, it
seems fair to assume that young Jefferson was lacking the paren-
tal care and affection all children need if they are to develop as
confident and happy individuals. An admired but severe and
remote father (remote in physical distance if not in emotional
warmth) and a mother of whom he had no loving or affectionate
word to utter were hardly ideal parents for a lonely and sensitive
boy.

Jefferson's unwelcome apprenticeship to the Reverend William Douglas was terminated by Peter Jefferson's untimely death
at the age of forty-nine. If that death released young Thomas
from his servitude to Douglas, it also left him profoundly bereft.
It would certainly not have been surprising if Jefferson, already
deeply wounded by his father's abandonment of him, had not
felt an even deeper sense of betrayal at his father's dying. Such
a feeling is more than hinted at in his autobiographical reflection
written many years later: "When I recollect that at fourteen

years of age the whole care and direction of myself was thrown on myself entirely, without a relation or friend qualified to advise or guide me, and recollect the various sorts of bad company with which I associated from time to time, I am astonished I did not turn off with some of them and become as worthless to society as they were." It is curious to reflect on the phrase "without a relation or friend qualified to advise or guide me." What, one asks, about his mother? That he could write as though the death of his father had left him an orphan tells us a good deal about his relation with his mother. As for friends to guide him, there were plenty of those among his dead father's friends, his mother's numerous relatives, and above all, the guardians appointed in his father's will, who took a keen interest in the tall, thin, red-haired young man with his pale, fair skin and almost feminine delicacy of features.

Peter Jefferson left a very substantial estate of some seventy-five hundred acres in four or five different parcels, twenty-one horses, a number of hogs and cows, and fifty-three slaves. To his wife he left the house and lands at Shadwell, one sixth of the household goods and slaves, two work horses, and a third of the livestock on the plantation. His six daughters each received a slave as a servant and £200 to be paid to them as a dowry or at twenty-two years of age. Tom and his brother, Randolph, who was as backward as Tom was precocious (indeed, there are numerous suggestions that he was retarded), inherited the remaining slaves. The livestock not left to his widow was to be sold and the money used for the education of the two boys. To Thomas went "my mulatto fellow Sawney, my Books, mathematical instruments, & my Cherry tree Desk and Bookcase."

Although the education of more than one young Virginia gentleman ended in the early teens, it had clearly been Peter Jefferson's intention that his sons be properly educated—in this case, graduated from the College of William and Mary at Williamsburg, the second oldest college, after Harvard, in the English colonies. Since Jefferson had no inclination to return to the care of Douglas, he looked elsewhere for instruction and found it in the person of another Anglican minister, James Maury, a

Jane Randolph, Jefferson's mother, belonged to Virginia's wealthy planter class, for whom fox hunting was a favorite pastime. Peter, Jefferson's father, was a self-taught surveyor. In 1751 he helped draft this map (right)—the first to show the Blue Ridge Mountains in parallel ridges.

Virginian who had himself attended William and Mary, been ordained a priest in England, and returned to take a parish in Fredericksville, not too far distant from the Jefferson plantation at Shadwell. Maury, who like Douglas depended on teaching planters' sons the classical languages and literature to eke out his meager salary as a frontier parson, was a rather morbid man, strained beyond his resources by the necessity of supporting eight children and attending to the needs of his far-flung parish. In compensation he had genuine intellectual gifts and interests. He was an adequate scholar in the classics, and he also aroused his young pupil's interest in science and natural history. It may very well have been from Maury that Jefferson imbibed his own basic philosophy of education—a rather incongruous combination of the classical and the practical. Maury believed that Greek and Latin were "absolutely necessary" but that they must be balanced by the study of geography, history, and a variety of more practical studies, including mathematics and agriculture.

Important for an introspective and moody young man was the homelike atmosphere of the Reverend Mr. Maury's large family, which threatened to burst the seams of the minister's modest quarters. In addition, Jefferson enjoyed the friendship of his tutor's son, James, Jr., several years younger but bright and companionable. The overworked senior Maury had three other pupils, James Madison, cousin of the future President, destined to become an Anglican bishop and president of the College of William and Mary; Jack Walker, the son of one of Jefferson's guardians, Dr. Thomas Walker; and Dabney Carr, a brilliant and captivating youth who became Jefferson's dearest friend.

Jefferson spent weekends at Shadwell, often taking his schoolmates home with him. He may well have been thankful to spend no more time there. The atmosphere at home must have been oppressive. His mother was not a cheerful and encouraging presence. In addition to the backward Randolph, one of Jefferson's sisters, Elizabeth, was perilously close to being mentally retarded. On the other hand there was the endless coming and going of visitors and relatives that characterized Virginia plantation life, so that Shadwell seemed to young Jefferson, who was already displaying those studious and reclusive tendencies that became so evident in his mature years, to present an endless round of distractions and meaningless activity.

At Shadwell Jefferson and his siblings learned to dance under the guidance of Alexander Ingles, and it may have been Ingles who taught him the rudiments of the violin, thus planting the seed of what was to become one of Jefferson's predominant passions, a love of music. He also became an expert rider with a lifelong devotion to fine horseflesh and to the particular pleasures of riding. It was in long, solitary, unattended rides, a practice so unusual that it was frequently commented on, that Jefferson could most easily indulge his desire to be alone.

There is no indication that Jefferson felt particularly close to his two older sisters, Jane and Mary, the former of whom died in 1765 at the age of twenty-five. Mary married John Bolling, who turned out to be something of an alcoholic. Although she occasionally visited Monticello over the years, usually with her numerous children, Jefferson's references to her are infrequent and without special warmth. He does note that her unforgiving attitude toward her husband's weakness was not the best inducement for him to reform. Martha was the sister to whom he obviously felt closest, and this tie was greatly strengthened when she married Dabney Carr in 1765.

After two years with James Maury, Jefferson apparently felt that he had exhausted his teacher's intellectual resources. He had improved the rather scanty Greek and Latin he had acquired from Douglas and profited from the intellectual stimulus of his companions. More important, he had already discovered in himself an unappeasable appetite for learning. So the immediate question was, what next? Was he to return to Shadwell and take up his duties as master of the plantation, to live with his mother and his six sisters and dull brother in a scene of both practical and psychological disorder or escape to a world more congenial to his already rather sophisticated tastes? During the Christmas vacation in 1759 Jefferson visited the home of a friend, Nathan Dandridge, in Hanover County, and there met for the first time among the holiday visitors who crowded the Dandridge house Patrick Henry, twenty-three years old. Henry, very much a frontier figure, stood out among the young gentlemen who made the Dandridge house their headquarters.

In Jefferson's view he had "something of the coarseness of the society he had frequented." But he had an undeniable vitality and a rough humor that made him the leader in the little circle. Again in Jefferson's words, "His passion was fiddling, dancing and pleasantry. He excelled in the last, and it attached every one to him." Apparently sometime during the holiday, Jefferson made up his mind that he wished to go to the College of William and Mary to continue his formal education. He therefore wrote to one of his guardians, John Harvie, enumerating his reasons for deciding that college was a logical next step. "In the first place as long as I stay at the Mountains the Loss of one fourth of my Time is inevitable, by Company's coming here & detaining me from School. And likewise my Absence will in a great Measure put a Stop to so much Company, & by that Means lessen the Expences of the Estate in House-Keeping. And on the other Hand by going to the College I shall get a more universal Acquaintance, which may hereafter be serviceable to me; & I suppose I can pursue my Studies in the Greek & Latin as well there as here, & likewise learn something of the Mathematics. I shall be glad of your opinion."

The letter is an interesting one. Jefferson does not put the argument for college on intellectual or academic grounds. Like millions of young Americans who were to go to college in the generations to come, he placed his primary emphasis on the advantageous social contacts that might be anticipated and indicated that, as for academic concerns, he could doubtless *do as well* at Williamsburg as at home. One might conjecture that he knew his guardian to be an eminently practical man who could be appealed to more readily on utilitarian than on intellectual grounds, or, equally possible, that meeting students of the college from time to time at the Reverend Mr. Maury's and at the Dandridges', he knew himself to be already their intellectual superior and thus expected little stimulation from an institution that was somewhat notorious for the casual character of its academic demands. It was part of the style of life of a Virginia planter to appear not to take the world too seriously. A smattering of polite learning was a necessary attribute of a gentleman, but to pursue learning with avidity was, if not out-and-out bad taste, a bit excessive. This atmosphere pervaded the college as it has most American institutions of higher education down to the present day. Gambling, drinking, card playing, and horse racing may be said to have made up the informal curriculum of William and Mary. In any event it was plain that Jefferson expected little more from the college than that it serve as a refuge from Shadwell.

If such was his attitude, he was pleasantly surprised. There are, of course, few institutions so benighted that they do not contain a few lively minds. Jefferson found such a mind in Dr. William Small, a Scotsman who was a temporary teacher at the college. Characteristically severe in his assessment of the intellectual level of his college mates, Jefferson declared that the low standards of admission "filled the college with children. This rendering it disagreeable and degrading to young gentlemen already prepared for entering on the sciences." But he became an immediate disciple and friend of Dr. Small, who among ill-prepared "children" undoubtedly welcomed a budding intellectual. In his autobiographical sketch made in later life, Jefferson wrote in classic terms of his relationship with Small: "It was my great good fortune and what probably fixed the destinies of my life that Dr. Wm. Small of Scotland was then professor of Mathematics, a man profound in most of the useful branches of science, with a happy talent of communication, correct and gentlemanly manners, & an enlarged & liberal mind. He, most happily for me, became soon attached to me & made me his daily companion when not engaged in the school; and from his conversation I got my first views of the expansion of science & of the system of things in which we are placed."

It is plain that Jefferson's education, under the direction of Dr. Small, took place far more outside the classroom than in. Small's term at the college was to be only two years longer than

Jefferson's. He fell out with the governing body of the college over the question of tenure and returned to England, where with Erasmus Darwin, Joseph Priestley, and other enlightened spirits he formed the Lunar Society of Birmingham, a group of skeptics who chose as one of their particular targets the religious establishment of their day. Small's involvement with this group suggests that it was probably he who first sowed the seeds of deism in young Jefferson's mind. Theism—belief in the truth of the Christian religion as contained in scripture, revelation, and the accumulated wisdom of the Church, whatever branch of it one subscribed to—was the dominant religious perception throughout the American colonies. While there were undoubtedly many nonbelievers scattered about at every level of colonial society, most of them found discretion the better part of valor and kept their doubts to themselves. Then as now, for a politician to express skepticism about the validity of the Christian religion was to doom himself to oblivion. Deism accepted the notion of God as a kind of general principle, the prime mover—or, in an image popular with deists, the Great Watchmaker—who created the universe, established the laws on which it was to run, and then left it to its own devices, so to speak, rather than, as the theists believed, actively and continually intervening. The deists thus rejected what was from the orthodox Christian point of view the most important single intervention of God into human history in the person of his Son, Jesus Christ. More specifically, they rejected the notion of the divinity of Christ and viewed him as simply a great and wise teacher. Historic Christianity seemed to the deists simply a mishmash of superstition and priestly obfuscation. Often they felt obliged to devote a substantial part of their energies to brushing away these cobwebs that impeded man's use of his reason. France was a hotbed of deism, and such philosophers as Voltaire, Diderot, and the so-called Encyclopedists (from their role as contributors to Diderot's great *Encyclopedia,* the first in history designed to organize human knowledge on rational principles) were the standard-bearers in the campaign of deism against Christian orthodoxy. Jefferson himself was a deist for years before revealing it generally through the publication of his *Notes on Virginia.* Benjamin Franklin and Thomas Paine were likewise tarred with the deist brush. Paine in his *Age of Reason* spelled out his own philosophy to his cost. Franklin was far more discreet and escaped becoming an object of public opprobrium because of his beliefs. These matters are important, both in regard to Jefferson's own intellectual development and to his political career. In the bitter presidential campaign of 1800 he was denounced as an infidel and heretic by his opponents, and throughout his life he was very tender on the subject of his deistic beliefs.

In addition to his friendship with Small, Jefferson delighted in the companionship of Dabney Carr and Jack Walker, who followed him to William and Mary, and in that of John Tyler of Gloucester County and John Page, heir of the ancestral Page mansion, Rosewell, across the York River. Rosewell was the greatest house in colonial Virginia. Several generations in the building, it bankrupted the family but served as a center of hospitality in the Tidewater because of its proximity to Williamsburg. Although John Page had those intellectual interests common to his class and became, in time, governor of Virginia, he had none of Jefferson's brilliance. As he himself put it, he never "made any great proficiency in any study, for I was too sociable and fond of the conversation of my friends, to study as Mr. Jefferson did, who could tear himself away from his dearest friends to fly to his studies."

Whatever the college's academic shortcomings—and they were doubtless numerous—Jefferson's two years there may well have been among the happiest of his life. Besides the friendship and intellectual stimulus of Small and his obvious pleasure in the company of such companions as Carr, Page, Tyler, and others, there were the traditional entertainments of college students, prominent among them "the regular annual riots and battles between the students of William and Mary with the town boys," in which Jefferson was an enthusiastic participant. In the words of a friend, "When young he adopted a system, perhaps an entire plan of life from which neither the exigencies of business nor the allurements of pleasure could drive or seduce him.

In March, 1760, at the age of seventeen, Jefferson left the frontier for Williamsburg and William and Mary College (right, records of his fees for room and board, and the main college building, designed by Christopher Wren). During Jefferson's two-year stay William Small (left), the only nonclerical member of the six-man faculty, encouraged his interest in mathematics and science and introduced him to his stimulating circle of friends.

Lewis & John Burwell .... Dr̄s

1760. July 28. To the Table for board &c. of each 126 Days   8 . 19 . 6

No certainty what is due, so that the Table
has its sight, no torch it, the whole to be
carried to the credit of Day, 1765.

1764. March 25th. To Stock (Led̄r. B. fol. 21) .... 8 . 19 . 6

1765. March 25. To D̄o. (D̄o. fol. 54) .... £ . 8 . 19 . 6

Thos. Jefferson .... Dr̄

1761. March 25. To the Table for board &c. one Year ..... 13 . —

1762. March 25. To D̄o. for D̄o. one Year .. 13 . —

April 25th. To D̄o. for D̄o. one Month .. 1 . 1 . 8

£ 27 . 1 . 8

Messr̄s. Jesse & Thos. Ewell Dr̄s

1761. March 25th. To the Table for board &c. 288 Days each . — 20 . 10 . 5¾

1762. March 25. D̄o. for D̄o. of Jesse 1 Year .... 13 . — .

March 15. D̄o. for D̄o. of D̄o. to this Day . — 17 . 1

30 Auḡt. 1768. Wrote to Bertrand &
Ewell :—   34 . 07 . 4½

drawn off

Much of his success is to be ascribed to methodical industry."

That passage raises a compelling question about the Jefferson psyche. First of all, Jefferson grew up in a culture, that of plantation Virginia, where, as we have suggested, seriousness of purpose was suspect. The leaders of the commonwealth were certainly intelligent and able men who often worked hard to build up and sustain the great plantations on which their wealth and influence rested; but they had, as a common characteristic, a lavishness of temperament, an impulse to self-indulgence—indeed often to reckless extravagance—similar to that of young aristocrats in most cultures. Curiosity, often of a very penetrating kind, and even learning lightly borne were by no means uncommon qualities of their class, but disciplined labor, frugality, and prudence were much more commonly found among New Englanders than Virginians. In his open-handed hospitality, his love of luxury, his self-indulgence, and his own often heedless extravagance, Jefferson was very much an upper-class Virginian. What puzzled his contemporaries was his obsessions. They were clearly his own. An observer, himself without a ruling passion, has no idea of what relentless taskmistresses the Muses are. They drive their votaries to serve them with a fierce energy no earthly taskmaster could command. In a certain sense Jefferson was the most self-indulgent of men, following every whim or mood or passion. But passions indulged are the groundwork of all greatness. Whims and moods are just that. One might put the question thus: "When is self-indulgence the avenue to greatness?" Answer: "When it rises to the level of passion—or compulsion. They are blood sisters for a certainty."

So we know that Jefferson, feminine in feeling, addicted to learning, passionate in his response especially to those Muses whose jurisdictions were music, painting, sculpture, and that most practical realm of art, architecture, had the soul of an artist: impulsive, intuitive, secretive, moody, irrational, devious in the way that artists are often devious, hiding some particular vulnerability, some truth too tender to expose to the world. How ironic that this least rational, most tenderly intuitive of men should have paraded all his life under the banner of rationalism, of the redemptive power, not of religion or of love, but of reason and reason's great handmaiden, science. Thus we have Jefferson the artist, living in a society that had no use for or understanding of the planter as artist, forced to masquerade first as a more or less typical Virginia planter—because that was the only type his fellows could recognize or respond to—and then as a politician, a role as uncongenial to him in essence as that of a canting New England parson. And all the while he lived in his own private purgatory, a purgatory invested with a suffocating awareness of death and insanity and evil that he dared not confront. The artist in him created the image of him with patient, exquisite strokes so skillfully laid on that few who came after could penetrate to the essential Jefferson and see him in that dark chamber of horrors he so often inhabited: the enigmatic mother, the retarded siblings, the dead sisters, and most of all the denying father, who betrayed him first by sending him away and then by dying too soon, thereby betraying him into the hands of his mother.

Jefferson's creation of the Jeffersonian image was by no means unique to him. One might indeed argue that every great figure contains an artist who instinctively or perhaps often self-consciously creates the public image of himself with which all future biographers have then to contend. One certainly senses that this was true of Washington, a masterful artist of the image, always aware of being at center stage in history. But Jefferson, conscious of his own emotional instability and the degree to which he was so often at the mercy of his nerves, was more artful. He covered his trail in innumerable ingenious ways and became in the last decades of his life less a person than a presence, inhabiting his own stage, occupying his own carapace, and living, finally, in some harmony with his demons.

It might be said that the biographer becomes in some strange way the friendly adversary of his subject if he does not more often become his accomplice. The simplest human life is not easy to penetrate and contains at its heart unfathomable mysteries. How much more so that of the great man. If he is the artist of his own image, the artful creator of his own life, he has left a thousand clues about, designed to confuse and mislead his biographer-lover-adversary. And so his biographer is required to be as coolly skeptical, as cautious and deliberate, as Sherlock Holmes. Indeed, the detective-story analogy is not inappropriate. Just when the trail seems plainest the biographer should be most on his guard.

2. Law and Love

Apparently on the advice of Dr. Small Jefferson decided to study law, less from a clear desire to be a lawyer than to remain in Williamsburg and continue to read, study, and talk. Small was a close friend of one of the leading lawyers of the colony, George Wythe. Wythe's gracious Georgian residence stood on the green, hardly a stone's throw from the governor's mansion, and Wythe was the center of a circle of cultivated and learned gentlemen of the town whose nominal head, at least, was Francis Fauquier, lieutenant governor of the province. Wythe, who looked rather like an intelligent gnome with a large head and diminutive body, was a power in the colony. He was noted for the austerity of his courtroom manner and was never guilty, his admiring pupil said, of a "useless or declamatory thought or word." To young Jefferson, Wythe was the ideal type of the ancient Roman lawmaker, "the Cato of his country," "my second father," "my antient master, my earliest & best friend."

In later life Jefferson described to a friend the course of study he pursued under Wythe. "When I was a student of the law . . . after getting through Coke [on] Littleton, whose matter cannot be abridged, I was in the habit of abridging and common-placing what I read meriting it, and of sometimes mixing my own reflections on the subject. . . . They were written at a time of life when I was bold in the pursuit of knowledge, never fearing to follow truth and reason to whatever results they led, and bearding every authority which stood in their way."

It was characteristic of Jefferson that he should cast himself in the role of ruthless pursuer of the truth and that he should believe that reason, relentlessly applied, would unerringly discover truth. These were the most basic convictions of the Enlightenment. The light of reason threw its beneficent rays over all subjects of human investigation; the most arcane secrets must in time yield to the cold scrutiny of scientific inquiry. Yet Jefferson's life seemed full of the anguish of the unknowable and uncontrollable. Perhaps the persistence of tragedy in his life made Jefferson so dogged in his devotion to what he believed to be reason. The Christian religion has its own forms of consolation to deal with the tragic and the incomprehensible; but Jefferson, like the greater portion of his countrymen in the generations to come, turned from the solace of traditional Christianity to the consolations of the new science, hardly conscious of the nature and certainly not of the consequences of the new faith.

For the American colonists Sir Edward Coke was probably the most important of all the great English legal theorists, and although Jefferson at times wished "the Devil had old Coke" and declared him an "old dull scoundrel," he came to draw heavily on him for guidance in revising the laws of Virginia years later. Jefferson's reference to his commonplace book, moreover, is worthy of note. At a time when books were expensive and libraries few and far between, many students kept a book or a succession of books in which they copied important passages—striking things they wished to have at hand, quotations from learned authorities, and increasingly in the period of pre-Revolutionary agitation, passages concerning the rights and liberties of a free people.

Jefferson's commonplace books, now in the Library of Congress, are a kind of map of the early development of his mind. A special favorite of Jefferson's was the eccentric Scotsman Henry Home, Lord Kames, who wrote voluminously on a wide variety of subjects from morality and natural religion to law and property. Kames was a severe critic of a social system that, by making land the monopoly of a few, kept the majority in poverty; Jefferson copied from Kames this sentence: "The perfection of human society, consists in that just degree of union among individuals, which to each reserves freedom and independency, as far as is consistent with peace and good order."

After his graduation from William and Mary, Jefferson joined a secret society limited to six members and known as the Flat Hat Club. The club was a typical association of high-spirited and doubtless, on occasion, mischievous young men, the counterpart and forerunner of innumerable such societies in virtually every institution of higher learning in the land. Fauquier shared Jefferson's passion for music, introduced string concerts in the Governor's Palace, and invited Jefferson to play his violin with the other gentleman musicians. While Small remained in Williamsburg, he, Wythe, Fauquier, and Jefferson often dined together. Such a talented quartet could perhaps have been rivaled only in a center of cultivation and learning as large and developed as Philadelphia, the third greatest city of the British Empire. Jefferson was an attentive listener and wrote later, "At these dinners I have heard more good sense, more rational and philosophical conversations, than in all my life besides. They were truly Attic societies," a reference to the learned gatherings of ancient Athens. To participate as an equal in such company was an extraordinary opportunity for a young man. Undoubtedly Jefferson learned as much from the flow of wit and reason around those candlelit dinner tables as from the learned tomes he so dutifully consulted, and he cherished the memory of those occasions for the rest of his life.

That Jefferson did not limit his activities to the intellectual and cultural pleasures afforded him by his friendship with his three older companions is suggested by the fact that his expenses constantly outran his allowance from his father's estate. He thus early established a pattern of indebtedness that was to plague him the rest of his life and that, again, was characteristic of his class.

Jefferson's interest in the opposite sex also manifested itself during the Williamsburg years. There is substantial evidence

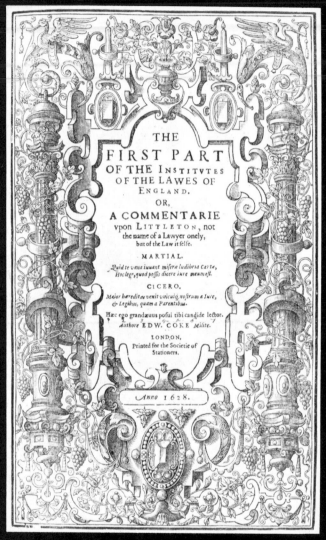

THE
FIRST PART
OF THE INSTITVTES
OF THE LAWES OF
ENGLAND.

OR,

A COMMENTARIE
vpon LITTLETON, not
the name of a Lawyer onely,
but of the Law it selfe.

MARTIAL.

Quid te vana iuuant miseræ ludibria Cartæ,
Hoc lege, quod possis dicere iure meum est.

CICERO.

Maior hæreditas venit unicuiq, nostrum a Iure,
& Legibus, quam a Parentibus.

Hæc ego grandæuus posui tibi candide lector.

Authore EDW. COKE *Milite.*

LONDON,
Printed for the Societie of
Stationers.

Anno 1628.

After graduation Jefferson took up the study of law under George Wythe (right), an outstanding classical scholar as well as a brilliant lawyer whose later students included John Marshall and Henry Clay. Although Jefferson complained often and bitterly during his five years of legal training about the dryness of Sir Edward Coke's texts (above, the title page from a 1628 edition), he later commended Coke's works revering common law as the basis of all legal study.

that despite having grown up in a largely feminine household he was shy and ill at ease with girls. It is clear that Jefferson, in common with youths of primarily intellectual and aesthetic bent, was slow to mature physically and psychologically. In any event, he fell in love with Rebecca Burwell, one of the young charmers of Williamsburg society and a member of one of the first families of Virginia. When he departed for Shadwell in the winter of 1762–63 for a concentrated session with his law books, Jefferson carried with him a silhouette of Rebecca in a locket. On his journey home he wrote John Page a letter describing the state of his heart. In the mode of the day he gave his loved one a pseudonym—Belinda—fearful perhaps that the letter might fall into alien hands, and sprinkled his epistle with Greek and Latin phrases. He had suffered, he wrote, mishaps more severe than "have befallen a descendant of Adam . . . since the creation of the world." Rats had gnawed up his pocketbook while he slept and stolen his "jemmy worked silk garters, and half a dozen new minuets I had just got, to serve [them], I suppose, as provision for the winter." Moreover the roof of his room had leaked, his watch had been soaked, and Belinda's picture was ruined. "It's my opinion," he added, "that the Devil came and bored a hole over it on purpose."

Back at Shadwell, where the atmosphere was so different from the life and gaiety of the capital, Jefferson inquired from Page anxiously about Rebecca and asked for advice on the best strategy. As a cure for love, he proposed to Page that they take a world tour, lasting two or three years, to England, Holland, Spain, France, Italy, and Egypt. But lovelorn as he professed to be, Jefferson neither returned to Williamsburg nor wrote to the object of his affections. He was burdened by "the loss of the whites of my eyes; in the room of which I have got the reds," he wrote John Page. Hearing that a friend was to be married, he complained to Page, "Why can't you and I be married too . . . when and to whom we would choose? Do you think it would cause any such mighty disorders among the planets? Or do you imagine it would be attended with such very bad consequences in this bit of a world, this clod of dirt, which I insist, is the vilest of the whole system? . . . I verily believe I shall die soon and yet I see no other reason for it but that I am tired of living."

But Jefferson remained safe at Shadwell, and even the news that a serious rival had appeared on the scene at Williamsburg failed to budge him. To Page's suggestion that he return to Williamsburg to defend his interests, he replied, "No, no, Page; whatever assurances I may give her in private of my esteem for her, or whatever assurances I may ask in return from her, depend on it—they must be kept in private." Anticipating rejection, he reconciled himself with the thought that "perfect happiness . . . was never intended by the deity to be the lot of any of his creatures in this world. . . ." For a man with such a stoic philosophy, "Few things will disturb him at all; nothing will disturb him much." Still seriously contemplating an extended European trip, Jefferson also toyed with the idea of returning to Williamsburg and building a small house there, "which shall contain a room for myself and another for you [Page], and no more, unless Belinda should think proper to favour us with her company, in which case, I will enlarge the plan as much as she pleases." An odd notion, a household made up of the two young friends and a new bride.

At last, after nine months, the lovesick youth returned to Williamsburg without having written to his beloved in the interval, danced with her in the Apollo Room of the Raleigh Tavern, and tried to get up courage to avow the seriousness of his intentions, which she would certainly have had to take on trust since she had seen no practical evidence of them. "I was prepared to say a great deal," he wrote Page. "I had dressed up in my own mind, such thoughts as occurred to me, in as moving language as I knew how, and expected to have performed in a tolerably creditable manner. But good God! When I had an opportunity of venting them, a few broken sentences, uttered in great disorder, and interrupted with pauses of uncommon length, were the too visible marks of my strange confusion!" The consequence was that he could never have imagined himself "so wretched as I now am!"

A few weeks later he tried again. His ardor was hardly

unconfined. Again he reported to Page, "I . . . opened my mind more freely, and more fully." He did not exactly propose but rather suggested that sometime in the future—presumably after he returned from a trip to England—he might propose. Rather than making her an offer she could not refuse, he had made her an offer that she could not accept. Having talked in what was obviously a rambling and rather incoherent way and having left poor Rebecca Burwell to guess at his intentions, he professed to await some word from her, which not surprisingly never came. Finally, some six months after his curiously veiled avowal, he heard through friends that she was engaged to another man. He responded to the news with a violent headache that lasted for days.

Allowing for a certain amount of youthful play-acting and self-deception in regard to love and for the conventions of courtship common to Jefferson's age and class, his romance with Rebecca Burwell, if it could be called that, was a strange one clearly directed more at forestalling marriage than consummating it. The plans for a *ménage à trois* with Rebecca and John Page in Williamsburg and for the extended European tour, the long, silent absence from his beloved, the nonproposal of marriage after which he waited for an answer to a question he had not really asked, all suggest more than the normal waffling and uncertainty of a young man in love for the first time.

These considerations, plus the intense headache that followed the news of her betrothal to another man, suggest that Jefferson was going through a severe psychological crisis. Bewildered Belinda, one suspects, was no more than an innocent bystander. Perhaps Jefferson was passing through that classic period of searching and uncertainty common to most young males which Erik Erikson has termed an "identity crisis." His confusion about the meaning and direction of his own life may have been mirrored in his confusion about his real feelings toward Rebecca Burwell. There is, for instance, the illusory trip. It made no sense for Jefferson to talk so casually, in the middle of his law training, about an extended and expensive trip (he was constantly pressed for funds). Even the letters to John Page expressing his doubts and uncertainties he forbore to mail for months on end, further emphasizing the turmoil of his own emotions. As Erikson has suggested, so far from being unusual, the search for one's own "identity" is a classic human experience at the threshold of manhood. Somewhat out of the ordinary is the manner in which Jefferson attached the problem to a particular girl. How odd the whole affair must have seemed to Miss Burwell! There is a hint of lingering resentment in the pleasure she seems to have taken years later at the charges of cowardice made against Jefferson during his term as wartime governor of Virginia. The charges were manifestly unfair, but she knew him already as a coward in affairs of the heart.

That Jefferson, after the Burwell affair, took on the mantle of a dedicated misogynist, sprinkling his commonplace books with quotations hostile to women, is not without significance. He still clung to the illusion that Belinda had wronged him and that the anguished emotions he felt were those of disprized love. In any event, these years about which we know so little were plainly difficult years for a man of Jefferson's temperament. He drifted back and forth between Shadwell and Williamsburg, an uneasy spirit living in a state of suspended animation while most of his friends married, established estates, begat children, and picked up those agreeable strands of life that constituted the style of the young Virginia gentleman.

Perhaps the moral of the Burwell romance was that Jefferson himself sensed that his remarkable talents and energies were not to be damped down by a conventional marriage, which would draw him at once into the pleasant but stultifying existence of his friends. Perhaps his ambivalence about Rebecca Burwell was, in practical fact, no more and no less than his ambivalence about his social class, his style of life, and his future prospects. It is no easy matter to imagine the extent that the members of a traditional aristocracy are bound by the situation into which they have been born. From the outside, and especially from the perspective of an age in which tradition has lost its hold over men's minds to a degree that could not have been conceived of in earlier periods, the ubiquitousness of class is

Francis Fauquier (above), royal governor from 1758 to 1768, was a member of the Royal Society and patron of the arts who cultivated Virginia's wealthy planters and intellectuals. Through William Small and George Wythe Jefferson came to dine regularly at the governor's palace (left) and played his violin or cello at concerts sponsored there by Fauquier.

hard to grasp. It almost completely circumscribes the lives of its members. That is how it defines itself: a system so rigid that its members are literally forced to conform or, as we say today, to "drop out." Thus the process of freeing oneself from its trammels (which are closely associated with its pleasures and prerogatives) is a painful and laborious one. We must believe that Jefferson—in those years when he seemingly loitered along in his legal training, steady only in the avidity of his reading and the passion of his sensuous involvement in the natural world— was struggling to extricate himself from or rise above the limitations of his particular class, spacious as that world was in some ways. A great destiny is, for the destined one, like a great pain, an undefinable cosmic ache, an urge only dimly understood. Jefferson's future friend John Adams had been shaken and obsessed by the same pain, the same yearning for the unperceived but believed-in future.

One is tempted to say that Jefferson was waiting for the sound of the drums of history that would waken him from his slumberous legal studies. But ambivalence was at the center of his being, so that his oscillation between Williamsburg and Shadwell symbolized his oscillation between the world of the artist-philosopher-farmer (at Shadwell) and the almost equally seductive social whirl at Williamsburg.

He had started his studies under the direction of George Wythe in 1762. He continued them until 1767—five years, almost as much time as it takes a modern graduate student to earn his Ph.D. Patrick Henry had studied law six weeks before being admitted to the bar. Jefferson's apprenticeship was not so much in the law as in the broader horizons of humane study. Law was the cover he used to repair his superficial studies at the college. Obviously he read a vast amount, thought a good deal, and suffered substantially.

If Jefferson remained in a kind of limbo, the world went on around him. Most important to him was the marriage of Martha, his favorite sister, to Dabney Carr, his old schoolmate and with the possible exception of John Page his closest friend. Dr. Small, as we have noted, returned to Scotland; Francis Fauquier, lieutenant governor of the colony, one of the most popular and successful of a long line of Englishmen who held that office, died in 1768.

Most momentous was a changing and hardening of the attitude of Great Britain toward her American colonies. In dire financial straits from the enormous cost of the Seven Years' War —or Great War for Empire—in which she had humbled the military might of Spain and France, the mother country was scratching about desperately for additional revenue. In the course of cleaning out the cupboard, her thoughts turned, not surprisingly, to her American possessions, prosperous and flourishing, the happy beneficiaries of the defeat of France and Spain. They were enjoying the advantages of a glorious victory; they should be willing to pay some of the costs. Hence there were a series of parliamentary acts designed to extract revenue from the colonies, the first being the Revenue Act, which placed a duty on molasses from the West Indies. Since it affected primarily New England merchants involved in trade with the Indies, this duty caused little stir in Virginia. But it was followed scarcely a year later by the Stamp Act, which placed a tax on newspapers, legal documents, college diplomas, and playing cards—thus affecting the lives of a large number of people in every colony, north and south. The principle of the thing was especially obnoxious: the idea that members of Parliament, thousands of miles away, could pass statutes that would take money out of the pockets of Americans without their leave.

Resistance to the Stamp Act was widespread and spontaneous. The Virginia legislature, the House of Burgesses, was at the end of its spring session when the official text of the Stamp Act reached Fauquier. Anticipating a hostile reaction from the assembly, he planned to withhold the contents of the bill until the assembly disbanded. Only 39 out of 116 legislators remained in Williamsburg when some member got his hands on the text. After it had been circulated among them, the remaining members immediately called for a discussion "of the Steps necessary to be taken in Consequence of the Resolutions of the House of Commons of Great Britain relative to the charging [of] certain

Stamp Duties in the Colonies and Plantations of America."

Patrick Henry, who must have been privy to some advance information, had already prepared seven resolutions, three of them of astonishing boldness. The first four simply stated the "privileges, franchises, and immunities"—in a word the rights —possessed by the colonies. These were the rights of any Englishman of the realm, initiated, so legend had it, at the time of the Magna Charta, extended and refined in the centuries that followed, and capped by the Glorious Revolution of 1688. The fifth stated unequivocally that "the General Assembly of this colony have the only and sole exclusive right and power to lay taxes and impositions upon the inhabitants of this colony, and that every attempt to vest such power in any person or persons whatever, other than the General Assembly aforesaid, has a manifest tendency to destroy British as well as American freedom."

This was strong stuff. It was, in plain fact, revolution. The Virginia assembly was being asked to say, in effect, that Parliament had no power in any case whatsoever to tax the colonies. It is hardly surprising that the more moderate members drew back in alarm. When the resolutions were reported out for debate, Jefferson and his friend John Tyler, also studying law in Williamsburg, were in the audience. The chamber was completely under the domination of the young frontier member, Patrick Henry. We have no text of what he said, and the secondhand reports that exist are contradictory. The familiar schoolbook story, that Henry, carried away by his own flight of oratory, compared George III to Tarquin, Caesar, and Cromwell and when challenged by more moderate members with cries of "Treason! Treason!" replied defiantly, "If this be treason, make the most of it," is refuted by the testimony of a French visitor who was present and noted that Henry had indeed launched himself on a comparison of the British monarch to the three historic tyrants, but when rebuked, he apologized and said that he was sorry if he had caused any offense. The Frenchman's version is certainly the most persuasive, particularly in view of the fact that the more familiar story never appeared in print until sometime after Henry's death in 1799.

But of one thing there is no question. Henry was marvelously eloquent. And in that moment the young Jefferson may be said to have become a revolutionary; he and his companion identified themselves wholeheartedly with Patrick Henry's fervent exordium. It was truly a remarkable performance by the frontier lawyer. Arrayed against him was much of the political power of the colony, men who were accustomed to running affairs unchallenged and now found themselves on the defensive as Henry demonstrated the superiority of passion over reason. Such men as Jefferson's cousin Peyton Randolph opposed the resolutions primarily on the grounds that they were hasty and intemperate and that the assembly had previously stated, politely but firmly, its view of its powers in a document to which its members were even now awaiting an answer. Jefferson heard Peyton Randolph exclaim as the votes went for the resolutions by increasingly narrow margins—the vote on the fifth resolution was 20 to 19—"By God, I would have given one hundred guineas for a single vote." Henry had in his pocket two more resolutions, Six and Seven, which were even more fiery than Five, but observing the resistance to Five he wisely withheld them and, having carried the day, departed for home. His opponents, it turned out, had not yet capitulated. Peter Randolph, a member of the conservatively inclined Governor's Council and another of Jefferson's numerous Randolph cousins, spent hours, according to Jefferson, looking through old records of the assembly for a precedent by which the offensive fifth resolution might be expunged.

The following day the assembly reconvened, and with Henry absent the managers tried to bully the members into repealing the resolutions of the previous day. They were successful only in regard to the fifth resolution. The offensive fifth was wiped from the record, but it was all too late. Part of Henry's haste in departing may have been due to his determination to disseminate his Virginia resolutions throughout the other colonies. Not only did all five go forth as the official act of the assembly, but Six and Seven were added, so that all seven ap-

Roman historian Cornelius Tacitus

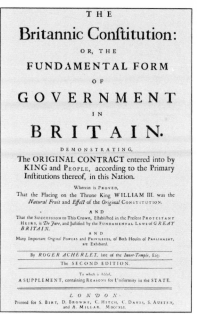

THE

Britannic Conſtitution:

OR, THE

FUNDAMENTAL FORM

OF

GOVERNMENT

IN

BRITAIN.

DEMONSTRATING,

The ORIGINAL CONTRACT entered into by
KING and PEOPLE, according to the Primary
Inſtitutions thereof, in this Nation.

Wherein is PROVED,
That the Placing on the Throne King WILLIAM III. was the
Natural Fruit and *Effect* of the *Original* CONSTITUTION.

AND
That the SUCCESSION to This Crown, Eſtabliſhed in the Preſent PROTESTANT
HEIRS, is *De Jure,* and Juſtified by the FUNDAMENTAL LAWS of *GREAT
BRITAIN.*

AND
Many Important *Original* POWERS and PRIVILEGES, of Both Houſes of PARLIAMENT,
are Exhibited.

By *ROGER ACHERLEY,* late of the *Inner-Temple,* Eſq;

The SECOND EDITION.

To which is Added,
A SUPPLEMENT, containing REASONS for Uniformity in the STATE.

LONDON:
Printed for S. BIRT, D. BROWNE, C. HITCH, C. DAVIS, S. AUSTEN,
and A. MILLAR. MDCCXLI.

Acherley's **The Britannic Constitution,** *1741*

Signing of the Magna Charta, 1215

British historian Sir Henry Spelman

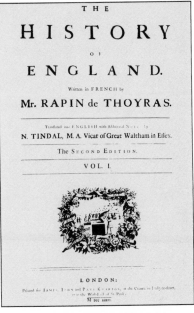

Rapin de Thoyras's History of England, *1723*

British jurist Sir William Blackstone

Jefferson and other Americans were inspired by British Whig writers who interpreted English history as a continuing struggle for liberty. These scholars accepted Tacitus's view of Saxon England as a society of free men and self-governing institutions. Beginning with the signing of the Magna Charta, Englishmen had fought to regain rights lost as a result of the Norman conquest.

peared to have passed. Seven went so far as to declare that anyone who failed to subscribe to the initial resolutions was a traitor to the Commonwealth of Virginia. That smacked of coercion on top of intimidation. Since popular sentiment is frequently ahead of official policy, the resolutions, if they offended the leaders in the provincial government and caused the governor to dismiss the house, added greatly to Henry's popularity and carried his name far beyond the boundaries of his native colony. Popular feeling was well reflected by Jefferson's teacher, the Reverend James Maury, who expressed his approval of the resolutions even though "some may brand us with the odious name of rebels."

Massachusetts, perhaps disconcerted at having the play taken away from it by its sister colony to the south, responded on June 8, 1765, with a call for a continental meeting, or congress, to gather in New York in the fall to discuss what action might be taken in opposition to the Stamp Act. When it convened in October, the Stamp Act Congress passed a number of resolutions of its own, none as bold as those of Virginia, but nonetheless speaking so plainly that all who chose could read the message: the colonists would not use stamps! It was as simple as that. Any lingering doubt was removed a few months later when Parliament directed that the stamps were to be put into use. There were no stamps, but there were riots in abundance. Parliament faced the kind of dilemma every legislature seeks to avoid, that posed by an unenforceable law. The Stamp Act, it seemed, would require a soldier for every colonist, or for every stamp. Even the most obtuse member (and obtuse members were numerous) could understand that the respective houses had no recourse (short of war) except to beat a hasty retreat, and they did so with as good grace as possible, covering their turnabout with the Declaratory Act, which in effect declared that although they were in this instance out of generosity and general benignity repealing an unpopular act, their loyal subjects should not assume that the members were thereby renouncing their right to levy taxes on them in the future, whenever and in whatever manner they wished.

The Stamp Act was, by any standard, an egregious error. More than a decade later when fighting had broken out, King George declared that his only regret, in reviewing the long contention between rights of the colonists and the authority of Parliament, was the repeal of the Stamp Act. He may have meant that if there was to have been war, or revolution, it would have been better for England if it had started then, at the time of the Stamp Act, when the colonies were unorganized and poorly prepared, rather than later, when the impulse to resistance had hardened into revolutionary fervor. Indeed the Stamp Act was like a wave that, having swept over the colonies and then receded, left behind it a residue of radical political notions that could not be readily subdued.

In the middle of the excitement over the Stamp Act Jefferson's oldest sister, Jane, died at the age of twenty-five. It was another of those untimely deaths that touched Jefferson's own life intimately and helped to account for the deep streak of morbidity in his nature. Such deaths were, to be sure, common in eighteenth-century America, but it is equally clear that Jefferson suffered a strange excess of them. Jane remains a dim figure. Her brother, whose silences were often so baffling, seems never to have written or spoken of her. We do not even know the cause of her death. It may have served to make Shadwell even less congenial to him than before. In any event the following spring he decided to make a journey to Philadelphia and New York, the great metropolises, along with Boston, of English America. The ostensible reason was to be inoculated for smallpox in Philadelphia, the most advanced center for the study of medicine, and so many other things, in all the colonies. The real reason was a natural youthful curiosity and desire to travel, which was not unrelated to his uncertain state of mind and general restlessness. Williamsburg, as lively a place as it must have been, especially during sessions of the assembly, was a small part of the great world. The Stamp Act controversy had stimulated Continental sensibilities and made those colonists most actively engaged in the resistance conscious that they shared common interests and concerns. So it was at least symbolically appropriate that young Jefferson should have signalized that wider consciousness by setting forth in a horse and carriage driven by one of the Shadwell slaves to see the world. Philadelphia was, as noted earlier, the third greatest city of the British Empire, ranking next to London and Birmingham in size and second only to London itself in the new spirit of enlightened learning.

3. Domestic Life

Jefferson made his way through Maryland, stopping at Annapolis, where the legislature of that colony was in session. To the young Virginian the Maryland legislators looked like an unruly mob. Having traveled on to Philadelphia, he took the smallpox inoculation, and after seeing the sights of that cosmopolitan city he continued on to New York, where in an inn on the Hudson he met Elbridge Gerry, a firm Massachusetts patriot.

In July Jefferson took a coastal vessel back to Virginia. There he resumed his legal studies, and some six months later George Wythe introduced him to the general court of the colony; he was briefly examined and at long last admitted to the bar. His first legal case involved transferal of a deed to land. More cases followed, and Jefferson rode the circuit with other members of the bar—to Staunton, to Culpepper, to Albemarle —handling the variety of cases that came a young lawyer's way. While he was thorough and meticulous in the preparation of his cases, he had little gift for the rough and tumble of courtroom advocacy. He could not and did not wish to learn to play upon the sympathies of a jury with the consummate skill of a Patrick Henry. In consequence he found himself preoccupied with the more routine cases for more modest fees. As Edmund Randolph put it, "Mr. Jefferson drew copiously from the depths of the law, Mr. Henry from the recesses of the human heart."

In his first year of practice he handled the respectable total of 67 cases for fees of £293, of which he was able to collect only £43. The next year he had 115 cases and the year following 198. The steady increase in the number of cases he handled was testimony to his ability as a lawyer. Obviously he gave his clients good service. Unfortunately most of them, casual in all things having to do with money, failed to pay their fees. In the first six years he practiced law he collected little more than a third of what was owed him.

Shadwell occupied the time not devoted to the law. There he planted vegetables and flowers—peas, asparagus, celery and onions, marigold, amaranth, and carnations, all recorded in his precise, neat hand. An hour or more a day was given to practicing on his beloved violin. Meanwhile, in the political realm matters moved intermittently toward some final confrontation. Not having learned the lesson that the Stamp Act should have taught him, Charles Townshend, "Champagne Charlie" as his enemies called him, now chancellor of the exchequer, egged on by George Grenville, who had had to see his cherished Stamp Act repudiated, won the approval of a supine Parliament to a set of duties, named after him, on tea, lead, paper, and a variety of other commodities. Passed in 1767, the Townshend Acts stirred up another furor in the colonies. This time the merchants took the lead in opposition, at least in the northern colonies, and their weapon was a pledge of nonimportation of British goods designed to create such economic pressure that Parliament must once more retreat. The colonial resistance was much more moderate than it had been at the time of the Stamp Act, but it was nonetheless resolute.

Jefferson seems to have been little involved in the controversy over the Townshend duties. He was at the beginning of his law practice, which with the development of Shadwell occupied most of his time. In addition he had acquired Andrea Palladio's *Four Books of Architecture*. Palladio, a sixteenth-century Italian architect whose renderings of buildings infatuated Jefferson, was famous for his villas and *palazzi* built in the neoclassical style. These marvelous volumes, perhaps the greatest work ever composed on the subject of architecture, became Jefferson's principal treasure. Poring over them he discovered, with the power of revelation, his lifelong avocation—architecture. When Palladio's work came into his hands he had already conceived a grand scheme, an elegant plantation house of his own on top of a mountain adjacent to Shadwell. Typically, the great Virginia mansions were built along rivers, where water was plentiful, the land was flat and fertile, and where, at least in the Tidewater, ships could pick up the tobacco that was the staple crop of most successful plantations. Thus to build on a hill or small mountain —Monticello—was itself unprecedented. Hilltop land was far less productive than valley land, water was often difficult to obtain, wells had to be sunk to great depths and even then were unreliable, unsurfaced hillside roads were especially subject to erosion and difficult to maintain. Mules or oxen had to haul everything needed for the building and supply of such a plantation house up a steep grade on rutted, bumpy roads.

In other words, to build a house on top of a hill was, in the eighteenth century, a reckless and quixotic act in terms of any sensible farm management. It was a decision prompted purely by aesthetic and perhaps psychological considerations, one bound to increase the cost vastly and in all ways complicate the original construction of the mansion and the subsequent daily life of its occupants. That a young man not yet in full possession of himself or his father's estate, without great financial resources, and with little practical experience in building or in fact in farming projected such an ambitious plan gives us a crucial insight into Jefferson. Indeed, if a clue to his enigmatic character is to be found anywhere, surely it must be on the site and in the structure that was to dominate his life more definitively than any other building has dominated the life of any other great public figure in our history. If Jefferson's genius were not striking enough to veil his eccentricity or make it subordinate to his remarkably diverse talents, we would be inclined, I suspect, to perceive him as a genuine oddity, an individual whose highly unorthodox impulses disposed him to at least one venture that was more than slightly mad.

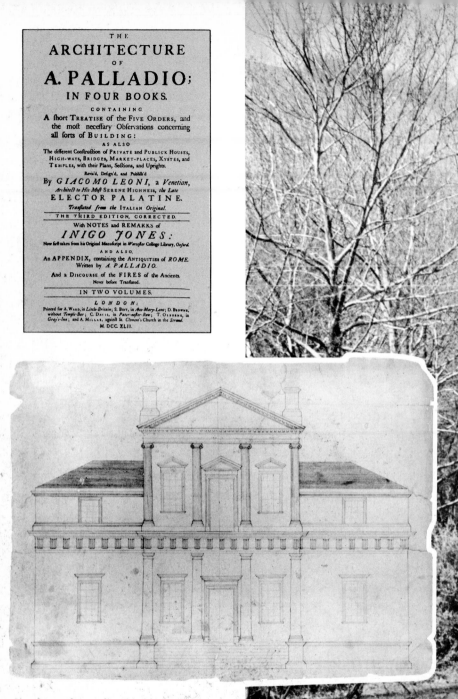

THE
ARCHITECTURE
OF
A. PALLADIO;
IN FOUR BOOKS.

CONTAINING

A short TREATISE of the FIVE ORDERS, and the most necessary Observations concerning all sorts of BUILDING:

AS ALSO

The different Construction of PRIVATE and PUBLICK HOUSES, HIGH-WAYS, BRIDGES, MARKET-PLACES, XYSTES, and TEMPLES, with their Plans, Sections, and Uprights.

Revis'd, Design'd, and Publish'd

By *GIACOMO LEONI*, a *Venetian*,
Architect to His Most SERENE HIGHNESS, the Late
ELECTOR PALATINE.

Translated from the ITALIAN Original.

THE THIRD EDITION, CORRECTED.

With NOTES and REMARKS of
INIGO JONES:
Now first taken from his Original Manuscript in *Worcester* College Library, *Oxford.*

AND ALSO,

An APPENDIX, containing the ANTIQUITIES of ROME.
Written by *A. PALLADIO*.

And a DISCOURSE of the FIRES of the Ancients.
Never before Translated.

IN TWO VOLUMES.

LONDON:

Printed for A. WARD, in *Little-Britain*; S. BIRT, in *Ave-Mary-Lane*; D. BROWNE, without *Temple-Bar*; C. DAVIS, in *Pater-noster-Row*; T. OSBORNE, in *Gray's-Inn*; and A. MILLAR, against St. *Clement's* Church in the *Strand*.
M. DCC. XLII.

Soon after ending his law studies Jefferson began a forty-year project—building Monticello, on a hill near Shadwell (right). His early designs were influenced by Palladio (top, the title page from a book Jefferson owned). The upper portico seen in the 1771 drawing above was never completed; the octagonal ends, which were built eventually, do not appear.

So Jefferson, the champion of reason, did another of the unreasonable things that had already become so much a part of the pattern of his life. Guided by Palladio, who advised that country houses should be built "in elevated and agreeable places . . . upon an eminence," and indifferent to all practical considerations, he proceeded with the plans and drawings for Monticello. Notions of light and space, so dramatically suggested by Palladio's drawings, obsessed him; airy vistas, the endlessly changing play of light and shadow on trees and hill and valleys, the great breathing spaces that stretched out to the horizons, enchanted him. Again one is tempted to speculate that the dark spaces of his inner world cried out for that splendid infinitude. Perhaps Jefferson built Monticello not as an assertion of vanity but as a means of survival. Certainly it became an essential refuge; was it also his sanitarium? His magic mountain? The only place where he could hold the world in some kind of precious if precarious balance?

The sketches began with ideas borrowed from Palladio and adapted to the site and, at least roughly, to Jefferson's means. The house grew, changed, unfolded, filled his mind, haunted his dreams. Before a spadeful of earth had been dug or a brick laid, he was describing the wallpaper for the dining room and listing the furniture—Venetian blinds, a backgammon table, a clavichord to be made to his specifications in Germany.

In 1767, the year of the Townshend Acts, Jefferson began to order materials for Monticello. He had decided to level off the top of his mountain—a herculean task—so that he might have wide lawns and gardens surrounding his aerie. Fruit trees were planted—apple, peach, cherry, pear and pomegranate, fig and almond. In the summer of 1769 he had work started on the south outbuilding containing a single room in which he intended to live while superintending the construction of the main house. The previous winter, with everything at sixes and sevens, he had presented himself at Charlottesville, the newly established seat of Albemarle County, as a candidate for the House of Burgesses. He and Dr. Thomas Walker, his former guardian, were chosen, and four months later, early in April, 1769, Jefferson traveled to Williamsburg for the meeting of the assembly. Francis Fauquier had died the year before, and the colony had a new lieutenant governor, Norborne Berkeley, baron de Botetourt, called Lord Botetourt. The only issue of any special significance before the assembly was an appeal by the Massachusetts legislature for common action against the Townshend duties.

This time the response of the Virginians was far more circumspect. As Jefferson later described the tactics of the warmer patriots: "Subsequent events favored the bolder spirits of Henry, the Lees, Pages, Masons, &c., with whom I went in all points. Sensible, however, of the importance of unanimity among our constituents, although we often wished to have gone faster, we slackened our pace, that our less ardent colleagues might keep up with us; and they, on their part, differing nothing from us in principle, quickened their gait somewhat beyond that which their prudence might of itself have advised, and thus consolidated the phalanx which breasted the power of Britain. By this harmony of the bold with the cautious, we advanced with our constituents in [an] undivided mass, and with fewer examples of separation than, perhaps, existed in any other part of the Union." And these tactics of caution and moderation the Virginians continued down to the outbreak of the Revolution. Their resolves were, in their view at least, correspondingly mild; but Botetourt, doubtless anxious to display an intention to rule firmly, called the leaders of the house to his palace the next day and notified them that he was displeased with their resolutions and was, in consequence, dismissing, or dissolving, them.

The members were indignant. Most of them gathered at the Raleigh Tavern, where they constituted themselves in effect an extralegal session of the assembly. Led by George Washington, they voted to join the Association for Nonimportation as part of a common colonial effort to force Parliament to repeal the Townshend duties.

The assembly that Botetourt had so highhandedly dissolved was re-elected by the voters almost to the last man. Thus rebuffed, the lieutenant governor was in a more tractable mood when the new (essentially the old) assembly convened in the fall. As in the case of the Stamp Act, colonial resistance had also produced a change in British practice if not in policy. Townshend had died, and Pitt's administration had been succeeded by that of Lord North. In the general exultation over the repeal of the Townshend duties, few people noted that North had failed to mention the tax on tea as among those duties that had been removed.

The events of 1767–69, specifically the passage of the Townshend Acts, the subsequent opposition to them in the colonies, Jefferson's own entry onto the political scene as a representative from Albemarle County, the proroguing of the assembly by Botetourt, and the retreat by the British government in face of the rather uneven pressure exerted by the colonies, had politicized Jefferson. He had, to be sure, been deeply stirred by Patrick Henry's eloquence at the time of the Stamp Act, but after its repeal he had returned to his studies of the law and pursued his own private visions.

Now, like so many of his counterparts in every colony, he began to turn his attention in a serious and sustained way to political theory. What were the rights of Englishmen under the unwritten British constitution? More broadly, what were the "rights of man"—those rights with which an individual was born and of which no earthly power could deprive him? How was a proper government constructed? And perhaps most important of all, under what circumstances did people have the right to resist unjust governments? Thus to his studies of architecture and music, ethics (moral philosophy), natural philosophy (science), agriculture, and law, Jefferson added what we might call political philosophy—the study of human societies, political principles, and political behavior.

Again one began with the ancients, with Thucydides and Polybius, the great Greek historians, with their Roman counterparts, Livy and Tacitus, and with such heroes of republican Rome as Cicero and Cato. In addition there were a host of more or less contemporary French, English, and most important of all, Scottish philosophers and political theorists who had written eloquently of the nature of government and the duties of the governors to the governed. Jefferson, already a deist, found such French writers as Rousseau, Voltaire, and Diderot most sympathetic. Among the English writers John Locke, with his famous treatises on government, was an essential mentor, but there were others, such as Algernon Sidney, who had paid with his life for his resistance to the unlimited powers of the Crown and who became one of Jefferson's particular heroes. And there were the modern Scottish writers, Francis Hutcheson, James Burgh, and Adam Ferguson, who shared the American perspective on a corrupt and decadent Parliament.

It was as though American political leaders everywhere were enrolled in a crash course on political theory. The Stamp Act had produced a wave of popular resistance. The Townshend duties had alerted the colonists that the Stamp Act could not be dismissed as an erratic, one-time error by Parliament. Even more than the Stamp Act, this fact served to turn practical politicians into political scholars. Jefferson thus turned from the architecture of buildings to the architecture of governments. Of what combination of ideas, principles, practical needs, and historical residues was a proper government constructed? He ordered from England a large batch of books on constitutional law and ancient history. His commonplace book ran over with reflections on the relation between people and their governors. He noted that it was the practice among the ancient Celts of Britain for the people to raise up and depose their kings. Likewise, among the earliest Greeks kings were elected "by the free consent of the people. They were considered chiefly as the leaders of their armies." When they abused their powers, "the people, as opportunity offered, resum'd the power in their own hands."

Among the modern works, Montesquieu's *Spirit of the Laws* exerted perhaps the greatest influence on Jefferson's thinking. Montesquieu was a great admirer of what he believed to be the British constitution, and his description of how he believed the executive, judicial, and legislative branches balanced and checked each other became an article of faith for Jefferson and other patriot leaders. In addition, Jefferson was instructed by the Frenchman's discussion of the source of all political power as residing in the mass of the people and by his views on the nature of federations of semiautonomous republics.

As with most lives, the public and the private life of Jefferson interacted. While he pushed ahead with his plans for Monticello, nurtured his growing law practice, and read about and reflected upon the nature of republics, Shadwell burned to the ground. He was in Charlottesville when a slave arrived with the news: "Master, the old place is burnt down. Everything's gone." "Everything? Didn't you save my books?" Jefferson asked. "No, Master, all lost." Then the slave grinned. "Not all. We saved your *fiddle.*" Jefferson wrote John Page, telling him of the death of his "favorite pullet" and then adding, almost offhandedly, "My late loss may perhaps have reached you by this time; I mean the loss of my mother's house by fire, and in it of every paper I had in the world, and almost every book. On a reasonable estimate I calculate the *cost* of the books burned to have been £200 sterling. Would to god it had been the money. *Then* it had never cost me a sigh. . . . Of papers too of every kind I am utterly destitute. All of these, whether public or private, of business or of amusement, have perished in the flames." Jefferson says nothing of the predicament in which his mother and his sisters and brother were left by the fire. He began immediately ordering books from England to replace those destroyed in the conflagration.

A few months after the fire Botetourt appointed Jefferson lieutenant of Albemarle County, the office his father had held. Since Jefferson was utterly unmilitary and had never shown the slightest interest in such matters, one wonders why the office was tendered and accepted. Meanwhile Jefferson, almost alone among his close friends, remained unmarried, and quotations from assorted authors on the fickleness, infidelity, and general inferiority of woman continued to appear from time to time in his casual jottings. In October, 1770, he visited The Forest, the plantation of a wealthy lawyer-planter, John Wayles. Wayles was an Englishman, amiable and enterprising, with a "handsome fortune." He was also engaged in the slave trade and that, evidently, was the primary source of his wealth. Not only did John Wayles deal in slaves; like many of his fellow planters he went to bed with the more desirable of his female chattels.

His daughter, Martha, had recently been widowed. She had married a young Virginian, Bathurst Skelton, at the age of eighteen, and he had died two years after their marriage, leaving her with an infant son, John. Martha Wayles Skelton was a thin young woman with hazel eyes, auburn hair, and a ruddy complexion. Her musical interests complemented Jefferson's own; she played the spinet and the harpsichord. So Jefferson, having met Martha Skelton sometime in 1770, became her rather leisurely suitor. While he labored over the building of Monticello, he paid court to her, stopping off at The Forest whenever business or the inclinations of his heart carried him in that direction. Unlike cruel Belinda, Martha Skelton was not, apparently, pressed by other suitors, so Jefferson could take his sweet time in getting to the point.

Much of his energy was given to Monticello, which went on, despite his constant attentions, if anything more slowly than his courtship. What he called the Southeast Pavilion, a one-room brick structure, was, as earlier noted, completed and put into use as the headquarters from which he directed the construction of the house. One reason for the slowness with which the building proceeded must have been the constant changes in Jefferson's plans. He made dozens of drawings, some rough, some worthy of a professional architect. Elevations, floor plans, architectural details, poured forth; even sketches for the color and design of curtains to hang at the windows.

The first drawings of the house showed a rather conventional structure with a central two-story portico with simple Doric columns, surmounted on the second story by fluted Ionic columns, which in turn supported a Greek pediment. Jefferson clearly had trouble with second floors. Here the rather small awkward windows appeared to be cut off by a heavy molding that ran around the house at the level of the first-floor portico. The chimneys rose at what seemed a quite impossible line from the edges of the central pediment. Indeed, the whole house seemed somewhat cramped in its feeling and hardly large enough for the scale of living that Jefferson projected. But then the oddest thing was perhaps the subterranean dimension. It was rather as though Jefferson had bracketed the hill (after its top had been so laboriously removed) with a huge U. The central branch of the U ran under the house. The north wing contained the stables and had an exposure northward. The southern wing contained kitchens and quarters for the household slaves, a smoke room, and a laundry. It also had an open side. The rooms that opened off the long underground corridor connecting the two lateral wings were primarily storage rooms—one for wine, another for beer, another for rum, one for meal, one for milk, a pantry, and a buttery. To get from the kitchen to the dining room, a slave had to travel along the corridor up a narrow flight of stairs to the dining room, at the opposite end of the house. Keeping food warm during that extensive trip was not a problem unique to Monticello. Most plantation kitchens were in dependencies, that is, outbuildings; chafing dishes in the dining room helped to reheat or keep hot dishes warm. But the striking thing about Jefferson's successive plans—the underground U was the most stable element in the plans for an obvious reason (once laid down at vast trouble and expense it could hardly be altered)— was the relation between what was visible and what was invisible. Contemplating that difference and imagining the house and its dependencies in full operation, it is impossible for this biographer not to perceive the house with all its architectural appurtenances as a symbol of the architect with his own strange, invisible inner life.

The modern dictum asserting that form follows function, now happily fading, would have left Jefferson unmoved. It was façades that captivated him. Function, however warped, must follow form. Stories might be crammed together, concealed, chopped off; stairways compressed to no more than the width of a man's shoulders; rooms buried beneath the ground; water hauled laboriously up the hill in carts or caught in complex systems of gutters and rainspouts and stored in huge cisterns.

No matter, it was the vista, the perspective, the unclouded brow of the hill, the unmarred façade of the house that was the important thing. But clearly that was not all of it. There was also an obsessive ingenuity. Everything was a puzzle: the way a door opened or a window closed, a closet, a toilet, a bed. What was this endless fascination with the machinery of the universe and the machinery of domestic life? It was as though the architect was determined to tinker tirelessly with his environment so that at last he might be living in a vast, intricate machine of his own devising, beautiful to contemplate, impossible to penetrate, perpetually tantalizing, a riddle harboring an enigma. Was ever human energy so tirelessly discharged against bricks and mortar? Did ever stones and bricks so become the colors of an artist's palette, worked and reworked, laid on and erased, studied, studied, studied? One sees him, in the mind's eye, stepping back to view the mansion's prospects—as an artist, brush in hand, steps back from his easel—in different lights and from different angles. To soften that line, to strengthen this, to raise that roof level, conceal that interior space. To block out or lower a bedroom window (what of the bedroom's occupant, another victim of art!), move a chimney, make a square room octagonal.

The grounds were somewhat more tractable. Here he would divert a much-needed spring to form a cascading waterfall flowing through a modest Greek temple. Or perhaps a Chinese pagoda. The French had made chinoiserie the rage. Adjacent to the temple would be a reclining marble figure and a Latin inscription translated into English that would read:

> Nymph of the grot, these sacred springs I keep,
> And to the murmurs of these waters sleep:
> Ah! spare my slumbers! Gently tread the cave!
> And drink in silence or in silence lave!

At the same time he made plans for a family graveyard. "Chuse out," he noted, "for a Burying place some unfrequented vale in the park where is 'no sound to break the silence.' . . . Let it be among antient and venerable oaks; intersperse some

Know all men by these presents that we Thomas Jefferson and Francis Eppes are held and firmly bound to our sovereign lord the king his heirs and successors in the sum of fifty pounds current money of Virginia, to the paiment of which well and truly to be made we bind ourselves jointly and severally, our joint and several heirs executors and administrators in witness whereof we have hereto set our hands and seals this twenty third day of December in the year of our lord one thousand seven hundred and seventy one The condition of the above obligation is such that if there be no lawful cause to obstruct a marriage intended to be had and solemnised between the abovebound Thomas Jefferson and Martha Skelton of the county of Charles city, widow, for which a license is desired, then this obligation is to be null and void; otherwise to remain in full force.

On January 1, 1772, Thomas Jefferson married Martha Wayles Skelton at her father's home, The Forest (above, an 1890 photograph). In the marriage bond (left), written by Jefferson and cosigned by a friend from school named Francis Eppes, the word *spinster* is crossed out, and *widow* has been inserted in another handwriting.

gloomy evergreens. . . . In the center of it erect a small Gothic temple of antique appearance, appropriate one half to the use of my own family; the other of strangers, servants, &c. . . . In the middle of the temple an altar, the sides of turf, the top a plain stone. Very little light, perhaps none at all, save only the feeble ray of an half extinguished lamp." In fairness to Jefferson it should be said that most young men of parts and culture in the Western world, Europe and America, were at the same time entertaining such morbidly romantic thoughts.

Jefferson's feelings about Martha Skelton are as obscure as many of his other feelings. Certainly his courtship seems not to have been an especially ardent one. The marriage bond was signed in November of 1771, more than a year after they first met (although again it must be said that long courtships were much more common in the eighteenth century than today), and a month later, on the first day of the new year, they were married. The wedding festivities at The Forest lasted for several weeks, and it was January 18 before the bride and groom set off in Jefferson's phaeton for Monticello. It began to snow as they rode along and finally the snow became so deep that they had to abandon the carriage and continue on horseback. They reached the top of the mountain late at night, the servants were all asleep in the unfinished house, and the story is told that rather than wake them Jefferson spent the first night with Martha in the Southeast Pavilion. John Skelton, Martha's four-year-old son, had been left behind at The Forest in the care of his grandparents. On September 27, nine months less three days after the wedding, the Jeffersons had their first child, named Martha after her mother and nicknamed Patsy. In the next ten years Martha gave birth to five more children, four daughters and one son; in addition she had at least two miscarriages. Of the six children only two survived: Martha, her first, and Mary or Maria (Polly), born in August of 1778. The birth of her last daughter, Lucy Elizabeth, who died three years later, undoubtedly helped to bring on her own death.

Whatever may have been Martha Jefferson's gifts or failings they remain obscure, since her husband destroyed the letters they exchanged during their courtship and never wrote or spoke of her except in passing. One thing does seem clear: she was physically very frail. To lose four out of six children, in addition to having several miscarriages, was an excessive mortality rate even in eighteenth-century Virginia. Since she was constantly pregnant during the ten years of her marriage, it seems likely that she was also "poorly" much of that time.

Within a year and a half after her marriage, her son had died; her husband's brother-in-law and closest friend, Dabney Carr, died May 16, 1773; and her father, John Wayles, died on May 28, 1773. Carr and Jefferson while still boys had made a compact that in the event of the death of either of them, the survivor would bury the other under a particular oak at Monticello. The first body thus to be placed in the Monticello burying ground was that of Jefferson's brother-in-law and dearest friend. While slaves were preparing the grave Jefferson took notes on the time required to turn the soil. Two men spent three and a half hours at the job; thus, Jefferson calculated, one man would take seven and could therefore be expected to turn an acre in four working days. Although one should not load its meaning excessively, the incident demonstrates again Jefferson's strange capacity for compartmentalizing his emotions; it is almost as though he had developed a technique for dealing with pain—to search out some item of practical trivia connected with the experience and concentrate on that. Jefferson was especially devastated by Carr's death. Not only did it leave his sister a widow, it also deprived him of a beloved friend from his childhood days.

The death of Martha's father brought her, in the settlement of his estate, eleven thousand acres of land and thirty-five slaves along with a heavy load of debts. Since it was notorious that John Wayles had had children by at least one slave woman, among the slaves inherited by Martha Wayles were several of her half sisters and brothers, not to mention her father's black mistress.

Something perhaps should be said here about Jefferson's relations with women. We have no reason to believe that his marriage to Martha Skelton was anything but a conventionally happy one. Indeed, his virtual collapse at her death would indicate the most profound emotional attachment. Yet against these conclusions must be placed his curious collection of misogynous musings about women and the fact that shortly before and after his marriage he made persistent sexual overtures to Betsey Walker, the wife of his old friend Jack Walker, who once during an absence left her and her young son in Jefferson's care. In view of his diffident courtship of Rebecca Burwell and his general aloofness toward women as well as his keen sense of personal honor, the recklessness of such an advance is hard to comprehend. It might be said to be one of those instances when "out of character" comes most readily to mind. Yet again the fact is that Jefferson, far more than most historical figures, is constantly stepping "out of character." So we must add another perhaps unanswerable question to those already confronting us. What curious combination of fear and dependence formed Jefferson's attitude toward women? Certainly we know nothing about Martha to suggest that she was in any way exceptional— a rather pretty young woman of average accomplishments, often in poor health. Perhaps the answer is that she was the first woman in his life who gave herself to him in complete trust and demanded nothing from him in return. A great man may need nothing so much as the simple, unquestioning love of a thoroughly unexceptional woman. To have that, finally, and then to lose it could be far more lacerating than losing the most brilliant and accomplished but demanding wife.

4. War

Jefferson was frequently in Williamsburg in connection with his duties as a member of the assembly. The agreement not to import British goods languished after the repeal of the Townshend duties. Although some of the more determined patriot leaders wished to maintain the policy until *all* taxes had been removed, that course proved to be too draconian for most Americans, especially those who depended upon trade with Great Britain for their livelihood. In Virginia the most "forward spirits," on the occasion of the burning of the British revenue sloop *Gaspee,* met at the Raleigh Tavern in Williamsburg and made plans for a committee of correspondence to exchange information with patriot leaders in the other colonies so that proposals for resistance might be properly coordinated if an occasion arose for common action. Jefferson was an active member of the group. A resolution was drafted to be presented to the assembly calling for such a committee "whose business it shall be to obtain the most early and Authentic intelligence of all such Acts and Resolutions of the British Parliament, or proceedings of Administration, as may relate to or affect the British Colonies in America, and to keep up and maintain a Correspondence and Communication with our Sister Colonies, respecting these important Considerations. . . ." The assembly passed the resolution without a dissenting vote. It was a small but significant step toward creating Continental solidarity.

Having contributed to the formation of the Virginia Committee of Correspondence, Jefferson once more withdrew to Monticello. This time his withdrawal was accompanied by the abandonment of his law practice. Although he had been reasonably successful, he was doubtless discouraged by the difficulty of collecting the fees owed him. Lacking a courtroom presence, he was necessarily confined to those aspects of the law where routine overshadowed drama. Perhaps most important of all, Monticello obsessed him. His new bride was there, and his extravagant dreams for his hilltop villa remained to be fully realized. He collected books and fine wines, supervised his acres, four plantations scattered over three counties, and worked hard at mastering the principles of scientific agriculture. The Virginia plantation was in fact the precursor of the modern agribusiness. By 1774 Jefferson had 187 slaves on his various plantations. He, like his fellows, ran less a farm than a business. Although the plantations had overseers, they nonetheless required constant supervision. Jefferson was, as we have already noted, an indefatigable record keeper, and his farm and account books reveal his attention to the minutiae required for running such an agricultural business.

On February 21, 1774, Monticello was shaken by a strong earthquake, which drove everyone from the house. In the excitement Jefferson's afflicted sister, Elizabeth, then in her thirtieth year, disappeared. It was two days before she was found, more dead than alive. She died a few days later and was buried in the family plot near Dabney Carr.

In 1773, scarcely a year after Jefferson had brought his half-frozen bride to Monticello through the snowdrifts, the North ministry, which replaced the Pitt-Grafton ministry, had decided to bail out the corrupt and bankrupt East India Company by imposing a tax on East India tea to be paid by the colonists. Millions of pounds of tea had accumulated in the company's warehouses, and North's notion was, in effect, to dump this tea in the colonies by reducing its cost so that even with the tax it would be a bargain. North and his ministers were beguiled by the idea that American women were addicted to tea and that this addiction would overcome any political scruples their notoriously henpecked husbands might have. Moreover, most members of the British government were convinced that throughout all the agitation over rights, the vast majority of Americans were interested only in the profit and loss columns; in the British view their actions were based on self-interest rather than principle. One prospective advantage of dumping East India tea in America at reduced prices was that it would demonstrate to the world the true nature of colonial rhetoric about freedom.

In every colony groups of patriots took action to prevent the tea's being landed or, if landed, sold. Most of the ships bearing tea turned back to England in the face of such determination. In Massachusetts, once the vessels carrying tea had entered the Boston harbor, Governor Thomas Hutchinson ordered British warships to close off the harbor mouth, barring the retreat of the ships. He was determined to force a showdown with the patriot groups in the colony. The Boston Tea Party followed and the North government, in retaliation, closed the Boston harbor, hoping thereby to starve the Bostonians into repentance and submission. The closing of the harbor was followed by a bill suspending the colony's government. Parliament then passed the Quebec Act, which among other things extended the jurisdiction of England's Canadian province to include the western boundaries of the American colonies. These acts of Parliament were called the Intolerable, or Coercive, Acts. The immediate question was whether Boston would be abandoned by the other colonies or whether they would make common cause with their beleaguered neighbor. Although some colonies, among them New York and Pennsylvania, showed an inclination to drag their feet, there was never any doubt about where Jefferson and most of his fellow Virginians stood.

On May 5, 1774, the Virginia assembly opened its spring session. Two weeks later word arrived from Boston of the closing of its port by British ships of war. The radical patriots of the assembly met to try to decide on the course of action that would most effectively awaken their colleagues and constituents to the

The House of Burgesses, to which Jefferson was first elected in 1768, was sometimes forced to meet at the Raleigh Tavern (below) to formulate plans of resistance. In May, 1774, the members unanimously voted for a day of fasting (right) to protest the Boston Port Act. The British cartoon at left portrays agitators threatening loyalists who refuse to cooperate.

TUESDAY, the 24th of MAY, 14 GEO. III. 1774.

THIS House being deeply impreſſed with Apprehenſion of the great Dangers to be derived to *Britiſh America*, from the hoſtile Invaſion of the City of *Boſton*, in our Siſter Colony of *Maſſachuſetts Bay*, whoſe Commerce and Harbour are on the 1ſt Day of *June* next to be ſtopped by an armed Force, deem it highly neceſſary that the ſaid firſt Day of *June* be ſet apart by the Members of this Houſe as a Day of Faſting, Humiliation, and Prayer, devoutly to implore the divine Interpoſition for averting the heavy Calamity, which threatens Deſtruction to our civil Rights, and the Evils of civil War; to give us one Heart and one Mind firmly to oppoſe, by all juſt and proper Means, every Injury to *American* Rights, and that the Minds of his Majeſty and his Parliament may be inſpired from above with Wiſdom, Moderation, and Juſtice, to remove from the loyal People of *America* all Cauſe of Danger from a continued Purſuit of Meaſures pregnant with their Ruin.

Ordered, therefore, that the Members of this Houſe do attend in their Places at the Hour of ten in the Forenoon, on the ſaid 1ſt Day of *June* next, in Order to proceed with the Speaker and the Mace to the Church in this City for the Purpoſes aforeſaid; and that the Reverend Mr. *Price* be appointed to read Prayers, and the Reverend Mr. *Gwatkin* to preach a Sermon ſuitable to the Occaſion.

Ordered, that this Order be forthwith printed and publiſhed.

By the HOUSE of BURGESSES.

GEORGE WYTHE, C. H. B.

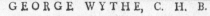

seriousness of Parliament's actions. Jefferson, Edmund Randolph, Patrick Henry, and Richard Henry Lee were among those meeting at the Raleigh Tavern. Apparently Jefferson and one of the Lees proposed a day of prayer and fasting to dramatize the plight of Boston and express solidarity with its citizens. If, as Edmund Randolph subsequently asserted, the idea was Jefferson's, it is an early indication of his flair for dramatic political action. Jefferson was, as we have observed, not a religious man. Therefore he clearly did not make the proposal because he believed in the efficacy of prayer and fasting, but rather because it seemed to him an appropriate political strategy, an act that the moderates would find difficult to oppose and that he hoped would have the effect of lifting the whole issue above partisan politics.

Since the radical strategists who had come up with the idea were not notable for their piety, they looked for a weightier and more respectable sponsor and found him in Robert Carter Nicholas, chairman of the assembly's Committee on Religion. The day appointed was June 1. Lieutenant Governor Lord Dunmore responded as the radicals had doubtless anticipated, by dissolving the assembly, which promptly adjourned to the Raleigh Tavern, by then almost as much the home of the legislature as the assembly chamber itself. At the Raleigh, after calling for a convention in August to name delegates to a continental meeting, the members adjourned. Jefferson returned posthaste to Charlottesville, where he joined with others of the community in the day of prayer and fasting, noting that its effect "through the whole colony was like a shock of electricity, arousing every man & placing him erect & solidly on his centre."

In anticipation of the nominating convention, Jefferson sat down and wrote an essay entitled *A Summary View of the Rights of British America.* The most original aspect of Jefferson's treatise was the forthrightness with which he engaged the subject of the king and the powers vested in him. The king, Jefferson pointed out, "is no more than the chief officer of the people appointed by the laws, and circumscribed with definite powers, to assist in working the great machine of government, erected for their use, and consequently subject to their superintendence." Jefferson placed strong emphasis on the argument that the colonists, like the ancient Saxons migrating to Britain, had in effect established a new society governed by such laws as seemed "most likely to promote public happiness." The American colonists had established themselves as individuals, and then, having carved out their own settlements and forms of government, they had entered into a kind of covenant, or agreement, with the mother country to accept a common head or sovereign as the symbol of their relationship. The king was "thereby made the central link connecting the several parts of the empire thus newly multiplied." It was an ingenious argument: that the colonies somehow had particular rights that derived from their own efforts and sacrifices in establishing themselves in the wilderness and that only after they had created their own societies did they enter into a kind of formal alliance, approaching England as equals.

Although few Englishmen, and perhaps not many Americans, could have been persuaded that such indeed had been the case, there was a symbolic rightness to it. It was an effective counter to the British argument that the colonies had always been dependent and subordinate. In fact they *had,* from the beginning, enjoyed a status in relation to the mother country that was unusual if not unique in the history of colonies. It was true enough that common sense and "the common feelings of human nature" ran counter to the notion that the American colonists "hold their political existence at the will of a British parliament." Were Americans to live "at the imperious breath of a body of men whom they never saw, in whom they never confided, and over whom they have no powers of punishment or removal, let their crimes against the American public be ever so great"? The Americans laid their case before the king and his ministers "with that freedom of language and sentiment which becomes a free people claiming their rights, as derived from the laws of nature, and not as the gift of their chief magistrate."

The *Summary View of the Rights of British America* anticipated Thomas Paine's *Common Sense* by personalizing the argument, so to speak. All discussions about the relations between the colonies and the mother country had previously concentrated on the misuse of power by the British ministry and a Parliament subservient to it. The king had enjoyed immunity from criticism, and indeed every official colonial protest had been prefaced by the most respectful references to His Majesty's benevolence. The colonists were constantly appealing *to the king* for redress of grievances charged to Parliament and the king's wicked ministers, ignoring the fact that the king himself was the most implacable enemy of what Americans conceived to be their liberties. The father-king, as the supreme symbol of the empire and indeed of all law and authority, had remained above criticism. The country was not yet ready for Jefferson's daring attack on the monarch himself. Although no one took up its challenge, the Virginian's essay pointed the direction in which public opinion was eventually to move.

A severe attack of dysentery prevented Jefferson from attending the August convention in Williamsburg that had been called to choose and instruct delegates to a Continental meeting. He sent two copies of his *Summary View,* one to Patrick Henry, who ignored it, and one to Peyton Randolph, speaker of the assembly, who did present it to the lawmakers. Edmund Randolph, who was present at a kind of preliminary reading of the document, reported that many of the paragraphs were applauded by the listeners. He noted, "The young ascended with Mr. Jefferson to the source of these rights; the old required time for consideration, before they could tread this lofty ground." The young radicals, Randolph believed, had moved "far beyond the politicks of the day." So the *Summary View* and the resolutions it proposed were set aside for more moderate statements. Nor was Jefferson among the delegates chosen to meet at Philadelphia in the fall. He had one rather considerable consolation, however; the report was printed as a pamphlet by his friends and received wide distribution. Arthur Lee, brother of Richard Henry, serving in England as a colonial agent, managed to get it published there, and it was read and applauded by the more ardent Whigs. If it did not succeed in stripping the king of his aura of majesty, the pamphlet established on a Continental scale his own credentials as a radical publicist and thus made him a prospective candidate for a future writing assignment of considerable importance.

In Virginia, as in the other colonies, following the recommendations of the Continental Congress, agencies of government were established under the names of various committees: committees of correspondence, of public safety, and of defense. These committees took over a variety of duties formerly performed by officials of the colony appointed by the governor or his council. The Richmond convention, in effect the assembly, prorogued by Lord Dunmore, debated the proper steps to put the colony in a posture of defense. When a resolution was proposed calling for the raising and arming of militia, the more conservative delegates protested that such action was tantamount to war. Upon which Patrick Henry rose to declaim: "Gentlemen may cry peace, peace—but there is no peace. . . . Is life so dear, or peace so sweet as to be purchased at the price of chains and slavery? Forbid it, Almighty God! I know not what course others may take; but as for me . . . give me liberty, or give me death!"

The resolution finally passed by a narrow margin, and Jefferson, who had strongly supported it, was appointed to a committee to implement it. The Richmond convention's next act was to suspend all legal proceedings in the colony, with certain necessary exceptions, and to vote a list of delegates for the meeting of the Second Continental Congress, scheduled to convene the following spring. Jefferson was not among the original delegates chosen, but he was selected as an alternate to Peyton Randolph in the event that delegate was unable to attend.

Even while the delegates to the convention at Richmond pushed ahead with their plans for the defense of the colony, events hurried them along willy-nilly. Expresses from Boston brought word from the Massachusetts Committee of Correspondence of the battles of Lexington and Concord and the heavy losses suffered by British regulars on their retreat to Boston. The war of the Revolution had clearly started. Lord Dunmore, faced at every turn by opposition and disobedience, de-

A
SUMMARY VIEW
OF THE
RIGHTS
OF
BRITISH AMERICA.
SET FORTH IN SOME
RESOLUTIONS
INTENDED FOR THE
INSPECTION
OF THE PRESENT
DELEGATES
OF THE
PEOPLE OF VIRGINIA.
NOW IN
CONVENTION.

BY A NATIVE, AND MEMBER OF THE
HOUSE OF BURGESSES.

by Thomas Jefferson.

WILLIAMSBURG:
PRINTED BY CLEMENTINA RIND.

Jefferson's first major literary contribution to the patriot cause was a twenty-three-page essay (left) written in July, 1774. He listed specific grievances and warned: "Let not the name of George the third be a blot in the page of history." A furious George III (right, his image on a gold medal) assured Parliament he would uphold its "supreme authority." By March, 1775, the House of Burgesses, inspired by Patrick Henry's oratory in Old St. John's Church (below), had voted to arm the state militia.

cided to reconvene the assembly. Peyton Randolph, still speaker of that body, felt that his first responsibility was to it. Jefferson thus succeeded to his place on the list of delegates to Congress.

Stopping in Williamsburg on his way to Philadelphia, Jefferson was enlisted by Randolph to draft a reply to Dunmore's opening address to the assembly, which urged moderation and passed on assurances from the British ministry that no further taxes would be laid on the colonists. Before Jefferson had completed the document the governor, having inflamed public opinion by seizing powder from the colony's armory, fled with his family to a British warship off Yorktown. A few days later, on June 12, 1775, Archibald Cary, a respected moderate, read Jefferson's reply, stating in emphatic terms that "the British Parliament has no right to intermeddle with the support of civil government in the Colonies. For us, not for them, has government been instituted here; agreeable to our Ideas, provision has been made for such Officers as we think necessary for the administration of public affairs, and we cannot conceive that any other legislature has a right to prescribe either the number or pecuniary appointments of our Offices." However they might be cloaked in deferential language, the facts were plain enough— Virginia was in a state of revolt against the authority of the mother country. Jefferson then went on to express the determination of the Virginians to stand by their sister colonies. Having heard the reading of his resolutions and the beginning of the debate on them, Jefferson rode on to take his place with his fellow delegates in the Continental Congress.

On June 21, 1775, Jefferson, having found lodgings with a cabinetmaker named Benjamin Randolph (no relation), presented his credentials and took his seat with the other members of the Virginia delegation. One of these, Richard Henry Lee, wrote that "there never appeared more perfect unanimity among any sett of Men than among the Delegates, and indeed all the old Provinces not one excepted are directed by the same firmness of union and determination to resist by all ways and to every extremity." Lee, always the optimist, painted rather too rosy a picture of the deliberations of the Congress, but it was certainly true that the delegates showed an encouraging disposition to stand as firm against British troops as they had against British statutes. A few days after Jefferson's arrival George Washington, appointed to command the Continental army—in truth a ragtag and bobtail collection of New England militia camped at Cambridge in appallingly dirty conditions—left to assume his new duties. Washington's appointment had been engineered by the two Adamses and Richard Henry Lee as a symbol, in part, of the alliance of Massachusetts and Virginia or, more broadly, of the northern and southern colonies.

In the Congress Jefferson found an ally in plain-spoken John Adams, Jefferson's counterpart in the breadth of his intellectual interests and the force of his mind. In temperament and appearance the two men made a dramatic contrast. Jefferson was tall and thin; Adams short and stout. Adams, while not notable for his eloquence, was a powerful and frequent speaker in Congress; Jefferson seldom uttered a word. Adams's manners were the somewhat stiff and awkward ones that characterized his fellow New Englanders; Jefferson had the easy affability of his class. Once past Adams's surface constraint, the man lay quite open, warm, humorous, affectionate; on the other side of the Virginian's graciousness lay a private territory to which few, if any, were ever freely admitted. While Adams, a thoroughgoing politician, plunged into every problem head-on, Jefferson preferred a more circuitous route. The tragedy of loss had dogged Jefferson from his youth. By contrast Adams had had a singularly happy and untroubled life. Both widely read, they differed profoundly in their view of human nature. Jefferson had a boundless faith in the basic goodness of man and in his ultimate perfectibility. Adams, by contrast, had imbibed a kind of Calvinistic pessimism with his mother's milk. It seemed to him that men and women had displayed in history a strong propensity to selfishness and, indeed, evil and that all human contrivances were little more than ingenious devices to minimize the "original sin" with which every human being was tainted.

If Jefferson was at heart the artist with a talent for brilliant effects, Adams was the more thorough and rigorous thinker, but he shared the Virginian's suspicion of formal religion and the doctrines of orthodoxy, most specifically the divinity of Christ. Like Jefferson, Adams ended his days an avowed deist, in his case a Unitarian.

Jefferson was a classic member of the Virginia planter class, a rural capitalist with thousands of acres of land, a great mansion a-building, and scores of black men and women in his service as slaves. Adams was a small-town lawyer living in a cottage on a modest farm. He shared Jefferson's passion for land and the proper cultivation of it, but he had infinitely less, only as much as he and a hired hand or two could plant and harvest. Yet, despite what might have appeared insurmountable incompatibilities, the two men became devoted and, except for an unhappy interlude of almost twenty years, lifelong friends. Such is the power of common principles and common actions that they are capable of overcoming the most profound contrarieties of background, personality, and disposition. Perhaps more than any other two single individuals of the generation of so-called founding fathers, Jefferson and Adams represented in principle the union of diversities and apparent contradictions that made possible the merging of thirteen states into a single nation. It was perhaps a final irony that Jefferson, the aristocratic planter, should have been the unflinching advocate of democracy, while Adams, the archetype of democracy in his own style of life, could never entirely overcome his distrust of those to whom Jefferson referred so confidently as "the people." Perhaps Adams knew them too well to cherish many illusions about them. In any event, the two men hit it off at once. In Adams's words: "Though a silent member of Congress, he [Jefferson] was so prompt, frank, explicit and decisive upon committees and in conversation . . . that he soon seized upon my heart."

As Adams's comments suggest, the two men were soon coconspirators plotting together how they might hurry along their less ardent compatriots. Soon after the news arrived of the Battle of Bunker Hill in June, 1775, Congress decided that it needed a declaration of some kind to explain to the world, or to whoever might be inclined to listen, why it had been necessary to take up arms against the mother country. The task was assigned initially to John Rutledge of South Carolina. Not satisfied with his hastily produced draft, the delegates added John Dickinson and Jefferson to constitute a committee of three charged with producing a more acceptable document. Jefferson took his turn. After having reviewed the provocations of General Thomas Gage and his troops, he added, "We should be wanting to ourselves, we should be perfidious to posterity, we should be unworthy that free ancestry from which we derive our descent, should we submit with folded arms to military butchery & depredation, to gratify the lordly ambition, or sate the avarice of a British ministry." Again the effect was not quite what the delegates wished. The rhetoric seemed overblown. "Submit with folded arms" was not a happy phrase. "Military butchery," "lordly ambition," did not convey the impression of a restrained and dignified statement. When the full committee, including William Livingston of New Jersey, met to review the draft, that document encountered heavy sailing. In Livingston's opinion it had "the faults common to our Southern gentlemen. Much fault-finding and declamation, with little sense or dignity. They seem to think a reiteration of tyranny, despotism, bloody, &c. all that is needed to unite us at home and convince the bribed voters of [Lord] North of the justice of our cause." So the task was passed on, finally, to John Dickinson, who incorporated much of Jefferson's language in a more closely reasoned and moderate statement. Jefferson, always extremely sensitive to criticism, a characteristic he shared with John Adams, was offended at what seemed to him the misuse of his handiwork; but he was soon at work on another committee drafting a reply to Lord North's so-called conciliatory proposals for ending the state of hostilities. Here he used substantially the same statement he had drafted a few weeks earlier for the Virginia assembly.

On the first of August Congress recessed and Jefferson headed for Richmond, where the Virginia convention—having abandoned Williamsburg—was assembled. He took with him in his carriage a number of books, including sheets of music he had

Soon after Jefferson reached the Pennsylvania State House, later renamed Independence Hall (left), for the Second Continental Congress, he befriended John Adams (seen here about 1775, when he was forty).

bought during his brief stay in Philadelphia, as well as an Indian tomahawk and a supply of strings for his fiddle.

At Richmond Jefferson was re-elected as a delegate to the next session of Congress. Only Peyton Randolph and Richard Henry Lee received more votes—89 and 88 respectively to Jefferson's 85. From an alternate delegate, Jefferson had risen dramatically to a full-fledged delegate, preferred by his colleagues over such respected figures as Richard Bland, Benjamin Harrison, and his old mentor, George Wythe.

Back at Monticello Jefferson was reunited with his family. Martha had just given birth to a daughter, christened Jane Randolph after Jefferson's mother. The infant was ailing and sickly and died a few days after Jefferson's return. Congress convened September 13, and Jefferson was already more than a week late when he started out for Philadelphia. He had had precious little time at home as it was. Martha, in uncertain health and depressed over the death of her daughter, had seen little of him since their marriage. In Philadelphia Jefferson was, for a time, a cipher. He was little suited for or interested in the tedious day-to-day business that occupied most of the time of the delegates. As though in recognition of this fact, few committee assignments came his way, and since the vast portion of the business of Congress was conducted by committees, Jefferson grew increasingly bored and restless. Although he wrote faithfully to Martha, he received no word in return. He wrote to Francis Eppes, Martha's half sister's husband, "I have never received the scrip of a pen from any mortal in Virginia since I left it, nor been able by any enquiries I could make to hear of my family. I had hoped that when Mrs. Byrd came I should hear something of them but she could tell me nothing about them. The suspense under which I am is too terrible to be endured. If any thing has happened, for god's sake let me know it."

Finally, toward the end of December, Jefferson left Congress and hurried back to Monticello. There he found Martha in reasonably good health but his mother ill. She died three months later, and he noted the fact in his account book without comment. So his mother passed from a scene where she had been as unsubstantial as a ghost. One cannot help but wonder what secret lay hidden there. Did her two retarded children, Randolph and Elizabeth, bear damaged genes that they had inherited from their mother? Virginia aristocrats interbred recklessly, not infrequently first cousins with first cousins, and the Randolphs had done their share of this. Insanity was as common among the first families of Virginia as it was in certain isolated villages of New England. Certainly for a son who wrote so voluminously never to write in any revealing way of his mother was unaccountable.

That we can make nothing of Jefferson's relationship with his mother is perhaps the ultimate measure of the inscrutability of his life. From his failure to speak of her as a son might be expected to speak of his mother, from the absence of any evidence of filial affection, his biographers have for the most part come to conclude reluctantly (since filial affection, besides being a natural human instinct, is a highly desired attribute in an American hero) that Jefferson disliked, or more probably hated, his mother. We say "hated" because the feeling of a son for his mother is seldom neutral, merely indifferent. On the other hand, we are by now familiar with Jefferson's impulse to hide or dissemble his deepest feelings. We know from the way he buried all traces of his relationship with his wife after her death that he was most apt to be silent when the pain was greatest. We know that he was an acutely sensitive person and what we might call love-dependent. His silence about his mother, like his silence about his dead wife, *may* have been the consequence of a dependence too profound for him to speak of. From his father he had some psychic distance; to whatever degree he might have felt abandoned by him he could at least mention him, if rather formally. Of his mother he simply could not speak.

What is the evidence? It is admittedly meager. His mother died on March 31, 1776. Her illness and death go further to explain Jefferson's long absence from Congress than any other assumption. In view of his virtual collapse after his wife's death, it does not seem far-fetched to speculate that his mother's death was almost equally devastating to Jefferson. Even if one does not love one's mother—perhaps especially if one does not love one's mother—her death—the death of the one who gave life—strikes at the very center of one's own mortality and thus, if for no other reason, is one of the most agonizing moments of existence. So Jefferson—loving or hating her (or coldly indifferent to her)—waited at Monticello for his mother to die and after her death became ill himself, so that it was a month or more before he was able to travel back to Congress or indeed to pay any serious attention to the revolution that he had so ardently promoted. If in addition, as some biographers have speculated, his illness marked the beginning of those migraine headaches that were to plague him for years, there is a fragment of additional evidence that his mother's death caused him acute suffering. Historians are so addicted to what is written down that their imaginations falter in the face of the blank record. Though millions of Americans suffer from them, migraine headaches are still, in large part, a mystery to the medical profession. But we do know that prominent among their causes, if by no means the exclusive reason for them, are states of extreme emotional stress —"anticipatory anxiety, repressed anger, or hostility and frustration." So many illustrious figures have suffered from them that we might indeed call them the great man's malady.

Jefferson's feelings toward his mother—which are not necessarily the same as his emotions upon her death—seem certain to remain veiled in that mystery which enshrouds so much of this strange man's inner life, but from all we know of him, that her death was a terrible trauma is more likely than that he viewed it with the dispassionate detachment suggested by the brief entry in his agricultural ledger. It is clear beyond question that he could not put down there or elsewhere those few simple, respectful, or affectionate sentences that he might have guessed would have been so reassuring to future biographers.

One thing more might be said. There is, in my opinion correctly, a certain wariness on the part of the general public toward excessive psychologizing about historical figures. Much of such interpretation is what I would call psychological reductionism, explaining many of the crucial actions of an important public figure by reference to a single principle—say, the Oedipus complex of Freudian psychology. There is, on the other hand, what I would call psychological enrichment—that is to say, an awareness of contradictions and complexities of character in the subject that, if they cannot be explained in any conclusive way, should at least be developed as fully as possible.

At any rate the country, meanwhile, was fighting for its life, and Jefferson was a delegate from the state of Virginia to the Continental Congress, a body with the staggering responsibility of managing a war against the greatest military power of the day. The delegates had to function as the legislative, executive, and judicial branches of government. They had to parcel out among themselves the duties of departments of war, navy, and foreign affairs. They had to procure money and supplies, arms, munitions, ships, all the vast paraphernalia of war. But instead of hurrying back to Philadelphia, Jefferson spent almost five months at Monticello, supervising the management of his plantations, laying in a stock of good Madeira wine, making a list of the horses he owned, playing his fiddle, and pushing along improvements to his mansion.

Certainly Jefferson's record of nonattendance was by no means unique. Delegates were often absent, called home by some crisis in their private concerns or by their constituents to fill some state office. Many were not as attentive to their duties as the urgencies of the times would have recommended. A war was going on and going badly for the Americans. The British, abandoning Boston, were about to establish themselves on Long Island, where they threatened New York. Benedict Arnold was in Canada with his tattered and heroic band. Washington struggled with endless problems of recruitment, training, and supply. There was agitation in Congress for a resolution declaring the states independent of the mother country, but a number of states shrank from so conclusive an act. During the spring of 1776 the picture of Achilles sulking in his tent while his fellows carried on the campaign against Troy might have occurred to certain critics. Perhaps it occurred to Jefferson himself. Now that matters had come to the crisis he had foreseen, the man who had been in the forefront of radical patriots went about his business as though no British soldier had set foot in America and no British warships menaced her shores.

Again, because we know so little of the nature of Jefferson's inner life, speculations must rest on the most meager evidence. He had left Congress precipitantly, as though in flight to his sanctuary. An infant daughter and then his mother had died not long after his return. He himself had suffered from an undiagnosed illness that if we accept the headache hypothesis as reasonable must have had psychosomatic origins. Rather than assume that Jefferson was indifferent to his state's and country's demands on him, we might more reasonably suppose that not for the first or last time he could not bring himself to leave his magic mountain. There he could fill his lungs with the restorative air that allowed him finally, like a diver whose blood has been sufficiently aerated, to descend once more into the dark waters of the world below.

5. The Declaration of Independence

Jefferson's return to Congress in mid-May, 1776, could not have been better timed. The most dramatic moment of his life awaited him; had he been a few weeks later he would undoubtedly have missed it. John Adams, who with his cousin Sam and Virginia coadjutor Richard Henry Lee had been laboring mightily to bring about independence, welcomed him back. Tom Paine's *Common Sense* had, for many Americans, cut the last cord that bound the colonies to the mother country. In his remarkable pamphlet, published anonymously, he had completed what Jefferson had begun in his *Summary View,* the destruction of the power of the Crown over the minds of the colonists, and thereby cleared the final obstacle to independence. Writing to Jefferson to recommend two friends for army commissions, John Page exhorted him: "For God's sake declare the Colonies independent at once, and save us from ruin. Adieu—written in haste. . . ." Jefferson needed no urging.

Late in May, in response to the proddings of Jefferson and his Virginia colleagues in Congress, word arrived at Philadelphia from the Virginia convention instructing its delegates to press for independence. At the same time the convention was engaged in the fascinating if arduous task of drafting a constitution for the new state of Virginia, the first former colony to undertake such a task. George Mason had written in the preamble to the bill of rights that prefaced the constitution, "All men

ORDINANCES, &c.

A DECLARATION *of* RIGHTS *made by the reprefentatives of the good people of* Virginia, *affembled in full and free Convention; which rights do pertain to them, and their pofterity, as the bafis and foundation of government.*

1. THAT all men are by nature equally free and independent, and have certain inherent rights, of which, when they enter into a ftate of fociety, they cannot, by any compact, deprive or diveft their pofterity; namely, the enjoyment of life and liberty, with the means of acquiring and poffefling property, and purfuing and obtaining happinefs and fafety.

2. That all power is vefted in, and confequently derived from, the people; that magiftrates are their truftees and fervants, and at all times amenable to them.

3. That government is, or ought to be, inftituted for the common benefit, protection, and fecurity, of the people, nation, or community, of all the various modes and forms of government that is beft, which is capable of producing the greateft degree of happinefs and fafety, and is moft effectually fecured againft the danger of mal-adminiftration; and that whenever any government fhall be found inadequate or contrary to thefe purpofes, a majority of the community hath an indubitable, unalienable, and indefeafible right, to reform, alter, or abolifh it, in fuch manner as fhall be judged moft conducive to the publick weal.

4. That no man, or fet of men, are entitled to exclufive or feparate emoluments or privileges from the community, but in confideration of publick fervices; which, not being defcendible, neither ought the offices of magiftrate, legiflator, or judge, to be hereditary.

George Mason (left) framed the Declaration of Rights (above, the first page), which was adopted unanimously by the Virginia constitutional convention on June 12, 1776. Jefferson, who incorporated many of Mason's thoughts in the Declaration of Independence, praised him posthumously as a Virginian "of the first order of greatness."

are by nature equally free and independent and have certain inherent rights, of which, when they enter into a state of society, they cannot, by any compact, deprive or divest their posterity; namely, the enjoyment of life and liberty, with the means of acquiring and possessing property, and pursuing and obtaining happiness and safety."

Even before he knew that the Virginia convention had launched itself on constitution making, Jefferson realized, belatedly but not surprisingly, that the real action was going on in Richmond, not Philadelphia. He wrote to his friend Thomas Nelson: "Should our Convention propose to establish now a form of government, perhaps it might be agreeable to recall for a short time their delegates. It is a work of the most interesting nature and such as every individual would wish to have his voice in. In truth it is the whole object of the present controversy; for should a bad government be instituted for us in future it had been as well to have accepted at first the bad one offered to us from beyond the water without the risk and expence of contest."

The letter is a poignant one that makes clear Jefferson's own preference. He considered himself above all a political theorist, a prospective maker of constitutions, and now one was being drafted in his own state and he was to have no part in it. In his dismay he went so far as to write to a friend in the convention urging him to try to postpone the drafting of a constitution for Virginia lest it be hastily and improperly done. There should be, he argued, a special convention composed of delegates elected specifically to draft a constitution. He followed up his plea to delay the framing of a constitution with a constitution of his own. Rather oddly, Jefferson's draft opened with a recital of the crimes of George III similar to that of the *Summary View*. Jefferson apparently did not know that John Adams had also prepared a constitution, which he had shown to Richard Henry Lee and which Lee in turn had forwarded to Patrick Henry and George Mason, who were managing affairs in the Virginia convention. Jefferson's draft is interesting primarily for his effort to extend the suffrage. A minimum number of acres—a quarter-acre lot in town or twenty-five acres in the country—would qualify its owner to vote for the lower house of the legislature, and any adult who did not own fifty acres of land would be entitled to receive that much from the public lands owned by the state.

In Jefferson's plan both the senate and the executive were creatures of the house of representatives, both appointed by that body and incapable of being reappointed. The executive was virtually powerless. Again we see Jefferson's bias against executive power, a bias that was apparently rooted in his hostility toward the British Crown. One of the provisions of Jefferson's draft that spoke most eloquently of his own enlightened spirit stated that the western lands claimed by Virginia should be made into new states "on the same fundamental laws contained in this instrument, and shall be free and independent of this colony and of all the world." The phrase "and of all the world" was one of the rhetorical flourishes to which Jefferson was addicted.

He summed up a bill of rights in these words: "No person hereafter coming into this country shall be held within the same in slavery under any pretext whatever. . . . All persons shall have full and free liberty of religious opinion, nor shall any be compelled to frequent or maintain any religious institution. . . . No freeman shall be debarred the use of arms. . . . There shall be no standing army but in time of actual war. . . . Printing presses shall be free, except so far as by commission of private injury cause may be given of private action." Each statement is in a certain sense autobiographical. Jefferson's commitment to democratic principles, and to the destruction thereby of the power of his class in Virginia, was spelled out in his proposed constitution, as were his deism, his uneasiness about slavery, his suspicion of power in all forms. We can only guess at the origin of Jefferson's suspicion of his own class. Doubtless it was related to his efforts to free himself from a life that he felt was both confining and superficial.

Jefferson sent his constitution to Richmond by George Wythe, but when Wythe arrived at the convention he found that the document that had been hammered out primarily by George

Mason was just being reported to the members for debate. It was too late to consider Jefferson's draft, but interestingly enough Mason's version was similar, especially in its limitations on the powers of the chief executive. In Mason's version, perhaps influenced by John Adams's, both houses were elected by the people, though the right of suffrage was to "remain as exercised at present." Both houses in turn chose the governor by joint ballot. While the powers of the governor were not as sharply limited as they had been in Jefferson's draft, he was advised by a privy council, and most powers of appointment were lodged in the legislature, commonly by a joint ballot of both houses. All laws were to originate in the house of representatives; they would then be approved or rejected by the senate or amended with the consent of the house. The governor could serve three consecutive one-year terms, but he was not thereafter eligible for re-election until a three-year period had passed.

That Jefferson's concentration of power in the lower house was not dictated entirely by faith in the wisdom of the people is indicated by his defense of the election of the senate and chief executive by the house of representatives, as expressed in a letter to Edmund Pendleton: "I had two things in view," he wrote, "to get the wisest men chosen, & to make them perfectly independent when chosen. I have ever observed that a choice by the people themselves is not generally distinguished for its wisdom. This first secretion from them is usually crude & heterogeneous. But give to those so chosen by the people a second choice themselves, & they generally will chuse wise men." It was a notion rather at variance with Jefferson's frequently avowed confidence in the wisdom of the people.

Meanwhile matters in Congress were moving, slowly but surely, to their denouement. On June 7 Richard Henry Lee proposed that "these United Colonies are, and of right ought to be, free and independent States, that they are absolved from all allegiance to the British Crown, and that all political connection between them and the State of Great Britain is, and ought to be, totally dissolved." While the debate on Lee's resolutions was going on, the advocates of independence succeeded in having a committee appointed to prepare a statement or declaration to accompany a formal resolution of independence. The committee, appointed on June 11, was made up of Roger Sherman, Robert Livingston, John Adams, Benjamin Franklin, and Jefferson. Jefferson was the youngest and least experienced member. Franklin was the best known as a writer, scientist, and patriot leader. Adams stood next in reputation as a politician and essayist. Roger Sherman, a delegate from Connecticut, was an able man but not renowned for his gifts as an expositor of the colonial cause. Robert Livingston was on the committee primarily to represent the more conservative delegates.

Jefferson's biographers have maintained that the choice of their subject to write the famous document was, in a manner of speaking, inevitable. Actually Jefferson came alarmingly close to missing the assignment entirely. He arrived in Philadelphia at very nearly the last moment to be eligible for election to the committee, since he needed a week or so to establish himself among his fellow delegates after an absence of almost five months. Once there, he did his best to persuade the Virginia convention to summon him home to work on the constitution of his native state, a task that seemed far more important to him than anything he might accomplish in Philadelphia. Assuming that the committee to draft a general statement to accompany the resolution on independence had to contain a member of the Virginia delegation, George Wythe, dean of the Virginia bar and a highly respected member of Congress, was the most likely candidate; but Wythe, who had labored through the long, tedious months that Jefferson spent at Monticello, had taken advantage of Jefferson's arrival to take a respite from his labors.

Another factor in Jefferson's appointment was that Richard Henry Lee, in the absence of Wythe Jefferson's principal rival for the committee membership, was intensely disliked by several members of the Virginia delegation. Equally important, his talents for political management were badly needed to round up votes for the resolution on independence. As Jefferson himself said, what was required in drafting a declaration was not bold new ideas but the articulation of generally accepted principles

The Com: of the whole Congress to whom was reported the resolution an ~~upon~~ the <u>Declaration</u> respecting independence. — 17

Resolved   That these ^{united} colonies are and of right

ought to be free and independant states;

that they are absolved from all allegiance

to the british crown and that all politicial

connection between them and the state of

great Britain is and ought to be totally

dissolved

that could be relied on to evoke a favorable response among all those groups and individuals disposed to support the American cause.

Even Jefferson's appointment to the committee did not by any means assure his designation as author of the statement. As we have noted, he was outranked, so to speak, by both Franklin and Adams. In any competition for the right to compose the statement, those two could claim precedence. Thus, one inevitably asks, why did Franklin and Adams, individuals with substantial egos and acknowledged forensic skills, allow their junior colleague to be the author of one of the most important documents in all history and thereby claim a secure place among the immortals? The answer is simple: no one had any notion that the declaration accompanying the resolution of independence would become such a historic document. Such men as John Adams and Richard Henry Lee were so preoccupied with preparing the resolution itself and with persuading reluctant delegates to vote for it and thus establish independence that they gave comparatively little thought to the rationale that would accompany it. The statement or declaration was, after all, only the latest in a series of petitions, complaints, and declarations that had flowed from the colonies since the days of the Stamp Act Congress without attracting any particular attention on either side of the Atlantic. There was no reason to believe that the latest one would be substantially weightier.

Franklin was inclined to be rather lazy and self-indulgent. He was busy operating as the resident sage of Philadelphia, entertaining delegates at his home and making wise and pithy observations on a wide variety of matters. Adams, always harassed and overworked (his New England conscience required it), was busy indoors and out with Sam Adams and Richard Henry Lee, buttonholing waffling delegates and trying to firm them up for independence. He had no time to give to labors of the pen; he was about more important business. So, assuming that any reasonably literate and eloquent statement of the American cause would have achieved a substantial degree of fame, John Adams handed that fame to his Virginia friend with hardly a thought for the consequences. Adams would hardly have been human if he had not had second thoughts when the declaration eclipsed the resolution as the full moon the brightest of the stars. As he told the story many years later, the committee of five met and decided on the basic form of the declaration. Jefferson and Adams (according to Adams) were then appointed a subcommittee to do the actual drafting. When they met, Jefferson, Adams wrote, "proposed to me to make the draught, I said I will not; You shall do it. Oh no! Why will you not? You ought to do it. I will not. Why? Reasons enough. What can be your reasons. Reason 1st. You are a Virginian and a Virginian ought to appear at the head of this business. Reason 2nd. I am obnoxious, suspected and unpopular; you are very much otherwise. Reason 3rd. You can write ten times better than I can. 'Well,' said Jefferson, 'if you are decided I will do as well as I can.' Very well, when you have drawn it up we will have a meeting." The passage is vintage Adams. The only problem is that Jefferson had a very different recollection. The committee had "unanimously pressed on myself alone to undertake the draught. I consented; I drew it. . . ."

The appearance of self-abnegation was almost as important to John Adams as fame. If he had passed up the fame, he could at least make it appear that he had done so in a remarkable gesture of modesty and self-sacrifice designed to promote harmony and good feeling. Hence the probably imaginary subcommittee. Which is not to accuse Adams of deliberate duplicity but only of a selective and corrective memory, a very common human quality. A similar conversation may well have taken place between the two friends in a different context. The point remains: Jefferson was given the task not primarily because the declaration was considered of such overriding importance but precisely because, compared to the resolution itself, it was perceived to be a relatively routine assignment. So what Jefferson had in a sense done his best to avoid by staying away from Congress until the last possible moment and, once there, by seeking to escape to the far more attractive enterprise at Richmond, overtook him. It was almost as though one of his beloved

Greek Fates had ordained that he should be wafted to Olympus in spite of himself. The Greeks had no place in their cosmology for "luck"; the gods managed all human affairs.

Whatever the combination of events and forces that thrust one of history's premier writing assignments on the tall sandy-haired Virginian, the most notable thing is that he was up to it. What Jefferson did, in essence, was to take George Mason's preamble to the Virginia Bill of Rights (which in turn was part of the constitution of that state in the process of being adopted by the convention at Richmond) and add to it a long list of the villainies (many of them imaginary) of George III. The part of the declaration most of us know is the first four sentences, beginning with, "When in the Course of human events. . ." and ending, "whenever any Form of Government becomes destructive of these ends, it is the right of the People to alter or abolish it, and to institute new government, laying its foundation on such principles, and organizing its powers in such form, as to them shall seem most likely to effect their Safety and Happiness."

After some prudential reflections on reserving such action as a last resort, Jefferson wrote, "The history of the present King of Great Britain is a history of repeated injuries and usurpations, all having in direct object the establishment of an absolute Tyranny over these States." Then followed a list of twenty-seven specific acts attributed to the malevolence of the king. Nowhere is there any direct mention of Parliament, previously described as the agent of all colonial woes. Moreover, in Jefferson's original draft almost a fourth of what we might call the "indictment section" was given over to an extensive attack on the king for all the evils of slavery. Reading the bitter and intemperate accusations on the matter of slavery, it is difficult not to feel that they reflected Jefferson's profound revulsion for the slave trade—which had been the basis of his father-in-law's fortune and of which he had been an indirect beneficiary through his wife's estate—and his own guilt at his involvement in a system he abhorred but from which he could not escape. Perhaps he was trying, by using the king of England as a scapegoat, to exorcise his own personal demons. The point worthy of comment is that Jefferson had been, as we have seen in his *Summary View,* the first colonial publicist to indict the king directly. At every subsequent opportunity he had repeated and amplified his charges. Paine, in *Common Sense,* had directed his fire primarily against the office rather than the person of the king. Now Jefferson returned to the attack on George III. If it was bad logic and worse history, it was good politics.

To direct hostility and resentment against a single figure is certainly far easier than to attack a system—a group of largely anonymous ministers or a body as large and amorphous as a parliament. But Jefferson's fury with King George seems to lie deeper than mere strategy. One senses in it a degree of animus more than political, something near the edges of pathology. Be that as it may, the delegates when they came to review Jefferson's initial draft cut out most of the references to the king's responsibility for slavery—that was a bit too thick. Enough remained, however, to make poor George a mythical monster, bloody-minded enough to rouse the ire of any loyal American. And that was, after all, the basic intention.

Of course the most famous and important words in the declaration are those beginning, "We hold these truths to be self-evident, that all men are created equal, that they are endowed by their Creator with certain unalienable rights, that among these are Life, Liberty and the pursuit of Happiness." George Mason had stated that "all men are by nature equally free and independent" and had described their inherent rights as "the enjoyment of life and liberty, with the means of acquiring and possessing property, and pursuing and obtaining happiness and safety." Nor were the words original with Mason. They were to be found in the *Second Treatise on Government* by the great English political philosopher John Locke.

Jefferson in effect did a skillful editing job on Mason's very recently written preamble. What used to be called rhetoric is a mysterious study. How is it that a word or two excised can transform a flabby sentence into a resonant, sinewy one? Jefferson was above all a stylist. A stylist is not necessarily a good writer in any conventional sense. He is simply a memorable writer. His thought may be as blurred as an unfocused photo or as muddy as the Mississippi, but if he has that indescribable (and unteachable) flair, his words will reverberate like a gong or an Aeolian harp. The modern philosopher Alfred North Whitehead wrote, "Style is the ultimate morality of mind." This somewhat inscrutable sentence seems to say that style is a strange fusion of the total experience of the individual, his or her *character*, and the power to express that totality through particular combinations of words. We speak typically of an artist's "style" as though it is his character projected through the visible world. Or, with a writer, through the written word. Whatever else about Thomas Jefferson may be obscure or debatable, it seems clear beyond cavil that he was a master stylist. I believe that his prose style was part and parcel of the style he displayed on his cherished fiddle, in his architectural drawings, and in the bricks and mortar of Monticello. At its best it was a style disarmingly simple and lucid, which in fact concealed as much as it revealed. At its worst it lapsed into angry ranting, but this latter deficiency grew increasingly rare. The declaration contains both elements in abundance. It is a schoolboy's task to pick holes in the author's reasoning—in, for example, his "self-evident" propositions or in the notion of "pursuing happiness"—but when the dissection and analysis are over the document remains what it has been from the first, a work of great power and eloquence that has moved the hearts of innumerable people in all ages and all parts of the world. The remarkable gifts of the stylist plainly triumphed over the failings of the logician.

Besides editorial tightening, Jefferson made a change in George Mason's litany of rights that seems to have been dictated by more than stylistic considerations. He omitted "property" as one of man's "unalienable rights." He never explained his reasons directly, so we must gather them by implication. Certainly there are, scattered through Jefferson's writings, many statements that indicate a profound uneasiness about the widely observed human tendency to use accumulations of property to limit and constrict the lives of those with less property or none at all. Jefferson was a close reader of James Harrington, the author of *Utopia,* who pointed out the relation between property and power. Property in fact was power. Power was always subject to abuse; it followed that the matter of property-power had to be approached with great circumspection. Inclusion of the right to possess property as one of the three most precious human rights might be taken by those disposed to use undue accumulations of property to exploit others as sanctioning such exploitation. While Jefferson, as we have noted, still accepted ownership of property as the basis of the suffrage, he wished to give property to those who did not own any and shrank from giving it equal standing with life and liberty. Having banished "property," Jefferson perhaps paused over "happiness" as an appropriate substitute rather than, as it had been with Mason, a kind of agreeable afterthought, a pleasant addition to the Lockean trinity—life, liberty, property. Jefferson tells us no more about the rational processes by which he arrived at the phrase "pursuit of happiness" than about his motives in dropping "property." Perhaps it is just as well. There may have been no rational processes; the substitution may have been simply an inspiration. Stylists clearly have to depend far more on the latter than the former.

Jefferson's original draft was apparently read by Adams and Franklin before it was reviewed by the committee as a whole. With a number of corrections and emendations it was then presented to Congress on June 28. Since the resolution of independence had not yet been passed, the declaration was premature and was "laid on the table" until that more urgent task had been accomplished. Finally, on July 2, with one crucial, mud-spattered vote—that of Caesar Rodney of Delaware, who arrived in the nick of time after an all-night ride—and with certain delegates whose consciences would not let them vote for independence remaining helpfully at home, as well as a good deal of additional arm twisting here and there, a majority of the delegates of each state, New York abstaining, voted for the resolution declaring the United States independent of Great Britain. John Adams wrote the next day to his wife: "Yesterday, the greatest question was decided, which ever was debated in America, and a greater, perhaps, never was nor will be decided among men. You will see, in a few days, a Declaration setting forth the causes which have impelled us to this mighty revolution, and the reasons which will justify it in the sight of God and man." (If Jefferson was the enunciator of general Revolutionary principles, John Adams was without rival as a trenchant commentator on the events of that Revolution.)

Congress, having settled the matter of independence once for all, turned its attention to the tabled declaration. For the better part of three days—July 2, 3, and 4—they picked away at Jefferson's handiwork (with the emendations of the committee of five). It was at this point that the greater part of Jefferson's indictment of George III for black slavery was excised. Significantly the delegates inserted several references to God and Divine Providence that were not in the draft copy. Although Jefferson suffered through what doubtless seemed to him mutilations of his writings without recorded protest, the draft, on the whole, profited from the delegates' collective editing. By the evening of July 4 it had taken on its final form. Congress ordered that a handsome copy be prepared for the signatures of the delegates and arranged for the printing and distribution of the text to the public. It was read in the State House yard on July 8 by John Nixon to the cheers of a large and enthusiastic crowd, and subsequently in every colony when copies of it arrived, independence and the declaration's proclamation of it were celebrated with patriotic ceremonies.

How much Jefferson resented the changes made by Congress in his declaration is quite strikingly indicated by the care he took to circulate to his closest friends copies of his draft along with the final declaration, so that they might observe how badly his prose had been damaged. He sent a set to Richard Henry Lee with a note asking him to "judge whether it is the better or worse for the critics," and Lee replied reassuringly, "I wish sincerely as well for the honor of Congress, as for that of the States, that the Manuscript had not been mangled as it is. It is wonderful [strange], and passing pitiful, that the rage of change should be

John Trumbull portrayed the drafting committee for the declaration (standing, from left to
right: John Adams, Roger Sherman, Robert
Livingston, Jefferson, and Benjamin Franklin)
presenting their work to John Hancock, president of the Continental Congress. Trumbull
began his work on this painting while in Paris
visiting Jefferson, who posed for him and gave
advice on other preliminary sketches.

so unhappily applied. However the *Thing* is in its nature so good, that no Cookery can spoil the Dish for the palates of Freemen.''

That he so resented the changes the delegates made in his manuscript is indicative of Jefferson's almost pathological sensitivity. Other documents of his drafting had suffered similar fates in the past, but he had not grown any more philosophical in consequence. Anyone who drafts a public paper must expect to have it modified by those who have commissioned it. The fact was that Jefferson's work was subjected to relatively mild treatment. Given the contentious and busybody nature of groups such as Congress, Jefferson had reason to be grateful that he had come off so well.

And when one considers that few figures in history have gotten so vast a return on so modest an investment of time, Jefferson had, with every passing year, more reason to be grateful for the opportunity. If he had done nothing else—died of consumption, drowned crossing the Rappahannock, or simply retired to Monticello—his drafting of the declaration, an accident that happened to him when he was barely thirty-three years old, would have secured him perpetual renown. He did, for a fact, seem favored by the gods. Compare, for example, the fate of George Mason, to whom Jefferson was so clearly beholden for the substance of the declaration. By and large, only professional historians and Virginians know of this rather obscure if remarkably gifted ''father,'' whose strictures on slavery, uttered eleven years later in the Constitutional Convention, constitute one of the most eloquent passages in all antislavery literature. Certainly the Declaration of Independence is stylistically superior to Mason's document, but the relative difference in fame of the two papers rests on quite other grounds. The most passionate and eloquent oration delivered on July 4 in a remote town will never emerge as a great historic utterance. History must conspire with the orator; the great words must illuminate a great occasion; they must intersect the currents of world history. Had fate assigned the writing of the Declaration of Independence to Mason and the preamble of the Virginia Bill of Rights to Jefferson, the differences in style would not have barred Mason's claim to fame or lifted Jefferson's sentences out of the relative obscurity suffered by Mason's. Such reflections need not lessen our admiration for the artistry of Jefferson's accomplishment. If you say "American Revolution" to the proverbial man or woman in the street, he or she is apt to think first of Washington and Jefferson. When one compares Washington's eight-year labor as commander in chief of the Continental armies under the most trying and arduous conditions imaginable with Jefferson's brief stint in composing the declaration, one is reminded once again of the ironies in which history abounds. That Muse clearly has no interest in any kind of evenhanded justice. Of course Jefferson's reputation does not rest exclusively on his authorship of the declaration (nor does Washington's on his role as general), but it is unquestionably the foundation stone and the essence of his fame.

Having been in Congress just long enough to assure himself of immortal glory, Jefferson was impatient to be back in Richmond, where it seemed to him the really interesting and important tasks lay—such as revising the laws of the commonwealth in the spirit of the Revolution—and where his sanctuary and sanitarium at Monticello lay within a day and a half's ride. He thus undertook a campaign to be relieved as a delegate to Congress and returned to the Virginia legislature. But again, predictably, even while pleading to be directed to return, he was upset at the news that among the delegates re-elected to Congress he had run fourth out of five.

Also, he was demoralized by Martha's failure to reply to the stream of letters he dispatched to Monticello. Thus before July was over, without waiting to hear whether he had been re-elected or replaced on the Virginia delegation, he wrote to Edmund Pendleton resigning from Congress and asking that he be replaced before the end of the year. A few days later he decided he could not wait. He made plans to return to Monticello immediately. However, since the only other Virginia delegate was Carter Braxton, who felt that he had served his turn and was himself planning to return home, Jefferson's departure would have left Virginia, the largest and most influential state besides Massachusetts, without representation in Congress. He thus remained, an unwilling prisoner, firing off desperate appeals to be relieved. To Richard Henry Lee, who had slipped away for a few weeks after months of yeoman service in Congress, he wrote imploringly, "For god's sake, for your country's sake, and for my sake, come. I receive by every post such accounts of the state of Mrs. Jefferson's health that it will be impossible for me to disappoint her expectation of seeing me at the time I have promised, which supposed my leaving this place on the 11th of next month [August]. I pray you to come. I am under a sacred obligation to go home."

There seems more than an ordinary note of desperation in Jefferson's letter. Compared with most of his fellow delegates he had served very briefly. Certainly his concern for Martha's health was a legitimate reason to wish to be home. But he had already used it as an excuse for decamping at the end of December, 1775, when the services of every delegate were desperately needed in Congress. Then as now he had complained bitterly at his wife's failure to write. Apparently she was not sick enough or lonely enough to urge him to hurry home. And when he did return she was not too sick to become pregnant soon thereafter. Again it is hard not to believe that Jefferson was the patient, and that his only medicine was Monticello.

6. Rusticating

By the end of August Jefferson was on his way home, explaining his hurried departure by his conviction that "our legislation under the regal government had many very vicious points which urgently required reformation, and I thought I could be of more use in forwarding that work." Well, perhaps, but Virginia had just drafted a constitution and was not likely to revise it at Jefferson's behest. Furthermore, for the author of the Declaration of Independence to profess to believe that the affairs of Virginia, still far removed from the active scenes of war, were more important than the country's desperate struggle for survival seems eccentric, to say the least.

Before he left Philadelphia, Jefferson gave John Hancock money that had been collected in Virginia for the poor of Boston and bought some new strings for his fiddle. He was home by September 9. He certainly did not find Martha seriously indisposed. She was able to accompany him a month later on October 6 when he traveled to Williamsburg for the opening of the fall session of the Virginia assembly, which was for the time being back in its familiar quarters. At Williamsburg word awaited him that he had been appointed by Congress as a commissioner to France with Benjamin Franklin and Silas Deane. The task of the commissioners was a delicate and important one—to negotiate an alliance with France against England. The appointment was reinforced by a letter from Richard Henry Lee, who had responded to Jefferson's frantic importunings to return to Congress so that he could go back to Monticello. "In my judgement," Lee wrote, "the most eminent services that the greatest of her sons can do America, will not more essentially serve her and honor themselves, than a successful negotiation with France. With this country, every thing depends upon it. . . ."

For three days Jefferson procrastinated and then declined, writing to John Hancock that "circumstances very peculiar to the situation of my family compel me to ask leave to decline a service so honorable and at the same time so important to the American cause."

Lee, who had been the promoter of Jefferson's appointment, clearly felt let down. "I heared with much regret that you declined both the voyage and your seat in Congress," he wrote. "No Man feels more deeply than I do, the love of, and the loss of, private enjoyments; but let attention to these be universal, and we are gone, beyond redemption lost in the deep perdition of slavery." If Jefferson was, as we have every reason to believe, a man of strict conscience with a strong sense of obligation, we must imagine that his failure to do what some of his closest friends and allies thought his duty must have cost him much anguish. Again one is tempted to feel that he dared not depart so far from his remedy—Monticello. If Jefferson believed that his own sanity was ultimately at issue, he could much more readily have made a decision that was difficult at best.

Again obscurity. Self-indulgence or self-preservation? In any event, he threw himself ardently into a project for establishing courts and revising the archaic, sometimes feudal, laws of his home state. The particular objects of Jefferson's reforming zeal were the Virginia laws, more honored in the breach than the observance, involving so-called entail and primogeniture. Entail allowed property owners to specify that their lands could not be divided among heirs but must remain intact. Primogeniture specified that where a property owner died intestate—without a will —his land would pass to his oldest male heir. Jefferson's own ideas about land tenure were radical for his day. His writings contain numerous statements on the general theme that land is the common property of society and should not be monopolized by any group of individuals. The right to labor "in the earth" was to Jefferson one of the sacred rights of all members of a society. He believed that if land was appropriated for commercial or industrial purposes, suitable work must be found for those displaced. Otherwise, he wrote, "the fundamental right to labor the earth returns to the unemployed."

Indeed, we might pause here to consider for a moment Jefferson's attitude toward the land. He had what we might call, for want of a better term, a romantic mystique concerning the land. It was, like music and architecture, one of his major obsessions. "The small landholders are the most precious part of a state," he wrote. And one of his most famous aphorisms reads: "Those who labour in the earth are the chosen people of God, if ever He had a chosen people." He could not stress sufficiently that "farmers whose interests are entirely agricultural . . . are the true representatives of the great American interest, and alone are to be relied on for expressing the proper American sentiments." Such statements fell sweetly on the ears of a people overwhelmingly agricultural, in a country where the few existing "large" cities numbered less than thirty thousand inhabitants each, small towns by modern standards. So Jefferson became the patron saint of the farmer, who in fact seldom corresponded very closely to Jefferson's idealized Virginia yeoman. Even more, Jefferson became a philosophical resource for the theoreticians and exalters of rural America and thereby helped to feed the paranoia felt by the country people toward the burgeoning cities, a paranoia that increased decade by decade as the farm and town lost ground to the metropolis.

To the degree that he romanticized the farmer and the land, Jefferson feared the European immigrant, whom Tom Paine, his intellectual ally on so many issues, summoned to America, "an asylum for mankind." Jefferson feared that immigrants from the teeming, corrupt cities of the Old World would contaminate the spirit of the new, bringing with them the servile and debased habits acquired in their native lands. Thus we might say that he was also the spiritual father of nativism, that mean and meager hostility to aliens that has from time to time asserted itself in the most unattractive kind of racism. Jefferson's suspicion of the immigrant, which if anything grew over the years, was undoubtedly related to if not rooted in his conviction that the purest vein of liberty and equality revealed in history was that enjoyed by the ancient Anglo-Saxons of Britain before they were corrupted by a far earlier invasion of immigrants, the Normans, with their authoritarian practices and institutions.

We certainly cannot give Jefferson all the credit (or blame) for the fact that Americans clung to the image of their rural purity long after it had ceased to correspond to the realities of a predominantly urbanized society. Perhaps he did no more than record the primary schizophrenia of the American people —a rural ethic in an industrial society. But things come back to us. What in Jefferson had come to seem archaic (or merely quaint)—the celebration of the farmer as pure and incorruptible —as we grew to be the industrial giant of the world has lately reasserted itself. The farms have become factories while the cities have become the jungles that the popular imagination once held them to be. We recently took for granted that our destiny was to be a network of huge metropolises fed by agricultural corporations. These farming corporations rivaled the greatest industrial empires, indeed were often owned by those same industrial empires, so that the agriculture Jefferson so loved and the industry he feared have finally merged in a strange new creation that suggests nothing so much as the evil monster of a fairy tale destroying the land and polluting its bounty. Echoes of Jefferson's eloquent phrases ring once more in our ears. Can a society in which ninety-five per cent of the people for all practical purposes are urban-based and only five per cent are engaged in agriculture (and the vast majority of those in what we have come to call agribusiness) be a sound and healthy society?

We recall that as recently as forty years ago twenty-five per cent of the population was engaged in farming, and we wonder if, predominantly urban and industrial as we are possibly fated to be, there may not be some critical minimum of small family farms below which we, for our own health as a society, dare not drop. Everywhere around the country groups are forming to press the issue of land reform, arguing for a more humane and just distribution of the land and celebrating the beauty and joy of its cultivation much as Jefferson did, indeed, invoking him, since we all need ancestors. A recent publication by the National Coalition for Land Reform entitled *The People's Land* opens with Jefferson's famous letter to James Madison dated October 28, 1785, in which he "makes the case for distributing the land to those who wish to till it." So we may expect to hear Jefferson quoted often in the days to come as we try to redress the balance between the cities that he feared and the land he loved.

While still in Congress, Jefferson had described the task he wished to undertake in revising the Virginia laws: "Our whole code must be reviewed, adapted to our republican form of government; and, now that we had no negatives of Councils, Governors, and Kings to restrain us from doing right, that it should be corrected, in all its parts, with a single eye to reason and the good of those for whose government it was framed." It was certainly a worthy undertaking, but one wonders if it had the urgency that Jefferson attributed to it and whether its principal attraction was not that it could be done at Monticello in the seclusion of his study.

The colony's criminal code specified capital punishment for a number of relatively minor offenses, but most of these were so out of keeping with the spirit of the times that they had become a dead letter. Jefferson excised them, leaving death by hanging for murder and treason (dueling was included under the heading of murder). Castration was prescribed for rape and buggery, and the "pretended arts of witchcraft, conjuration, enchantment, or sorcery, or by pretended prophecies, shall be punished by ducking and whipping, at the discretion of a jury, not exceeding fifteen stripes," a puzzling stipulation for an enlightened lawmaker. Most other crimes were to be punished by differing periods of labor on public projects. Negro slaves convicted of any criminal act were to be sold into slavery in other

I. Crimes whose punishment extends to **Life.**

1. High treason. Death by hanging ~~...~~
   Forfeiture of lands & goods to Commw.

2. Petty Treason. Death by hanging
   Dissection.
   Forfeit ~~of half lands goods~~ to ~~paved~~
   -sntatives of person killed

3. Murder. 1. by poyson. Death by poyson.
   Forfeit.ᵉ of one half as before.

   2. in Duel. Death by hanging
   gibbeting, if the challenger.
   Forfeit.ᵉ of one half as before us.
   - less the challeng.ᵈ pᵗ then to
   Commw.

   3. any other way. Death by hanging
   Forfeit.ᵉ of half as before.

4. Manslaur. 2ᵈ offence is murder.
   ~~labor 7 years.~~
   ~~Forfeit one half as before.~~

II. Crimes whose punishment goes to **Limb.**

1. Rape. ⎫
   ~~Polygamy⎬~~ } Castration.
2. Sodomy. ⎭

3. Maiming ⎫ } Retaleation.
4. Disfiguring ⎬ } forfeiture of half to sufferer.

III. Crimes punisheable by **Labor &c.**

1. Manslaur. 1ˢᵗ offence. Labor VII years.
   Forfeit.ᵉ half as before.

2. Counterfeiting. Labor VI. years.
   Forfeit whole to Commw.

3. Arson. ⎫ Labor V. years.
4. ~~Asportation of vessels~~ ⎬ Reparation threfold

5. Robbery ⎫ Labor IV. years
6. Burglary ⎬ Reparation. double.

7. Housebreaking. ⎫ Labor III years
8. Horse-stealing ⎬ Reparation.

9. Grand Larceny. Labor II. years
10. Reparation
    ~~...~~ pillory ½ an hour.

10. Petty Larceny. Labor I. year.
    Reparation
    ~~...~~ pillory ¼ of an ho...

11. Witchcraft &c. Ducking
    15. stripes.

12. Excusable homicide. ~~...~~
    nothing.

13. Suicide. nothing

0

From 1776 to 1779 Jefferson headed a committee to revise the laws in Virginia. The criminal code seemed unjustly harsh (above, a public punishment). Jefferson substituted "life" and "limb" penalties for more than twenty felonies that had been subject to the death penalty (left, his draft). The code was defeated in 1786 because, James Madison explained, Virginians preferred "our old bloody code."

countries, while blacks who bought their freedom or were eman-
cipated by their masters were required to leave the state within
a stated time. A white woman with a mulatto child was also
required to leave or become a slave herself.

The two bills from his pen by which Jefferson placed the
greatest store were those for "establishing religious freedom"
and for "the more general diffusion of knowledge." It was not
surprising that he should espouse freedom *from* religion as well
as freedom *of* religion for his fellow countrymen. His faith in
reason when enlightened by education was a fundamental tenet
that became, along with his romantic feeling for the land, a basic
article of the American faith.

In his *Notes on Virginia,* written for the instruction of the
French plenipotentiary to Congress, Jefferson spelled out his
religious views in some detail. "The error seems not sufficiently
eradicated that the operations of the mind, as well as the acts of
the body, are subject to the coercion of the laws. But our rulers
can have authority over such natural rights, only as we have
submitted to them. The rights of conscience we never submitted, we could not submit. We are answerable for them to our
God. The legitimate powers of government extend to such acts
only as are injurious to others. But it does me no injury for my
neighbor to say there are twenty gods, or no god. It neither picks
my pocket or breaks my leg. . . . Reason and free inquiry are the
only effectual agents against error. . . . Had not the Roman
government permitted free inquiry, christianity could never
have been introduced. Had not free inquiry been indulged, at
the aera of the reformation, the corruptions of christianity could
not have been purged away. If it be restrained now, the present
corruptions will be protected, and new ones encouraged. . . . It
is error alone which needs the support of government. Truth
can stand by itself."

The accuracy of some of Jefferson's statements might be
questioned—for instance, the assertion that "truth has only
flourished where free inquiry was permitted." Certainly new
ideas and new religions have often thrived in the face of the most
determined persecution. Perhaps it would be more accurate to

say that persecution cannot stifle ideas, whether "true" or not, "whose time has come." It would be more difficult to quarrel with the proposition that "the legitimate powers of government extend to such acts only as are injurious to others," although we are just beginning to accept that principle two hundred years after Jefferson stated it.

But again, such arguments are more or less beside the point, which is that Jefferson had a remarkable gift for expressing the best hopes and aspirations of his age, many of which became in time those of his country. He displayed that gift strikingly in his preamble to his Bill for Establishing Religious Freedom. It is one of those inspired utterances that seize on a part of our consciousness and, from having been simply part of a program of reform, become a cherished and inviolable principle. "Well aware," Jefferson wrote, "that the opinions and belief of men depend not on their own will, but follow involuntarily the evidence proposed to their minds; that Almighty God hath created the mind free, and manifested his supreme will that free it shall remain by making it altogether insusceptible of restraint; that all attempts to influence it by temporal punishments, or burthens, or by civil incapacitations, tend only to beget habits of hypocrisy and meanness, and are a departure from the plan of the holy author of our religion. . . . That to compel a man to furnish contributions of money for the propagation of opinions which he disbelieves and abhors, is sinful and tyrannical; that even the forcing him to support this or that teacher of his own religious persuasion, is depriving him of the comfortable liberty of giving his contributions to the particular pastor whose morals he would make his pattern . . . that our civil rights have no dependance on our religious opinions, any more than our opinions in physics or geometry; that therefore the proscribing any citizen as unworthy the public confidence by laying upon him an incapacity of being called to offices of trust and emolument, unless he profess or renounce this or that religious opinion, is depriving him injuriously of those privileges and advantages to which, in common with his fellow citizens, he has a natural right . . . that the opinions of men are not the object of civil government, nor under its jurisdiction . . . that truth is great and will prevail if left to herself; that she is the proper and sufficient antagonist to error, and has nothing to fear from the conflict unless by human interposition disarmed of her natural weapons, free argument and debate. . . ."

It is probably not too much to say that the matter of religious freedom has never been more eloquently expressed. The passage, and particularly certain sentences in it, have been repeated thousands of times. If one might question whether truth pursued in untrammeled freedom always triumphs over falsehood, the vast majority of Americans accept, at least in theory if not always in practice, the notion that right thought cannot be coerced and that it is never the function of the state to do more than protect the right of all religious groups to worship as they please. Indeed it is worth noting that our courts have probably gone further in the direction of the principles laid down by Jefferson in the last twenty-five years than in the preceding hundred and seventy.

The bill to which the words just quoted were a preface had slow going in the Virginia legislature, which was perhaps the greatest tribute to the degree that it was in advance of the thinking of the day. Not until 1786 was it finally guided through both houses by Jefferson's disciple, James Madison. The education bill had rougher going. Thus Jefferson, having cast his lot with the Virginia assembly rather than with Congress, had a mixed success in the session of 1776. His bill to abolish entails was passed and the work of revising the Virginia laws got an impressive start, but his bills on religion and education were rejected. It was again a measure of Jefferson's preference of the theoretical to the practical that he plunged with such passion into issues not directly connected with securing American independence.

When the session of the assembly ended, Jefferson hurried back to Monticello, where Martha was pregnant. There, not for the last time, he paid the price of locating on a hilltop. His wells and cisterns ran dry and water had to be hauled up the hill from the river. He immersed himself in the details of running his plantations. Congress, driven out of Philadelphia by the British, was lodged resentfully in Baltimore, "a boggy hole" as one delegate called it. American arms had a striking success at Trenton just before the turn of the year, but there had been bitter setbacks in the loss of Forts Lee and Washington on the Hudson, and Washington's dwindling and chilblained army was in desperate straits before the spectacular raid on Trenton restored American morale.

The spring session of the Virginia assembly was scheduled to begin on May 5, 1777. Jefferson arrived in Williamsburg a day or so later and nominated George Wythe as speaker. Having performed one or two other minor chores, he returned to Monticello after barely two weeks' attendance. Once more Jefferson had evaded what might not unreasonably be considered his duty to his state and country. Even John Adams wrote him with an implicit rebuke: "We want your Industry and Abilities here extreamly. . . . Your Country is not yet, quite secure enough, to excuse your Retreat to the Delights of domestic Life. Yet, for the Soul of me, when I attend to my own Feelings, I cannot blame you." It is clear, nonetheless, that he did, and so did many of Jefferson's compatriots. But Jefferson's sanity lay at Monticello, and that was the one argument he was unable to advance for his remissness.

On May 28 Martha gave birth to a son, but the child died two weeks later. When the fall session of the assembly convened early in November, Jefferson took his seat with the other members. His principal contribution at this session was a bill sequestering all property in Virginia belonging to British subjects while also allowing Virginia debtors of English merchants to pay off their indebtedness with greatly depreciated state money. When the bill passed, Jefferson was among those who discharged their debts at a fraction of their real value by taking advantage of its provisions. Two years later the assembly had second thoughts about this financial sleight of hand and repealed the act. This turnabout, which was due to the promptings of both conscience and good policy, greatly complicated Jefferson's own financial situation and contributed to the burden of debt from which he never succeeded in disentangling himself.

Back at Monticello at the end of the session, he threw himself into extensions of and additions to the house. He ordered three stone columns for the front portico and 100,000 more bricks. When he returned to Williamsburg for the spring session of the assembly in 1778, he was nominated for speaker but was defeated by Benjamin Harrison. The session was uneventful, and by July Jefferson was back at Monticello keeping a careful eye on his new fruit trees and pursuing his researches in law and constitutional theory. He carried on his usual extensive correspondence, writing a lyrical letter to an Italian freethinker, Giovanni Fabbroni. "Tho' much of my time is employed in the councils of America, I have yet a little leisure to indulge my fondness for philosophical studies," he wrote. What he most envied the Italians was their music. "This is the favorite passion of my soul, & fortune has cast my lot in a country where it is in a state of deplorable barbarism." His own resources were too modest to do what he would wish—employ "a domestic band of musicians" to play for the master of Monticello and his mistress and their friends. Yet he was unwilling to abandon the notion that "a passion for music might be reconciled with that economy which we are obliged to observe." He had the idea that Italian aristocrats might well have among their domestic servants and field hands "a band of two French horns, two clarinets, & hautboys and a bassoon, without enlarging their domestic expenses." If Jefferson were to guarantee the employment of such men for "a half dozen years, and at the end of that time to find them if they choose a conveyance to their own country might induce them to come here on reasonable wages. Sobriety and good nature would be desireable parts of their characters." While his countrymen struggled to expel the English invaders, Jefferson dreamed of imported Italian musicians, his own in-house orchestra at Monticello.

Preoccupied with such thoughts he wrote the astronomer David Rittenhouse, creator of the famous orrery, or planetarium, which Jefferson had so admired at Philadelphia, a revealing letter that may well have contained more than a measure of Jefferson's own rationale for spending so much time on his private affairs when his countrymen were in desperate straits. Rittenhouse and Franklin, he noted, were too gifted to waste their time on political matters. Congratulating Rittenhouse on the British evacuation of Philadelphia and reporting on Virginia's view of the Great Eclipse, Jefferson noted: "There is an order of geniuses above that obligation, & therefore exempted from it. Nobody can conceive that nature ever intended to throw away a Newton upon the occupations of a crown. . . . Cooperating with nature in her ordinary economy we should dispose of and employ the geniuses of men according to their several orders and degrees. I doubt not there are in your country many persons equal to the task of conducting government; but you should consider that the world has but one Ryttenhouse, & that it never had one before. The amazing mechanical representation of the solar system which you conceived and executed, has never been surpassed by any but the work of which it is a copy." The fact was that both Franklin and Rittenhouse were thoroughly involved in the American cause, while one constantly feels that although Jefferson was deeply absorbed by the abstract political and legal implications of the struggle for independence, he had little patience with the day-to-day labors and sacrifices required to make that theoretical independence a reality. The often painful and bitter details of the war itself were an unwelcome intrusion into the study of the scholar or the dreams and visions of the artist.

In August, 1778, when her first daughter, also Martha, nicknamed Patsy, was almost six, Martha gave birth to her second daughter, Mary (Polly), and Jefferson occupied himself with those scientific and agricultural matters that were such balm to his spirit. He also, under the influence of an Italian friend, Philip Mazzei, surrendered to an enthusiasm for all things Italian, going so far as to write to Richard Henry Lee that he thought Virginia would be a much more prosperous and advanced country if the early immigrants to the colony had been Italians rather than settlers "from the more Northern countries." Wine, oil, and silk seemed to Jefferson ideal crops for the more southerly

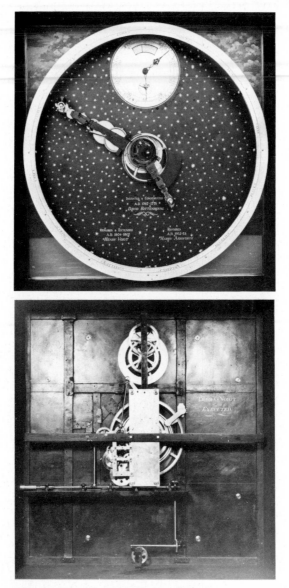

Throughout the war Jefferson kept in touch with David Rittenhouse (right, a 1791 portrait by Charles Willson Peale), the pre-eminent scientist in revolutionary America. He was particularly fascinated by Rittenhouse's orrery (above, front [top] and back views), an instrument designed to simulate the motions of bodies in the solar system.

climates. So life went, practical problems of the plantations alternating with visionary schemes that involved the recruitment of Middle Eastern farmers together with "many useful plants, esculant, medicinal and for manufacture, and arts useful tho' as yet unknown to us."

It is clear that Jefferson was what in his own time was commonly called an enthusiastic visionary, and it is plain enough that this quality which seized on everything novel or eccentric was directly related to his faith in science.

7. Governor of Virginia

In January, 1779, the British and Hessian troops captured at Saratoga arrived in Albemarle County after several months of marching and were quartered near Charlottesville. Jefferson found the Hessian officers excellent company. They were cultivated men and women (their commander, Major General Baron Friedrich Adolph von Riedesel, had his outspoken wife and three children with him), who discussed philosophical questions and had a knowledge of the wider world that captivated Jefferson. He played duets on the violin and violoncello with a young Hessian officer, and the baroness sang to their accompaniment. One officer wrote home, "My only Occupation at present is to learn the English language. It is the easier for me, as I have free Access to a copious & well chosen Library of Colo. Jefferson's. . . . He is now finishing an elegant building, projected according to his own fancy. In his parlour he is creating on the Cieling a Compass of his own invention by which he can know the Strength as well as Direction of the Winds. I have promised to paint the Compass for it. . . . As all Virginians are fond of Music, he is particularly so. You will find in his House an elegant Harpsichord, Pianoforte & some Violins. The latter he performs well upon himself, the former his Lady touches very skilfully & who, is in all respects a very agreeable, sensible & accomplished Lady."

When the spring session of the assembly began in May,

Rules

FOR

playing in a true Taste

ON THE

Violin German Flute Violoncello

AND

Harpsicord particular Thorough Bass

Exemplifyd in

Subjcts of English and Irish.

F.

Printed with His Majesty

Since college days music had been a "favorite passion" of Jefferson's. He played the violin and cello and was often accompanied by his wife on the harpsichord or pianoforte. His music library was extensive (left, the title page from an instruction book; below, a detail from the frontispiece of *The Compleat Tutor for the Harpsichord or Spinnet*, and a pattern for tuning a harpsichord). Jefferson said during the war that music in America was in a state of barbarism.

1779, Jefferson took his seat, but he once more tried to beg off, a plea to which Edmund Pendleton replied sternly, "You are too young to Ask that happy quietus from the Public, and should . . . at least postpone it 'til you have taught the rising Generation the forms as well as the Substantial principles of legislation."

Events were to turn out otherwise. Jefferson, along with General Thomas Nelson and his old friend John Page, was nominated for governor of the state to succeed Patrick Henry, who had served three terms and was thus ineligible to be chosen again. On the first ballot Jefferson led with 55 votes to 38 for Page and 32 for Nelson. Most of Nelson's supporters then switched to Page, but 12 swung to Jefferson, enough to make him governor by 67 to 61.

Thus there fell to Jefferson, whose principal concern from the early days of the war had been to extricate himself from practical politics, an almost impossible office, one so hedged about with restraints that even had Jefferson had the inclination to grasp it firmly and make of it what he could he would doubtless have encountered numerous frustrations. Not only did he not grasp it firmly; at times he seemed hardly to occupy the office at all. Indeed, it is plain that his attitude toward power was ambivalent in the extreme. We see ample evidence of his suspicion of power in his early attack on the authority of the Crown. We see it more formally presented in his own draft of a constitution for Virginia, which made the governor thoroughly subservient to the legislature and thus ran counter to the Montesquieuian principles of a proper balance between the three branches of government. He had accepted, if he had not sought, the position of colonel of the Albemarle militia, but he had never really exercised the office. He accepted the governorship of Virginia, but he seemed determined not to exercise even the nugatory powers of that office.

Unfortunately, power not used inevitably produces confusion and disorder, and this was very clearly the case with Jefferson's tenure as governor of his native state. One is led to speculate about that strange primness or reserve in regard to the use of power that Jefferson so frequently demonstrated, whose roots seem to lie deeper than principle or doctrine, indeed in some profound revulsion over the implications of power in the world. Certainly his writings abound in warnings about the dangers attendant on all accumulations of power, but then so do the writings of many of his contemporaries. In most instances their anxieties about the misuse of power stemmed from their belief in some version of the doctrine of original sin: that men have a radical propensity to selfishness, to vanity, and to what the eighteenth century called self-aggrandizement. This being the case, it had to be assumed that anyone, or any group, that accumulated undue power would use it to his or their advantage and, correspondingly, to the disadvantage of those without power.

But the roots of Jefferson's anxiety about power seem to have lain elsewhere. He had, after all, a decidedly optimistic view of human nature, at least most of the time. He was convinced that man and society were perfectible through the use of reason and the progressive advancements of science. Why then his ambivalence about power? One of the attributes of power is that it is confirmatory for the individual who acquires it. It comes to him, at least in the area of democratic politics, as a mark of the esteem of his fellows. It is clear that Jefferson acutely needed this kind of confirmation. The reader will recall that he did not wish to serve as a delegate from Virginia to the Continental Congress, but when he heard that he had been re-elected to the delegation by a portion of votes that left him second from the last, he expressed indignation.

The same reaction can be seen in his acceptance of the governorship, of which he seemed unwilling or unable to make effective use. He wished for the recognition of election to the office. At the same time it must be said that Jefferson's reluctance to carry what appeared to many his fair share of the load never seemed in the long run seriously to diminish the respect in which his peers held him. Despite periodic grumblings among his colleagues and open admonishments from the bolder, they kept choosing him for important and responsible offices, which suggests that he had a remarkable gift for drawing people to him. Indeed we must assume that he had charm, or charisma, a quality of tact and a delicacy of feeling that made his friends willing to overlook rather substantial deficiencies. Charisma is often characterized by passions under somewhat precarious control—one is tempted to say that a burning inner intensity is an essential element in this strange and ultimately inexplicable power that certain people exercise over others. Those qualities of morbidity and remoteness in Jefferson may well have attracted people to him. Great capacity for suffering, or, one might almost say, the emanation of suffering that some men and women exude like a subtle and troubling perfume, has similarly a strong power of attraction.

In any event Jefferson succeeded to the governorship of his state in the midst of a horrifying inflation, when six handkerchiefs for Martha cost the new governor £159 or roughly $300, when supplies of all kinds were desperately hard to find, when the Continental army was wretchedly equipped, unpaid, and mutinous, when there were bitter divisions among the patriots in Virginia, and when, most ominous of all, there was for the first time since the beginning of the war a serious threat of invasion of the state by British soldiers. Small wonder that Jefferson found the situation unmanageable and retreated into a kind of self-imposed exile. But first he struggled to bring some order out of the finances of the state. Writing to Richard Henry Lee, he spoke of the "intense labor and great private loss" he must experience as governor, adding, "It is a cruel thought that when we feel ourselves standing on the firmest ground in every respect, the cursed arts of our secret enemies, combining with other causes, should effect by depreciating our money, what the open arms of a powerful enemy could not. What is to be done? Taxation is become of no account, for it is foreseen, that, notwithstanding its increased amount, there will still be a greater deficiency than ever. I own I see no assured hope, but in peace, or a plentiful loan of hard money."

Of course Jefferson was not alone among patriot leaders in blaming the sad state of monetary affairs on "secret enemies," presumably the Tories. "They," whoever "they" were, were to blame. While it was true that some individuals took advantage of shortages to monopolize critically needed commodities and charge exorbitant prices for them, or, even more insidiously, ship them to foreign ports where they were paid for in hard money instead of inflated Continental paper, the blame in fact resided far more in Congress and the state governments for their lack of resolution to raise money by a fair and rigorous program of taxation.

But if Jefferson was inept at dealing with the immediate problems of wartime Virginia, he showed considerable enterprise in the matter of the western lands claimed by the state, encouraging the enterprises of George Rogers Clark that had started under Patrick Henry's governorship. Clark wished to build a fort at the confluence of the Ohio and the Mississippi, and Jefferson sent him detailed plans for such a fort as well as instructions for dealing with the Indians and the French settlers in the area. Jefferson enjoined thrift: "I must confide in you to take such care of the men under you as an oeconomical householder would of his own family . . . calling for as few supplies as possible. . . . We approve very much," he added, "of a mild conduct towards the inhabitants of the French villages. It would be well to be introducing our Laws to their knowledge and to impress them strongly with the advantages of a Free Government." The friendly Indians were to be enlisted, if possible, against the British Indians. "As to the English, notwithstanding their base example we wish not to expose them to the inhumanities of a savage enemy. Let this reproach remain on them, but for ourselves we would not have our national character tarnished with such a practice."

It was typical of Jefferson that he should be more attracted to the grand and remote—to the prospect of seizing Detroit and with it control of the whole northwest frontier—than to the local and immediate problems of the war. General Horatio Gates after his triumph at Saratoga, one of the few clear American victories of the war, was considered by Congress the hottest military property in the Continental army (there were members of Congress who talked of deposing Washington in Gates's favor). He was dispatched to the South to check the British inva-

The successful Virginia-sponsored expedition led
by George Rogers Clark (right) presented Governor
Thomas Jefferson with his first difficult executive
decision. After accepting the surrender of Colonel
Henry Hamilton at Vincennes in February, 1779
(above), Clark took his prisoner to Williamsburg.
Jefferson decided that Hamilton, known on the
frontier as Scalp Buyer, should be put in irons,
confined in the dungeon of the public jail, and denied writing and visiting privileges.

sion of the Carolinas, and he in turn appealed to Jefferson for men and supplies to assist him. Jefferson's response was to offer Virginia militia "provided they can be induced to go willingly. The length of their march heretofore and having been some time in service seems to give them a right to be consulted." To introduce democracy into the military forces in such a fashion, needless to say, seemed quixotic to the beleaguered Gates. To add to Jefferson's perplexities, a group of Virginia Tories along the New River, encouraged by the British invasion of the South, took up arms and threatened the Virginia lead mines, a crucial source of bullets for the Continental armies. When the uprising was suppressed, Jefferson instructed Colonel Charles Lynch, the officer in charge of the court-martial, to be ruthless in his punishment of the Tory leaders; that gentleman complied so enthusiastically that his name—Lynch—came to stand for lawless violence.

The Virginia legislature, like its corresponding numbers in other states, was notably behindhand in providing money, recruits, and munitions for the army of the Southern Department under Gates. Charleston was captured by the British and many of Virginia's best troops were caught in the net. Then on August 16 Gates suffered a crushing defeat at Camden. Having fled for his life, Gates was thoroughly discredited and the whole South laid open to the victorious British under the command of Charles Cornwallis. To add to Jefferson's woes, word came that Sir Henry Clinton, commander in chief of the British forces in America, was planning an attack on Virginia. The Virginia militia that Jefferson tried to muster to oppose the invasion were wretchedly armed and equipped, many without muskets or ammunition. They constituted a pitifully inadequate force. The state was saved, for the moment, more by British ineptitude than by Virginia valor. After a few desultory raids the invaders withdrew, Clinton's excuse being that Cornwallis failed to move north to support him.

With the British gone Jefferson appealed to the assembly to raise "a standing body of forces for the defence of this state." But the assembly refused to comply. They had already voted to raise three thousand men for the Continental army to serve for three years or the duration, offering as inducement "a healthy, sound negro between the ages of ten and thirty years, or sixty pounds in gold or silver. . . ." They had voted to issue £6,-000,000 in inflated paper currency and authorized Jefferson to issue another £4,000,000 if he deemed it advisable. While the invasion had proved abortive, the threat remained. Nathanael Greene, one of the few American generals with a legitimate claim to military prowess, had succeeded Gates after the Camden debacle and was in the process of putting together the *third* Continental army of the Southern Department from the shattered remnants of Gates's command and new levies that trickled into his camp.

There were a thousand things to be done to implement the enactments of the assembly and to make up the very considerable deficiencies of that body, which seemed in many instances to be passing the buck to the governor. The governor, in turn, showed no hesitation in passing the buck back to the assembly. In any event, in the midst of vast confusion and demoralization, Jefferson received a letter from François, marquis de Barbé-Marbois, the French emissary to Congress, with a number of queries about Virginia and sat down immediately to answer them. "I am at present busily employed for Monsr. Marbois," he wrote a correspondent in November, 1780. He was, he observed, grateful to the French minister for stimulating his researches into his native state and was ready to "acknolege to him the mysterious obligation for making me much better acquainted with my own country than I ever was before." He could do only so much in Richmond. Some information he could find only at Monticello, "where alone the materials exist which can enable any one to answer them."

Just as earlier he had hardly arrived in Congress before he was contriving to get away to Monticello, so a few months into his second term of office, on September 13, 1780, he indicated in a letter to Richard Henry Lee that he wished to resign. The reason, at least in part, seems to have been that he and his friend John Page wished to be free to pursue the researches that had been stimulated by Barbé-Marbois's letter. General Greene, who had hoped to make Richmond the base of operations for his campaign against Cornwallis, abandoned the notion after a visit convinced him that little help could be expected from Jefferson's largely moribund administration. He left as his representative the amiable Baron Friedrich von Steuben, who had already given hints that he was much better at drilling than fighting.

As though these dilemmas were not enough, word came from Washington in October that another British expeditionary force was being prepared in New York for a large-scale foray against the southern states, most probably with Virginia or the Carolinas as the principal target. Accompanying the dispatch was a warning to remove all military supplies to a safe location. On the last day of the year Jefferson received word from General Thomas Nelson that a British fleet had been sighted in Hampton Roads. The news called for all available forces to be mustered immediately, for word to be dispatched through the state, and for the highly vulnerable public stores concentrated at Richmond to be moved to some safer location—in short, for a prompt and energetic response. Instead Jefferson reacted like a sleepwalker. A friend visiting him shortly after Nelson's message arrived found him taking a walk. He expected no more than a raid. He did not intend to take any action until he received word confirming Nelson's warning. Two days passed without any action. By that time the British force, under the command of the traitor Benedict Arnold, was already in the James River, and transports were unloading troops twenty-five miles from Richmond.

At last Jefferson was galvanized into action. Word was sent out to muster all available militia; supplies were loaded on boats for shipment across the river; and Jefferson, the council, and the assembly all abandoned Richmond to Arnold's forces, which arrived on January 5, 1781. Arnold blew up the powder magazine with its precious supply of powder and sent a raiding party to nearby Westham to destroy an arms foundry there. This mission accomplished, and a number of buildings set afire, Arnold began his withdrawal to the British vessels anchored at Westover, burning buildings in Richmond and taking with him a number of slaves, including ten of Jefferson's. The slaves were lodged at Yorktown, retrieved after the surrender of Yorktown the next fall, and returned to Jefferson.

What made Virginia's humiliation all the more bitter was that Benedict Arnold had been the instrument of it. Like Washington, Jefferson hatched a plan to try to capture Arnold, using men from "West of the mountains," frontiersmen, for the mission and establishing a reward of five thousand guineas for Arnold alive and two thousand for him dead. The plan was never carried into operation and Washington wrote Jefferson that, devastating as the raid might have been, his primary goal must be to supply Greene's army opposing Cornwallis in North Carolina. There the outcome of the southern campaigns (and as it turned out, the war) would be determined. The assembly was not in session and the council was disposed to turn everything over to Jefferson. Cornwallis had burned his heavy equipment and started for Virginia with Greene withdrawing before him, not strong enough to risk his army in a showdown battle.

With Cornwallis advancing from the south and Arnold's expedition still in the offing, news came that a large French fleet had arrived off Hampton Roads. In addition, the marquis de Lafayette appeared with a hastily assembled corps to block Arnold's force.

Still the pressures on Jefferson persisted. Steuben wanted militia to defend the river against further raids. Jefferson explained that if the militia were disinclined to go, there was nothing he could do to force them to turn out. Greene importuned for more men and supplies to check Cornwallis's advance, and Lafayette had to feed his own men. Jefferson told an indignant Steuben that as to the militia "there is no hope of being able longer to keep them in service. The precedent of an actual mutiny would be so michevous as to induce us to believe an accommodation to their present temper most prudent. . . . You will judge from the temper of these Militia, how little prospect there is of your availing yourself of their aid." Jefferson and the council indeed insisted they be dismissed when their own commander attempted to march them to Steuben's aid. And so it went. The French fleet was driven off by the arrival of a larger British squadron. Lafayette, unable to rally any support in Virginia, withdrew northward, and Arnold once more landed his troops and marched for Williamsburg; once more Jefferson sent out a frantic call for the militia to assemble. But none showed up and Williamsburg was seized and supplies there destroyed. Again Richmond was threatened. An appeal to the militia was renewed. Two hundred responded, and an additional three hundred came without guns. Lafayette appeared just in time to save Richmond from a second investment by Arnold; but by the end of May the arrival of Cornwallis had enabled the British to renew their probes into the interior regions of the state, and the assembly voted to move the seat of government to Charlottesville.

In effect no government existed; Jefferson and a remnant of his council met and issued orders that no one obeyed. On June 1, 1781, he resigned his post, the end by his calculations of his second one-year term as governor. During most of his tenure the state had been virtually paralyzed. How much of this was attributable to Jefferson has been debated endlessly. For the most part, historians writing general histories of the Revolution have given Jefferson low marks for his performance as governor. Even his most ardent biographers can offer only lame defenses of their hero's discharge of his duties. There is no question that patriotic zeal was at a low ebb in Virginia. The individualism on which the state prided itself was ill-adapted for those common efforts required in wartime. Certainly Jefferson was as much the victim as the instrument of his state's impotence. Yet there is no doubt that a bolder and more active spirit could have accomplished far more than Jefferson did, as Thomas Nelson soon demonstrated, and it is hard not to be impatient with Jefferson's insistence that Virginians could never be required to do anything they did not wish to do.

That there was widespread criticism of Jefferson's administration is indicated by a move in the assembly to conduct an investigation of his performance as governor. Jefferson reacted to the investigation with the excess of sensibility that he invariably displayed when his motives or acts were questioned. A brief and halfhearted investigation cleared Jefferson of the charges; certainly it was no time for making a scapegoat of him. The depth of his feeling about the assembly's inquiry into his conduct is indicated by a letter to Edmund Randolph: "I have taken my final leave of every thing of that nature [politics], have retired to my farm, my family & books from which I think nothing will ever more separate me. A desire to leave public life with a reputation not more blotted than it has deserved will oblige me to emerge at the next session of the assembly . . . but as I go with a single object [to clear his name], I shall withdraw when that shall be accomplished."

A most interesting fact about Jefferson's poor record as governor of Virginia is that it, no more than his brief attendance in Congress and later in the Virginia assembly and his disposition to retreat to Monticello, failed to jeopardize seriously his "public image," his standing with his Virginia colleagues, or his subsequent assignment by Congress to important and responsible tasks. Failings and mistakes that would have spelled an end to the careers of other men were no impediment to Jefferson's.

Ironically, the most severe criticism directed at him concerned an episode in which he was guiltless. A few days after he had resigned as governor, word reached Monticello that a British cavalry raid, led by the famous Banastre Tarleton, had been dispatched to Charlottesville by Cornwallis to capture the assembly, council, and governor. Jefferson received the news calmly, had a leisurely breakfast, sent his family off in a carriage with some of his more precious papers, and prepared to leave himself. A unit of the British cavalry was in sight of Monticello when Jefferson finally mounted and rode away to join his family. Jefferson's enemies attempted to depict his flight as an act of cowardice, though it is not clear what they would have wished him to do. He could hardly have been expected to hold off a detachment of British cavalry single-handed.

Tarleton's raid was the last offensive move Cornwallis was

WILLIAMSBURG, *January 28th 1780.*

To Capt. ... Worthington of the Illinois Battalion!

Gentlemen:

YOU are appointed, and forthwith are to proceed, to recruit men to serve in the *infantry* — of this commonwealth.

Each man is to receive at the time of enlistment a bounty of seven hundred and fifty dollars to serve during the war, and the following articles of clothing, that is to say: A coat, waistcoat, a pair of overalls, two shirts, a pair of shoes, and a hat; to be delivered at the place of rendezvous, and with the like articles every year after during his service, to be delivered at his station; and will be entitled to the same pay and rations as are allowed by Congress to the like soldiers in continental service, and during his continuance in the service will be supplied with goods by this state, at the following rates, viz. Osnabrugs at 1s. 6d. per yard, coarse hats at 7s. 6d. each, coarse shoes at 8/ per pair, coarse yarn stockings at 5s. per pair, rum or brandy at the rate of 10s. per gallon, whiskey at the rate of 5s. per gallon, and such other imported articles as may be necessary at the rate of 120 per centum upon the first cost. At the end of the war he will be entitled to one hundred acres of unimproved land, within this commonwealth. All soldiers who may be disabled in the service will be entitled to receive pensions during life. You are to be allowed one hundred and fifty dollars for each able bodied soldier you shall enlist and pass with the officer of review to be appointed for that purpose. You are to make return of your enlistments within *two months* from the date hereof, in person, or by letter, and continue to make *monthly* returns thereof afterwards. So soon as you shall have enlisted and passed ... The men you are to enlist are to be rendezvoused at ...

Jefferson made several attempts to raise militia
(above, a commission for a recruitment officer), but
he was criticized for not defending Virginia against
troops commanded by Benedict Arnold (above,
right) and cavalrymen under Colonel Banastre
Tarleton, the so-called Butcher, (below, attacking
surrendering troops at the Waxhaws).

to make. Lafayette inhibited, if he could not check, the movements of the British. Cornwallis established himself at Yorktown, anticipating that Clinton would dispatch a fleet to take his army back to New York. Washington and his French allies slipped away from Clinton and hurried to Virginia, where they arrived, by the happiest of coincidences, shortly after a large French fleet had sealed off Cornwallis's escape route. The British surrender at Yorktown marked the end of the war for all practical purposes, but almost two years remained before a formal treaty was drafted recognizing American independence and officially bringing the war to an end.

The conclusion of the fighting brought problems almost as severe as those of the wearisome war years. The British had been fought to a standstill and peace and independence seemed secured, but it was far from certain whether the states allied under the uncertain banner of the Continental and then the Confederation Congress would coalesce into a nation. The spirit of parochialism was deep-rooted, as Virginia's reluctance to comply with the requisitions of Congress made clear. Animosities among states, dating from colonial times, still smoldered in many instances. Congress was, as one delegate put it, "a rope of sand." There was no provision under the Articles of Confederation, finally ratified by all the states in the closing months of the war, for a powerful executive to carry on the affairs of government. The whole matter of America's relations with the nations of the world remained to be resolved.

Having declared to Pendleton his intention to return to the assembly to defend his performance as governor, Jefferson changed his mind when the time came and refused to take his seat. James Monroe was prompted to write him a bold if restrained letter of rebuke, stating that he felt obliged to inform Jefferson of the views of his constituents. "It is publickly said here," Monroe wrote, "that the people of your county inform'd you they had frequently elected you in times of less difficulty and danger than the present one to please you, but now they had call'd you forth into publick life to serve themselves." A few days later John Tyler wrote as speaker of the house to reinforce

Monroe's exhortation and add the hint that if Jefferson did not appear voluntarily the "House may insist upon you to give attendance without incuring the Censure of being siezed," a plain threat to send the sergeant at arms after their delinquent member.

The letters provoked a bitter outburst from Jefferson. He had already "been thirteen years engaged in public service" and had during that time "so totally abandoned all attention to my private affairs as to permit them to run into great disorder and ruin. . . ." Nonetheless he now stood accused of "treasons of the heart and not mere weakness of the head. And I felt that these injuries . . . had inflicted a wound on my spirit which will only be cured by the all-healing grave." What followed was a laborious discussion of whether in fact the state had the right to require the services of any citizen even under the most desperate circumstances.

Jefferson, like most other planters, had suffered heavy losses at the hands of the British. Two of his four plantations had been raided: Elk Hill on the James River, Martha's inheritance from her father, and Cumberland. Jefferson calculated he had lost twenty-nine slaves, fifty-nine head of cattle, sixty hogs, and many of his crops. Since he was never really out of debt, the ravages of war added substantially to his financial burdens. But back at Monticello he resumed his building, and the marquis de Chastellux, visiting there in the spring of 1782, described the building and then the architect. "This house . . . is constructed in an Italian style, and is quite tasteful, though not without some fault; it consists of a large square pavilion, into which one enters through two porticos ornamented with columns. The ground floor consists chiefly of a large and lofty *salon,* or drawing room, which is to be decorated entirely in the antique style; above the *salon* is a library of the same form; two small wings, with only a ground floor and attic, are joined to this pavilion, and are intended to communicate with the kitchen, offices, etc., which will form on either side a kind of basement topped by a terrace." It was evident to the Frenchman that "Mr. Jefferson is the first American who has consulted the Fine Arts to know how he should shelter himself from the weather."

The builder of Monticello was "not yet forty, tall, and with a mild and pleasing countenance, but whose mind and understanding could serve in lieu of all outward graces; an American, who, without ever having quitted his own country, is at once a Musician, Draftsman, Surveyor, Astronomer, Natural Philosopher, Jurist, and Statesman, a Senator of America." In addition, he had "a gentle and amiable wife, charming children, whose education is his special care, a house to embellish, great estates to improve, and the arts and sciences to cultivate. . . ."

An observation is perhaps in order. The marquis's description suggests that he was slightly put off by his host's manner, since he found his "mind and understanding . . . ample substitutes for every exterior grace." The missing "exterior graces" were those forms of politeness observed by most members of Jefferson's class. The marquis's observations were reinforced by similar comments from other visitors to Monticello. Jefferson stressed informality. He was casual and offhand with visitors even to the point of rudeness, but when his conversational appetite was whetted he became irresistibly animated, lively, and enthusiastic.

The Monticello that Chastellux described was a relatively rudimentary form of the structure that ultimately emerged many years later, rather like a butterfly that keeps discarding chrysalises and appears each time in a more elaborate form. Building a handsome house from plans one has developed by consulting various great architects is one thing. Making certain additions and modifications from time to time is not unnatural; but to be some forty or fifty years building and rebuilding, putting up and tearing down, undertaking the most extensive revisions only in turn to revise *them,* and to do all this at enormous expense when already deeply in debt, demonstrates more than a keen interest in architecture: it displays an obsession whose mysterious depths lie beyond exploration. Again what is involved, one suspects, is therapy, not architecture—or therapy that happens to take the form of architecture. To wish to finish something that one has begun is a normal human impulse; Jefferson clearly wished *not to finish*. So we must be attentive to this matter. We must envision the piles of lumber, bricks, stones, and construction materials of all kinds that were constantly in sight, the appearance of disorder, the simple inconvenience of the perpetual building, tearing down, and rebuilding. We must imagine the dust, the powder of plaster, the wet paint, the general disruption of life occasioned by interminable construction.

Anyone who has built a house or lived in a portion of a house while another portion was being built or rebuilt will have a very sharp picture of what life at Monticello was like much of the time. And amid this confusion—of building materials, Indian relics, musical instruments, dinosaur bones, pieces of sculpture, pictures, opened and unopened crates from England or France or Italy, papers and innumerable books on shelves, tables, piled in corners—amid all this confusion, the philosopher pursued his studies, made his endless architectural sketches for the next modification or improvement, maintained a voluminous international correspondence, noted every mundane detail of plantation life in his precise, neat hand, and told us not a thing about his own deepest feelings except as they related to the sensuous and material world, to art, music, architecture, or the stars. All the rest is silence, a silence profound and baffling.

That the confusion and disorder of Monticello were often too much for Jefferson himself to endure is perhaps best indicated by the fact that he had another retreat, Poplar Forest, a plantation of some four thousand acres given over primarily to the raising of wheat and tobacco, to which he fled when Monticello was so filled with people—family, friends, visitors, and slaves—that he could not have that peace of mind necessary for quiet contemplation and serious writing. Poplar Forest was in Bedford County, approximately seventy miles from Monticello, several days' ride by horseback or carriage. So the retreat had a retreat. It was almost as though the distance from Monticello to Poplar Forest measured some internal distance that Jefferson could travel when he needed to escape from the rather inaccessible Monticello.

8. Notes on Virginia

As soon as he had resigned as governor and while the tides of war still flowed through his state, Jefferson escaped to Poplar Forest. It was not a casually undertaken journey. Jefferson had to gather up all relevant books and pamphlets, several hundred at least judging from his bibliography, pack them, and transport them by carriage to the Bedford County plantation. There, convalescing from a broken arm suffered in a riding accident, Jefferson plunged once again into his answer to the questions posed by François de Barbé-Marbois. The plan of work, dictated by specific questions that the French emissary had asked, was simple enough. It began with a review of the geography of the state —the rivers, the ports, the mountains, the flora and fauna (vegetable, mineral, and animal, as Jefferson called them)—then on through a discussion of the climate to a long section on the Indians, followed by chapters on the constitution, the laws, "Colleges, Buildings and Roads," the treatment of Tories, religion, manners, manufactures, commerce, weights, measures and money, and, finally, the bibliographical section entitled "Histories, Memorials and States-Papers."

In his section on the animals of Virginia, Jefferson disputed the theory of the great French naturalist the Count de Buffon that "the animals common both to the old and new world, are smaller in the latter." This proposition was of a piece with Buffon's opinion that all life in America was a degenerate form of life found on the continent of Europe. An important bit of evidence in Jefferson's countertheory was the bones of the mammoth, a huge prehistoric elephant whose descendants, according to the accounts of some Indian tribes, still lived in the Great Lakes region. Included was a table that triumphantly demonstrated the far greater size of American specimens of species found in Europe. Heading the list was an animal with no European counterpart—the bison, supreme and magnificent in its estimated weight of 1,800 pounds. European bears were listed as a puny 153 pounds, as opposed to 410 for their American counterparts. In virtually every category from elk to dormouse, rat, squirrel, dog, and cat, the American versions were, by Jefferson's calculations, larger and more vigorous.

Jefferson's ire was especially aroused by what he considered Buffon's slurs on the American Indians. The Frenchman had written: "Although the savage of the new world is about the same height as man in our world, this does not suffice for him to constitute an exception to the general fact that all living nature has become smaller on that continent. The savage is feeble [this would have been news to most frontiersmen] and has small organs of generation; he has neither hair nor beard, and no ardor whatever for his female . . . he is also less sensitive, and yet more timid and cowardly. . . ." The reason for all these deficiencies, Buffon stated, was that "the most precious spark of the fire of nature has been refused them; they lack ardor for their females, and consequently have no love for their fellow men: not knowing this strongest and most tender of all affections, their other feelings are cold and languid."

Jefferson was at his reasonable best in answering Buffon's charge that the small number of children to be found in Indian tribes was proof of their general inferiority, especially in regard to sexual "ardor," a deduction Buffon seems to have made largely from the absence of body hair on the Indian. "Negroes," Jefferson pointed out, "have notoriously less hair than the whites; yet they are more ardent," that is, more sexually potent. In his section on the Indians Jefferson retrieved a famous story of white injustice to a Mingo chieftain named Logan. Jefferson

In his *Notes on the State of Virginia* (above, his copy of the first edition), Jefferson exuberantly praised the Natural Bridge, located on property he owned: "The most sublime of nature's works . . . so beautiful an arch, so elevated, so light, and springing as it were up to heaven! the rapture of the spectator is really indescribable!"

used the account of Logan's speech upon the murder of his family by white renegades as an example of the remarkable oratorical powers of the Indians and as proof that their sensibilities were as keen as those of the whites. Finally, after arguing the case for the Indian with considerable resourcefulness, Jefferson directed a blow or two at another presumptuous Frenchman who considered himself an authority on America, the Abbé Guillaume Raynal, who in an incautious moment had written: "One ought to be astonished that America has not yet produced a good poet, an able mathematician, a man of genius in a single art, or a single science." Such a question might be reasonably asked, Jefferson replied, when America had existed as long "as the Greeks did before they produced a Homer, the Romans a Virgil, the French a Racine and Voltaire, the English a Shakespeare and Milton." Young as it was, America had nothing to apologize for. "In war," Jefferson wrote, "we have produced a Washington, whose memory will be adored while liberty shall have votaries, whose name shall triumph over time, and will in future ages assume its just station among the most celebrated worthies of the world. . . . In physics we have produced a Franklin, than whom no one of the present age has made more important discoveries, nor has enriched philosophy with more, or more ingenious solutions of the phenomena of nature. We have supposed Mr. Rittenhouse second to no astronomer living: that in genius he must be the first, because he is self-taught." Finally a swat or two at the British: "The sun of her glory is fast descending to the horizon. Her philosophy has crossed the Channel [to France, presumably], her freedom the Atlantic, and herself seems passing to that awful dissolution whose issue it is not given human foresight to scan."

In his chapter on population Jefferson expressed a classic uneasiness about America's "present" policy, which he described as designed "to produce rapid population by as great importation of foreigners as possible." America, in his view, had a government "more peculiar than those of any other [society] in the universe. It is a composition of the freest principles of the English constitution, with others derived from natural right and natural reason." If immigrants, familiar only with the monarchical governments of Europe, were allowed to enter the United States in large numbers, "they will bring with them the principles of government they leave, imbibed in their early youth; or, if able to throw them off, it will be in exchange for an unbounded licentiousness, passing, as is usual, from one extreme to another. It would be a miracle were they to stop precisely at the point of temperate liberty." It should be said in Jefferson's defense, if he needs one, that his strictures were directed not at the admission of immigrants, especially "useful artificers" who came on their own initiative, but at the rounding up of foreigners willy-nilly, primarily to populate vacant lands and make profits for land speculators.

In his initial mention of slaves Jefferson pointed out that one of the first acts of the Virginia assembly had been to forbid the importation of slaves into the state. "This will," he wrote, "in some measure stop the increase of this great political and moral evil, while the minds of our citizens may be ripening for a complete emancipation of human nature."

Having discussed the general characteristics of Indians while giving the lie to Buffon, Jefferson devoted a chapter (or section) to the Indian tribes of Virginia. Here again he could not forbear to point a moral. The Indians' way of dealing with crime seemed to him far more human than that of the presumably more civilized whites. Crimes were rare among them, Jefferson noted, adding, "Insomuch that were it made a question, whether no law, as among the savage Americans, or too much law, as among the civilized Europeans, submits man to the greatest evil, one who has seen both conditions of existence would pronounce it to be the last: and that the sheep are happier of themselves, than under the care of the wolves. It will be said, that great societies cannot exist without government. The savages therefore break them into small ones."

Jefferson listed thirty tribes known to have existed in the territory claimed by Virginia. His knowledge of and fascination with the "American aborigines" were striking. He showed the best instincts of the anthropologist in extrapolating from the archaeological evidence and trying to explain the migration of the Indians from Europe and their dispersion over the American continent. Language might have provided the answer, but unfortunately many tribes had already disappeared "without our having previously collected and deposited in the records of literature, the general rudiments at least of the languages they spoke." Jefferson's infatuation with the Indians led him to propose "a perpetual mission among the Indian tribes, the object of which, besides instructing them in the principles of Christianity [Jefferson was not opposed to the 'principles' of Christianity, it must be remembered, but only to its dogmas], . . . should be to collect their traditions, laws, customs, languages, and other circumstances which might lead to a discovery of their relation with one another, or descent from other nations." His insatiable curiosity about Indian remains and relics led him to perform excavations of Indian burial mounds on one of his own plantations and also to formulate a basic principle of archaeology, to wit, that those objects found in the lower sediments of soil were of more ancient origin than those near the surface. Although the observation seems simple enough, Jefferson was the first person, so far as history knows, to state it, and only many years later did it become an accepted rule of archaeology.

In reply to Marbois's question about the "constitution of the state," Jefferson gave an account of the original settlement of the colony with its several charters and its transformation from a private trading company to a royal colony. A major part of this section was devoted to a critique of the Virginia constitution of 1776. "This constitution," Jefferson wrote, "was formed when we were new and unexperienced in the science of government. It was the first too which was formed in the whole United States. No wonder then that time and trial have discovered very capital defects in it." Jefferson's principal criticisms were directed at the limitations of the franchise in the form of property qualifications, which by his calculations excluded "the majority of the men in the state, who pay and fight for its support. . . ." He also took a dim view of the election of the two houses of the Virginia legislature "by the same electors, at the same time, and out of the same subjects." Jefferson preferred the system adopted by a number of other states whereby the lower house represented the "persons" and the second the "property" of the state.

Jefferson also felt that the powers of the executive and judicial branches of the government were too dependent upon the legislative branch and that there did not, in consequence, exist that *separation of powers* that had long been considered the prerequisite of good government. Finally, there was the fact that the legislature in ordinary session could amend the constitution itself rather than being required to call a convention to do so. On this particular deficiency Jefferson expatiated at the greatest length.

The section on laws was, as one might expect, the same length as that on the constitution (the two sections together made up slightly less than a fourth of the entire work). After describing the administration of justice—the courts and the basic laws—Jefferson mentioned that the work of revising the laws of the colony to conform more closely to the requirements of a republican people had been undertaken "by three gentlemen," of whom Jefferson, of course, was one. He then listed "the most remarkable alterations proposed." Among these was the establishment of "religious freedom on the broadest bottom" and the emancipation of "all slaves born after passing the act." This plan for gradual emancipation, Jefferson had to admit, had not been included in the proposed changes, but a bill to that effect had been prepared and would be inserted if it appeared that there was a chance of favorable action by the assembly. The bill, Jefferson wrote, directed that all slave children be kept with their parents until they were eighteen and twenty-one for females and males respectively. They were then to "be brought up, at the public expense, to tillage, arts, or sciences, according to their geniuses" and finally "colonized to such place as the circumstances of the time should render most proper, sending them out with arms, implements of household and of the handicraft arts, seeds, pairs of useful domestic animals, &c., to declare them a free and independent people, and extend to them our alliance and protection, till they shall have acquired strength. . . ." Their places would then be taken by "an equal number of white inhabitants" recruited from various foreign parts.

If he were asked why not simply incorporate these independent blacks, educated and equipped at the public expense, into the general population of the country, Jefferson's answer was that "deep rooted prejudices entertained by the whites; ten thousand recollections, by the blacks, of the injuries they have sustained; new provocations; the real distinctions which nature has made; and many other circumstances, will divide us into parties, and produce convulsions, which will probably never end but in the extermination of one or the other race."

If he had stopped there, Jefferson might have appeared as an enlightened advocate of emancipation under a very generous plan, one that in actual fact was adopted by such radical black leaders as Marcus Garvey early in the twentieth century, that has appeared from time to time in various black manifestoes, and that indeed gave birth to the African state of Liberia. Several points are worthy of comment. One is that Jefferson spoke of the ex-slaves' "ten thousand recollections . . . of the injuries they have sustained" and the temptation for them to revenge those injuries as the major impediments to the two races living in harmony together "equally free and independent." The passage shows that Jefferson was not deceived by the "happy slave" illusion in which so many plantation owners found solace. He believed that the crimes committed by white masters against their slaves made any peaceful accommodation impossible. In addition, the reader must keep in mind that the population of Virginia numbered approximately 560,000, of whom roughly half were slaves, most of them illiterate and unable to fend for themselves in the white world that surrounded them. So Jefferson's program might be said to be both sensible and humane given the relationship between the races in his native state; a reasonable if not an ideal attempt at the solution of a basically insoluble problem. The most important difference between Jefferson's proposed solution—separation—and that of certain black leaders is that black advocates of separation have usually demanded that the United States set apart a state or states, or in earlier days still unsettled territory, for them to colonize rather than consigning them to Africa. It is hard to understand why Jefferson, aware of the almost limitless stretches of land that lay westward, did not make a similar proposal—to colonize unoccupied American lands. Perhaps the answer lay, in part, in his conviction that blacks were physiologically better suited to an African than an American climate.

Jefferson did not, as we know, stop with his visionary project for emancipation, which was, in any event, hopelessly impractical if for no other reason than that it would have bankrupted any state attempting to implement it. He went on to describe at considerable length the differences between white and black and the great superiority of the white over his black brother. This recitation must be an embarrassment to any decent-minded white person who reads it today and an affront to any black. It is a kind of catalogue of all the physical differences between the races that the vast majority of whites, through successive generations of American history, have taken as the measure of the irredeemable inferiority of black people—"the eternal monotony" of "that immovable veil of black which covers all the emotions of the other race."

The white has flowing hair as opposed to the short, kinky hair of the black, "a more elegant symmetry of form," which makes black men prefer white women just as the "Oran-ootan," believed by Jefferson to be a primitive wild man, preferred "black women over those of his own species." Blacks had a "very strong and disagreeable odour"; they needed less sleep than whites (which might have had a positive rather than a negative connotation).

The inventory was not all negative: Jefferson believed blacks to be "at least as brave, and more adventuresome" than whites; able to pass through danger with "more coolness and steadiness than the whites"; "more ardent after their female" but less capable of tenderness, less affected by grief. "In general," Jefferson added, "their existence appears to participate more of sensation than reflection." They seemed to Jefferson

Mannahoacs

	Tribes	Country	Chief Town	Warriors 1607	1609
Between Patowmac and Rappahanoc	Whonkenties	Fauquier			
	Tegninaties	Culpeper			
	Ontponies	Orange			
	Tauxitanians	Fauquier			
	Hassinungaes	Culpeper			
Between Rappahanoc and York	Stegarakies	Orange			
	Shackaconies	Spotsylvania			
	Mannahoacs	Stoff. & Spotsylva.			

Monacans

	Tribes	Country	Chief Town	Warriors 1607	1609
Between York and James	Monacans	Ja⁰ R. ab⁰ the Falls Fork of James R.			30
Between James and Carolina	Monasiccapanoes	Louisa Fluvanna			
	Monahaboes	Bedf. Buckingh᷑			
	Massinacacs	Cumberland			
	Mohemenchoes	Powhatan			
Eastern Shore					

Powhatans

Tribes	Country	Chief Town	Warriors 1607	16
Tauxenents	Fairfax	ab⁰ G᷑ Washington's	40	
Patowomekes	Staff. King Geo	Patowmac Cr.	200	
Cuttatawomans	King George	ab᷑ Lamb Cr.	20	
Pissasecs	K. Geo. Richm᷑	ab᷑ Leeds T.		60.
Onaumanients	Westmoreland	Nomony R.	100	
Rappahanoes	Richm᷑ county	Rappahanoc Cr.	100	
Moraughtacunds	Loncast. Richm᷑	Moratico R.	80	
Secacaonies	Northumberl᷑	Coan R.	30	
Wighcocomicoes	Northumberl᷑	Wicocomico R.	130	
Cuttatawomans	Lancaster	Corotoman	30	
Nantaughtacunds	Essex Caroline	Port Tobacco Cr.	150	
Mattapaments	Mattapony R.		30	
Pamunkies	King William	Romuncock	300	
Werowocomicoes	Gloucester	ab᷑ Rosewell	40	
Payankatanks	Piankatank R.	Turk. ferry, Grimesby	55	
Youghtanunds	Pamunkey R.		60	
Chickahominies	Chickahomin᷑ fh.	Orapaks	250	
Powhatans	Henrico	Powhatan mayne	40	
Arrowhatoes	Henrico	Arro...	30	
Weanoes	Charles City	Weynoke		
Paspaheghes	Cha. City, Ja᷑ City	Sandy point		
Chiskiacs	York	Chiskiac		
Kecoughtans	Elizabeth City	Roscow	20	
Appamattoes	Chesterfield	Bermuda H...		
Quiocohanoes	Surry	ab᷑ tp᷑ Chipoak		
Warrasqueaks	I. of Wight	Warrasqueac		
Nansamonds	Nansamond	Im᷑ mouth West Bra	200	
Chesapeaks	Princess Anne	ab᷑ Lynhaven R.	100	
Accohanoes	Accom᷑ Northamp	Accohanoc R.	40	
Accomacs	Northampton	ab᷑ Cheriton	80	

Jefferson's interest in Indian culture had been stimulated by the visit of these three Cherokee leaders to Williamsburg before their trip to London in 1762. In *Notes on the State of Virginia* Jefferson charted his knowledge of Virginia's Indians (left, his manuscript copy) and tried to correct European misconceptions about their customs.

much inferior in reasoning power, but it must be said that they had had inferior opportunities for enlightenment.

After making some comparisons between blacks and Indians that were unfavorable to the blacks, he added, "In music they are more generally gifted than the whites with accurate ears for tune and time, and they have been found capable of imagining a small catch. Whether they will be equal to the composition of a more extensive run of melody, or of complicated harmony, is yet to be proved." After further reflections on slavery in ancient and modern times, Jefferson added, cautiously, that it was very difficult to judge with any confidence what was innate in blacks and what was the consequence of the degraded condition in which they had been kept, noting, in a poignant aside, "as a circumstance of great tenderness, where our conclusion would degrade a whole race of men from the rank in the scale of beings which their Creator may perhaps have given them. . . . I advance it therefore as a suspicion only, that the blacks, whether originally a distinct race, or made distinct by time and circumstances, are inferior to the whites in the endowments both of body and mind."

Many things might be said of these sentences; I will say only a few of them. Jefferson considered himself a scientist as well as a humanitarian idealist. He was unequivocal on the evil of slavery, yet when he contemplated the consequences of emancipation his resolution faltered. The basis for his speculations was those blacks with whom he came into daily contact, his slaves, among whom were some of his own in-laws, the children of his wife's father, thus her own half sisters and brothers, whose color proclaimed unmistakably what plantation wisdom confirmed: they were the children of this impossible union. Characteristically, Jefferson could seldom bring himself to speak of these white-blacks or black-whites. Their daily presence posed a perpetual, unanswerable riddle, a question that burned beneath the genteel surface of every southern plantation and tormented the waking hours and the dreams of an infinite number of white wives with its consuming, unquenchable query: what of us? we who are neither black nor white, whose presence mocks all logical propositions and demonstrates how passion breaks through all formal arrangements and denies logical and dispassionate discourse, we who do not smell, whose hair is sometimes as long and straight as yours, whose feelings are as tender?

So while Jefferson, sequestered at Poplar Forest, speculated in his study, he was surrounded by the endlessly enduring, respectful, silently observing company, whose music and laughter drifted up from their quarters on breathless southern nights to trouble their master's sleep—they who needed so little sleep. That laughter was reassuring, threatening, mocking, speaking of the rich, "ardent" life, of "eager desire," of sensation, that lay beyond the circle of the great house where white folks lived their own strange—often, as it seemed to their slaves, cold and joyless —life of power and privilege. Cold and joyless: why else did they summon slave women to share their beds except to drop into that warm, sensuous, unspoiled black flesh where servitude was powerless to destroy spontaneity. To change their luck, the luck of being a white man in a mysteriously rustling, pulsating black world, constantly oscillating between delight and misery.

If Jefferson could not bring himself to speak of that variety of black who had already escaped from his carefully contrived theoretical propositions, he had left black men and women who were substantially as he described them, who smelled unpleasant to a white nose and were not given to reading ancient philosophers or calculating the transit of a star. We might as well indict him for his ideas as for his candor in expressing them. We do not scorn him for his eccentric notion that the fossils he found on nearby mountaintops were simply imitations of shell forms; no more should we convict him of racism (in Jefferson's day an as yet undiscovered category) because he expressed the convictions of the most liberal spirits of his time, convictions based, as they believed, on simple observation. The fact was that belief in the equality of black people, where it was to be found, was an article of faith, not the consequence of observation.

If the dominant group is allowed to describe the norm, it can always, and almost invariably does, designate the subordinate group as inferior. We must honor Jefferson for, as far as he goes, the tentativeness of his conclusions and the obvious effort it cost him to arrive at them; that and his unwavering conviction, in opposition to his upbringing and the canons of most members of his class, that human servitude was morally wrong and must be eradicated one way or another. That he could not face the implications of miscegenation for his carefully worked out theories is hardly surprising.

Under the heading of laws Jefferson included the essence of his own proposals for a system of public education in Virginia. His bill would require all county districts, or hundreds, of five or six miles square to establish a school for teaching reading, writing, and arithmetic. All residents of the district would be entitled to send their children "three years gratis, and as much longer as they please, paying for it." Each year a visitor would choose from each school "the boy of best genius . . . of those whose parents are too poor to give them further education and to send him forward to one of the grammar schools of which twenty are proposed to be erected in different parts of the county, for teaching Greek, Latin, geography, and the higher branches of numerical arithmetic." After several years' trial at the grammar schools, "the best genius" would again be selected to continue another six years "and the residue dismissed. By this means," Jefferson concluded, "twenty of the best geniuses will be raked from the rubbish annually, and be instructed, at the public expence. . . ." At the end of six years, half of the pupils would again be dropped and the remainder, chosen "for the superiority of their parts and disposition," were to go on to the College of William and Mary for three years of advanced instruction. "The general objects of this law," Jefferson wrote, "are to provide an education adapted to the years, to the capacity, and the condition of every one, and directed to their freedom and happiness."

Jefferson added a few observations on the curricula of these ideal schools. In the district schools, "wherein the great mass of the people will receive their instruction," the children instead of having the Bible imposed on them "at an age when their judgments are not sufficiently matured for religious inquiries" should be taught "the most useful facts from Grecian, Roman, European and American history." There they would also be taught that happiness in life does not depend on wealth, "but is always the result of a good conscience, good health, occupation, and freedom in all just pursuits. . . . By that part of our plan," Jefferson added, "which prescribes the selection of the youths of genius from among the classes of the poor, we hope to avail the State of those talents which nature has sown as liberally among the poor as the rich, but which perish without use, if not sought for and cultivated."

Basically the initial curriculum would be historical, for "history, by apprizing [the students] of the past, will enable them to judge of the future; it will avail them of the experience of other times and other nations; it will qualify them as judges of the actions and designs of men; it will enable them to know ambition under every disguise it may assume; and knowing it, to defeat its views. In every government on earth is some trace of human weakness, some germ of corruption and degeneracy, which cunning will discover, and wickedness insensibly open, cultivate and improve. Every government degenerates when trusted to the rulers of the people alone. The people themselves therefore are its only safe depositories. And to render even them safe, their minds must be improved to a certain degree. . . . The influence over government must be shared among all the people. If every individual which composes their mass participates of the ultimate authority, the government will be safe. . . ."

These passages have been quoted at considerable length because they give us a solid grasp of Jefferson's most essential philosophy and remind us of the degree to which he articulated a peculiarly American creed, or, one might even say, *the* American creed. First, that the people in general not only could be safely entrusted with the ultimate authority in government but that it was essential that they be so trusted—a trust, then, in "the people," with the belief that they contained a vast reservoir of untapped talent that could be utilized by "education." Indeed, in no other way could the mass of the people be prepared to share the responsibilities of republican government.

Moreover, it was possible to devise a particular curriculum or series of curricula, featuring history and science, that would accomplish the desired end. Also Jefferson (and most Americans subsequently) believed in a hierarchy of intellect. Thus, while rejecting the ancient hierarchies of class and caste, he proposed a new hierarchy to rest on the ability to conjugate Latin verbs and master Euclidean geometry, never questioning that honor, civic virtue, and common sense might not necessarily be the inevitable corollaries of learning. Jefferson clearly believed that ruthless intellectual competition would bring the natural aristocracy of talent and ability to the surface, thus serving the best interests of the individual and society at the same time.

American education has been astonishingly Jeffersonian though not, to be sure, in direct emulation of the principles laid down by the Virginian. In modern times the competitive element in American education has diminished (although substantial residues of the competitive-selective system remain), in recognition, one would hope, that the critical-analytical intelligence, epitomized by book learning, is not the only important and useful form of intelligence. In the last generation or so England, ironically, has most nearly reproduced Jefferson's ideal system of public education based on intense academic competition.

Jefferson's insistence that the pupils in the county hundred (or elementary) schools be taught great doses of history was typical of his preference for the theoretical over the practical. The notion that what the sons of poor Virginia farmers needed most was Greek and Roman history was almost as bizarre as the idea that they were capable at such a tender age of absorbing those sophisticated (and perhaps questionable) lessons Jefferson was so confident that the study of history would teach them.

Jefferson's belief that knowledge of the Bible was of less consequence than the study of Greek civilization, when it became generally known upon the publication some years later of his *Notes on Virginia*, proved a red flag to most devout Christians. But Jefferson did not stop there. In a section on religion, he not only wrote in detail of his own efforts to promote religious

toleration but stated his skepticism about the doctrines of orthodox Christianity. He incorporated into this section the greater
part of his preamble to the statute he had prepared on religious
liberty and added to it some equally eloquent observations.
Galileo, Newton, and Descartes had all introduced new truths,
and all efforts to suppress those truths, however they outraged
orthodoxy, had proved fruitless. "Reason and experiment have
been indulged, and error has fled before them. . . . Subject
opinion to coercion: whom will you make your inquisitors? Falli-
ble men; men governed by bad passions, by private as well as
public reasons. And why subject it to coercion? To produce
uniformity. But is uniformity of opinion desirable? No more
than of face and stature. . . . Is uniformity attainable? Millions
of innocent men, women, and children, since the introduction
of Christianity, have been burnt, tortured, fined, imprisoned; yet
we have not advanced one inch towards uniformity. What has
been the effect of coercion? To make one half the world fools,
and the other half hypocrites. To support roguery and error all
over the earth. Let us reflect it is inhabited by a thousand millions of people. That these profess probably a thousand different systems of religion. That ours is but one of that thousand.
That if there be but one right, and ours that one, we should wish
to see the nine hundred and ninety-nine wandering sects gathered into the fold of truth. But against such a majority we cannot
effect this by force. Reason and persuasion are the only practica-
ble instruments. To make way for these, free inquiry must be
indulged; and how can we wish others to indulge it while we
refuse it ourselves?"

At the end of the section on religion Jefferson revealed the
source of his impatience to remodel obsolete and oppressive
laws. "From the conclusion of this war," he wrote, "we shall be
going down hill. It will not then be necessary to resort every
moment to the people for support. They will be forgotten,
therefore, and their rights disregarded. They will forget themselves, but in the sole faculty of making money, and will never
think of uniting to effect a due respect for their rights. The
shackles, therefore, which shall not be knocked off at the conclu-

Although Jefferson owned hundreds of slaves (right, a page from his Farm Book listing his possessions; below, a slave ship unloading; above, Isaac, one of his slaves, from an 1840's daguerreotype), he detested the institution. In his *Notes*, Jefferson proposed a gradual emancipation leading to colonization.

Squire ♂ Mar. 20. 1810.
Goliath ♂ May 5. 1810.
Phill ♂ Sep. 1810.
Caesar 1820
Molly ♂ Apr. 21. 1811
3. John
5. Davy
6. Amy
7. Doll
Isabel ♂ 1819.
9. Betty Brown
0. Ned
Lewis
61. Nance
64. Jenny Ned's
68. Isaac
Bagwell
Jenny. Lewis's
9. Critta
70. Peter Hemings
71. Minerva
73. Sally
75. John Hemings
76. Jamey
Davy Jerry's ♂ 13
77. Rachael
Cretia
Frances
80. Mary. Moses'
Joe
81. Wormley
82. Shepherd
93.

1793. Edwin
Virginia. Bagw'
Sukey Doll
94. Scilla. Ned's
Dolly. Doll's
Solomon
95. Thruston
James. Lew'
Esther.
96. Philip
Nace
James. ned'
Sucky. Jerry's
97. Sanco.
Indridge
Evelina.
Maria.
Bec
98. Beverly. run away 22.
Aggy. Ned's

1800.
Nanny. Bagw'.
Isabel. Lew'.
Thrimson. Isabel'.
Israel. Ned'
Isaiah. Jerry's.
01. William. Moses' B.R.
Harriet. Sally'. run 22
Mary. Bet'
Joe. Rachael
Louisa Isabel 1816.
02. Jerry. Jerry'.
Randal. Cretia'.
03. Davy. Moses'.
Moses. Ned's.
04. Jupiter. Jerry',
Edy'.
Sally'.

1811. Apr. 1. Cornelius. Ursula',
Sep. Jamey. Scilla',
Dec. Jenny. Fanny',
Oct. Matilda. Cretia',
Dec. 25. Robert. Virginia',
1812. Oct. 27. Zacharias. Moses',
Dec. 6. Betsy. Ann. Edy',
1813. January. Lindsay. Esther',
1 May. Edmund. Rachael B.
Sep. Fanny. Scilla's ♂ mar 1
Sep. Mary. Cretia' ♂ mar
Oct. 1. Thomas. Ursula',
1814. May. Marshal. Maria'; [i. e. Lazari
Molly
June. Moses. Fanny's
1815. June 5. Peter. Edy',
July. James Band. Cretia'
Aug. Patsy. Moses's
Sep. Amanda. Virginia's
1816. Jan. 21. Louisa. Ursula',
April. 15. Martin. Maria'
July. Miles. Scilla'
Jennet. Sally'
Lindsay. Rachael's B.
1817. July 11. Melinda. Fanny'
Aug. Fossett. Mary'
1818. Jackson. Melly'
Lucy. Scilla'
James Hamilton. Maria'
Caroline. Ursula',
Lovenza. Sally'
1819. Jan. 7. Isabella. Edy',
Apr. 3. Indridge. Fanny',
Aug. Nancy. Cretia'
Oct. 15. Fontaine. Mary Mos'
1820. Jan. 27. Critta. Ursula',
Mar. Martha. Beck'
July. Amy. Isabel'
1821. Apr. Aggy. Scilla'
May. Sally'
William. Edy'
Nov. Virginia'
1822. Sep. Melinda. Fanny'
Dec. Gilly. Aggy'
1823. Martha. Maria' (Re
Manuel. Eve's
May. Isabella. Sally's. Cha'
girl. Virginia'
George. Ursula'

sion of this war, will remain on us long, will be made heavier and heavier, till our rights shall revive or expire in convulsion."

One of Barbé-Marbois's last queries was about "the particular customs and manners that may happen to be received in that State." It is worthy of note that Jefferson took advantage of this opportunity to write one of the most trenchant indictments of slavery ever penned: "There must doubtless be an unhappy influence on the manners of our people produced by the existence of slavery among us. The whole commerce between master and slave is a perpetual exercise of the most boisterous passions, the most unremitting despotism on the one part, and degrading submissions on the other. Our children see this, and learn to imitate it. . . . If a parent could find no motive either in his philanthropy or his self-love, for restraining the intemperance of passion towards his slave, it should always be a sufficient one that his child is present. But generally it is not sufficient. The parent storms, the child looks on, catches the lineaments of wrath, puts on the same airs in the circle of smaller slaves, gives a loose to his worst of passions, and thus nursed, educated, and daily exercised in tyranny, cannot but be stamped by it with odious peculiarities. A man must be a prodigy who can retain his manners and morals undepraved by such circumstances."

As for the slave himself, he must prefer any other situation "to that in which he is born to live and labour for another: in which he must lock up the faculties of his nature [and] . . . entail his own miserable condition on the endless generations proceeding from him. With the morals of the people their industry also is destroyed. For in a warm climate, no man will labour for himself who can make another labour for him. . . . And can the liberties of a nation be thought secure when we have removed their only firm basis, a conviction in the minds of the people that these are of the gift of God? Indeed I tremble for my countrymen when I reflect that God is just; that his justice cannot sleep forever: that considering numbers, nature and natural means only, a revolution of the wheel of fortune, an exchange of situation, is among possible events: that it may become probable by supernatural interference! The Almighty has no attribute which can take side with us in such a contest. But it is impossible to be temperate and to pursue this subject through the various considerations of policy, of morals, of history natural and civil. . . . I think a change is already perceptible, since the origin of the present revolution. The spirit of the master is abating, that of the slave rising from the dust, his condition mollifying, the way I hope preparing, under the auspices of heaven, for a total emancipation, and that this is disposed, in the order of events, to be with the consent of the masters, rather than by their extirpation."

This passage too is justly famous. Jefferson's emphasis on the effect of a slaveowner's behavior on his children is a touch of genius, as is his point that the slave must prefer any country in the world to the one in which he was born and labors. Equally somber is his premonition that revolutionary violence and the destruction of white masters will follow if the slaves are not freed. The section demonstrates in the most dramatic manner the anguish felt by a man of particular sensibilities at the "peculiar institution" of which he was almost as much a victim as the slave.

In the section on manufactures Jefferson gave vent to his anxiety about the development of an industrial society where immigrants would provide a docile and underpaid labor force. Industry was a necessity in Europe, since there was not enough land to enable everyone to farm. But in America the situation was different. There was enough land for everyone. "Is it best then," Jefferson asked rhetorically, "that all our citizens should be employed in its improvement, or that one half should be called off from that to exercise manufactures and handicraft arts for the other? Those who labour in the earth are the chosen people of God, if ever He had a chosen people, whose breasts He has made His peculiar deposit for substantial and genuine virtue. . . . Corruption of morals in the mass of cultivators is a phenomenon of which no age nor nation has furnished an example . . . generally speaking, the proportion which the aggregate of the other classes of citizens bears in any state to that of its husbandmen, is the proportion of its unsound to its healthy parts, and is a good-enough barometer whereby to measure its degree of corruption." Manufacturing should be left to Europe, with its depressed masses. "The mobs of great cities," Jefferson concluded, "add just so much to the support of pure government, as sores do to the strength of the human body. It is the manners and spirit of a people which preserve a republic in vigour."

It is not hard to imagine what Jefferson would think of present-day America, with its vast industries polluting the atmosphere, turning workers into slaves of an assembly line, and making life in our great cities a feat of survival.

9. Death Again

Jefferson wrote the greater part of his *Notes on Virginia* at Poplar Forest, that ultimate retreat. He returned to Monticello at the end of July, 1781, with his papers and books and resumed his direction of the improvements on the house. Again he was importuned to assume his share of public duties. Although the fighting of the war was over, enormous tasks remained to be accomplished, not least of which were the negotiation of a proper peace treaty and the establishment of a new nation on a sound footing. So Jefferson's friends began to press him to be a candidate for election to the assembly at the very least. Jefferson demurred. He wrote to Madison complaining that the assembly had impugned his character and that he was still determined to withdraw from politics.

Edmund Randolph, to whom Madison showed the letter, made a shrewd diagnosis: "The pathos of the composition is really great and the wound, which his spirit received by the late impeachment, is, as he says, to be cured only by the all-healing grave." But at least he might triumph over his enemies if he were "to resume the legislative character; for in the constant division between the two leaders, Henry and Lee, he might incline the scale to whichsoever side he would" and thereby come to manage the political fortunes of his state. In addition he had a large amount of unfinished business: he had drafted bills that had yet to be taken up by the assembly. Young James Madison, so perfectly attuned to Jefferson's thought and personality that he was like an alter ego, replied to Randolph: "Great as my partiality is to Mr. Jefferson, the mode in which he seems determined to revenge the wrong he received from his country does not appear to me to be dictated either by philosophy or patriotism. It argues, indeed, a keen sensibility and a strong consciousness of rectitude. But this sensibility ought to be as great towards the relentings as the misdoings of the Legislature, not to mention the injustice of visiting the faults of this body on their innocent constituents." To Madison, Jefferson's attitude appeared primarily vindictive.

But the pleas of his friends and political coadjutors left Jefferson unmoved. He remained at Monticello, where life was complicated by the arrival of his sister, Martha, Dabney Carr's widow, and her six children. His own Martha gave birth to another daughter, Lucy Elizabeth, after a difficult confinement. Doubtless Martha Carr's arrival at Monticello was occasioned by Martha Jefferson's poor health and the need for a woman's hand to assist in the domestic affairs of Monticello. As his wife's health failed, Jefferson became, with his sister, her constant companion and nurse. His daughter Patsy, then ten years old, wrote years later, "No female ever had more tenderness or anxiety. He nursed my poor mother in turn with Aunt Carr and her own sisters—setting up with her and administring her medecines and drink to the last. For the four months that she lingered, he was never out of calling; When not at her bed side, he was writing in a small room which opened immediately at the head of her bed. A moment before the closing scene, he was led from the room almost in a state of insensibility by his sister Mrs. Carr who with great difficulty got him into his library, where he fainted, and remained so long insensible that they feared he would never revive. . . . He kept his room for three weeks and I was never a moment from his side. He walked almost incessantly night and day only lying down occasionally when nature was completely exhausted. . . . When at last he left his room he rode out and from that time he was incessantly on horseback rambling about the mountain in the least frequented roads and just as often through the woods. . . . I was his constant companion. . . ."

The long solitary rides became part of the pattern of Jefferson's life at Monticello. The crippling grief occasioned by his wife's death on September 6, 1782, took him years to overcome; he never did completely—he could not bring himself to speak or write of Martha again and destroyed every letter that had passed between them. Patsy's account of her father's despair—it might indeed be called an illness—reminds us of his reticence about his father and his failure ever to speak of his mother. Indeed, his reaction to his mother's death might, if we are to judge by his subsequent undefined illness and the apparent onset of migraine headaches in the weeks following her death, have been very similar to his reaction to Martha's death, though not as intense. Certainly, his grief was out of proportion to any extant evidence about their relationship during the ten years of their marriage. True, Jefferson was always in a fever of impatience to get back to Monticello, but our argument is that it was the place to which he was so essentially attached and that the concerns expressed about Martha's health were often little more than excuses to return to his sanctuary. In other words, we have virtually no evidence by which to measure Jefferson's devotion to Martha (other than his tender care of her during her last illness) except his emotional collapse after her death. I believe that in addition to his deep and genuine affection for her, Jefferson was excessively love-dependent and found in Martha's death simply the latest example of the determination of a malign fate to strip him of every relationship upon which he depended for his own emotional health. If it ever could be said of any man that death was too much with him, it must be said of Jefferson. And while it may be dangerously presumptuous to say what constitutes "excessive grief," surely Jefferson's had in it substantial elements of pathology.

Martha Jefferson was buried not far from Dabney Carr in the Monticello burial ground. The lines inscribed on her tomb were not from the Holy Scriptures but from the *Iliad,* and they expressed that dark pessimism in the face of death that was characteristic of much Greek thought: "If in the house of Hades

The Commonwealth of Virginia to Th: Jefferson Dr.

1783.   Dollars
Oct. 25–Nov. 3. To travelling to Prince town. 10 days. — — — 80.
              To attending on Congress from Nov. 4. to Mar. 11 inclus. days 130 1520.
                                                                          1600.

Cr.

1783.
Sep. 30. Pr cash by Colo Monroe 13. guineas = 60⅔ Dollars
                                 7. Louis = 32. Doll — — — — — 92⅔
1784.
Feb. 14. Pr mr Harrison's bill on Holker for — — — — — 433⅓
Mar. 6. Pr do. — — — — — on do. — for — — — — 333⅓
Apr. 30. Pr do. — — — — — on Morris for — — — — 333⅓
May 11. Pr my draught in favor Ja Madison esq. — — — 407⅓
                                                      1600.

Sir,
    Be pleased to pay to James Madison esq. four hundred
and seven dollars and one third, being the balance due to me as
one of the delegates in Congress for the Commonwealth of Virginia,
and you will oblige Sir

The Honble   your very humble servt
  Jaquelin Ambler   Th: Jefferson
    Treasurer of Virginia.   Annapolis May 11. 1784.

In June, 1783, Jefferson accepted an appointment to the Confederation Congress meeting in Philadelphia. That same month rebellious troops drove Congress to Princeton, and in November it adjourned to the State House in Annapolis (left), where it met for nine months. Jefferson served until May, 1784 (above, his expenses).

men forget their dead, / Yet will I even there remember my dear companion." Jefferson's friends, deeply concerned about the reports of his profound withdrawal, plotted to draw him out of his retreat and once more into the world. With some management by the Virginia delegates, Congress appointed Jefferson minister plenipotentiary to join Franklin, Adams, and John Jay in the final phases of the peace negotiation in Paris. As soon as he got word of his appointment, Jefferson sent his acceptance and began to make plans to sail for France. He left the overall management of his affairs in the hands of his brother-in-law, Francis Eppes, husband of one of his dead wife's sisters, and another friend, Nicholas Lewis, and the household affairs in the capable hands of his sister, Martha. Young Martha (Patsy) accompanied him, while Polly and the infant, Lucy Elizabeth, remained with their aunt.

When Jefferson got to Philadelphia he found that the ship on which he was to sail was frozen in the ice of the Chesapeake at Baltimore. When the ice melted, the voyage was further delayed by news that British warships were lying in wait at the mouth of the bay. And then finally word came that the peace negotiations were virtually completed and Jefferson's services would not be needed.

On his way back to Monticello, Jefferson stopped at William and Mary to receive a Doctor of Laws degree and then went on to Richmond to repair his political fences and indicate that he was ready to take up a public life once more, especially if there was a likelihood of revising the Virginia constitution and getting some of his cherished reforms through the assembly. Back at Monticello Jefferson prepared the draft of a new constitution for Virginia. In it he provided for what was, in effect, universal manhood suffrage as well as the cessation of the slave trade and the freeing of all blacks born after December 31, 1800, much as he had proposed in the *Notes*.

In June the Virginia assembly appointed him a delegate to Congress to take his seat in November, 1783. In the intervening months Jefferson occupied himself with the education of his children, Martha and Mary, and the children of Martha Carr. In addition he drew up a catalogue of his library of 2,640 volumes. Included were a number of works of music by such composers as Purcell, Vivaldi, Corelli, Bach, and Haydn, and an increasing number of volumes on architecture.

In October Jefferson set out with Patsy for Philadelphia. There he discovered that Congress, threatened by mutinous soldiers demanding their back pay, had departed for Princeton and thence to Annapolis, where Jefferson finally caught up with it, having left Patsy in the charge of a family friend in Philadelphia. From Annapolis he wrote Patsy sketching out a formidable course of study for her to "render you more worthy of my love." From 8 to 10 she should study music, "from 10 to 1 dance one day and draw another . . . from 3 to 4 read French, from 4 to 5 exercise yourself in music, from 5 till bedtime read English, write &c." She was to render to her father a running report on the books she had read and the tunes she had mastered and, in addition, was to write once a week to each of her three aunts, with a copy to Jefferson. "Take care," her father added, "that you never spell a word wrong. . . . It produces great praise to a lady to spell well. I have placed my happiness on seeing you good and accomplished, and no distress which this world can now bring on me could equal that of your disappointing my hopes. If you love me then, strive to be good under every situation and to all living creatures, and to acquire those accomplishments which I have put in your power, and which will go far toward ensuring you the warmest love of your affectionate father."

This was a severe regimen to prescribe for a ten-year-old, and to reinforce it with the threat of withheld love must have made it doubly onerous for Patsy. Her father's determination to dominate her life, while not precisely to the modern taste, was quite typical of father-daughter relationships in the eighteenth century. Nonetheless it is hard not to feel considerable sympathy for Patsy, reading the demands her father placed upon her. The fact that, according to her own testimony, she had been his constant companion and, one might almost say, nurse in the period following her mother's death made the tie between them a particularly close one. While once again it is impossible to calculate the effect that her father's collapse must have had on her, coming on top of the shock of her mother's death, to say it must have been profound seems safe enough. Jefferson had at that moment displayed a dependence on his older daughter that was to last as long as he lived. She at least never failed him. After her marriage to her cousin, Thomas Mann Randolph, she came with her whole family to Monticello. Moreover she never deserted him, either by leaving or dying, and it is hard not to feel that she, forever aware of the precariousness of his psychic health, and always tender, solicitous, and loving (he demanded periodic avowals from her that she loved him more than anyone else, including, presumably, her husband and children), was not the real heroine of the remarkable drama of his life. If at the age of ten she had aided him in recovering his equilibrium, one senses that for the next fifty years she faithfully assisted him in maintaining it, she and Monticello in a strange alliance.

In Annapolis Jefferson found Congress with too few delegates to constitute a quorum; the session could not convene until mid-December. He was dismayed over the "situation of the army, the reluctance of the people to pay taxes, & the circumstances under which Congress removed from Philadelphia. . . ." Its prestige, in his opinion, was at an all-time low, and in its impotence the simplest questions (which were far outnumbered by extremely complicated questions) seemed impossible of resolution. During Jefferson's relatively brief sojourn there he drafted one of the most important documents to issue from his pen.

In October, 1780, Congress had passed a resolution, "Public Lands and New States," in an effort to quiet the fears of the states without land claims that they would be overshadowed by those with substantial western claims. All land, the resolution declared, that was ceded to the United States "by any particular States . . . shall be disposed of for the common benefit of the United States, and be settled and formed into distinct republican States" with "the same rights of sovereignty, freedom and independence, as the other States."

Working from this text, Jefferson drafted a bill that provided for the establishment of such states, indicating their boundaries and even proposing names—Michigania and Illinoia, Cherronesus, Assenisipia, Metropotamia, Polypotamia, Pelisipia, Sylvania, Saratoga, and Washington. He incorporated the provisions of the resolution of 1780 in requiring that all new states have republican forms of government and added a stipulation from his draft of a new Virginia constitution that after 1800 there should be no slavery in these states. In Congress the Southern delegates defeated the antislavery provision but accepted the rest of Jefferson's bill with minor changes. Jefferson also brought in a lengthy report providing for a committee of state to act as an executive body during the periods when Congress was in adjournment.

While Jefferson was in Annapolis he met a young Dutch nobleman, Count Gijsbert Karel van Hogendorp. The two men quickly became friends. The count wrote that Jefferson's conversation was "more usefull to me than that of any Gentleman in town." Hogendorp sensed Jefferson's deep melancholy and wrote to him later, "I pitied your situation for I thought you unhappy. Why, I did not know; and though you appeared insensible to social enjoyments, yet I was perfectly convinced you could not have been ever so. One evening I talked of love, and then I perceived that you still could feel, and express your feelings."

"Your observation on the situation of my mind is not without foundation," Jefferson wrote in reply. "Yet I had hoped it was unperceived, as the agreeable conversations into which you led me, often induced a temporary inattention to those events which have produced that gloom you remembered. . . . I have known what it is to lose every species of connection which is dear to the human heart: friends, brethren, parents, children— retired, as I thought myself to dedicate the residue of life to contemplation and domestic happiness, I have been again thrown by events on the world without an object on which I can place value." Jefferson did not refer to his wife's death as the cause of his gloom but rather to the fact that he had lost "every

In 1784 Jefferson chaired a committee of Congress charged with settling western land disputes (right, territories claimed by various states in 1783). The committee recommended the cession of all territories to the Congress and provided for successive stages of self-government, ending with statehood. Jefferson even drew up a map showing possible state boundaries (above, David Harley's map integrating Jefferson's plan). Although not all the recommendations were adopted—an antislavery provision was thrown out—they did form the basis of the Northwest Ordinance of 1787.

species of connection which is dear to the human heart," and then, as he planned to retire to a "life of contemplation and domestic happiness," the death of his wife had foreclosed that possibility and left him "without an object on which I can place value," a sentence that seemed to take no account of his surviving sisters or his three children, not to mention the Carr children, who were like his own. Yet, the last despairing sentence aside, it is plain enough from the content of the letter that he had suffered excruciatingly over those deaths he could not bring himself to speak of directly.

10. Paris

Early in 1784 Congress decided to send Jefferson to France to join Franklin and Adams in negotiating commercial treaties with the various European powers. He accepted the assignment and began to make preparations to sail. In addition to Patsy and several household slaves, he took with him as his secretary William Short, a fellow Virginian for whom Jefferson had high regard.

Jefferson picked up Patsy in Philadelphia and proceeded on to Boston, whence he was to sail, by way of New York, where he spent a week, and then New Haven. Ezra Stiles, the president of Yale, noted in his diary: "The Gov. is a most ingenous Naturalist & Philosopher, a truly scientific & learned Man—every way excellent." Jefferson, in turn, inquired of Stiles concerning the giant mammoth. At Boston, Jefferson had several weeks to wait before he could get passage, and the leading patriots of the city vied for the honor of entertaining the author of the Declaration of Independence.

When he arrived in Paris Jefferson found quarters at the Hôtel d'Orléans and then outfitted himself and Patsy in handsome clothes of the latest fashion. In addition he laid in glass, china, and silverware, an extensive stock of fine French wines, and books in abundance. He also procured a coach and a proper retinue of servants. He put Patsy in an expensive girls' school run by Catholic nuns and flung himself with gusto into the rich

My dear Patsy   Toulon April 7. 1787.

I received yesterday at Marseilles your letter of March 25. ~~I say~~ I received it with pleasure because it announced to me that you were well. experience learns us to be always anxious about the health of those whom we love. I have not been able to write to you so often as I expected, because I am generally on the road; & when I stop any where, I am occupied in seeing what is to be seen. it will be some time now, perhaps three weeks be--fore I shall be able to write to you again. but this need not slacken your writing to me, because you have leisure, & your letters come regularly to me. I have received letters which in--form me that our dear Polly will certainly come to us this summer. by the time I return it will be time to expect her. when she arrives, she will become a precious charge on your hands. the difference of your age, and your common loss of a mother, will put that office on you. teach her above all things to be good: because without that we can neither be valued by others, nor set any value on ourselves. teach her to be always true. no vice is so mean as the want of truth, & at the same time so useless. ~~teach~~ teach her never to be angry. anger only serves to ~~hurt~~ hurt ourselves, to divert others, and alienate their es--teem. and teach her industry & application to useful pursuits.

I will venture to assure you that if you inculcate this in her mind you will make her a happy being in herself, a most inesti- mable friend to you, and precious to all the world. in teaching her these dispositions of mind, you will be more fixed in them your- self, and render yourself dear to all your acquaintance. prac- tise them then, my dear, without ceasing. if ever you find your- self in difficulty and doubt about how to extricate, yourself, do what is right, & you will find it the easiest way of getting out of the difficulty. do it for the additional incitement of increasing the happiness of him who loves you infinitely, and who is my dear Patsy

yours affectionately

Th. Jefferson

Martha, Jefferson's oldest child (left, a 1789 miniature), was just twelve when she accompanied him to France in 1784. He placed his dear "Patsy" in a Paris con- vent school with a genteel reputa- tion. Jefferson failed to write to her for the first month of his tour of southern France; this letter is his response to her complaint.

and varied social and cultural life of the great city. Reading his carefully kept account books, one is struck by the extravagance of many of Jefferson's purchases. His Virginia plantations had never produced the income that they might have under more systematic management. While Jefferson was an indefatigable farmer, his interests ran largely to experimental rather than practical agriculture. Because he was far more interested in cultivating exotic plants and vegetables than in running a productive farm, he was invariably in debt. The income allowed him by Congress was a truly republican one—far too modest to support the style of life Jefferson chose to live. Among his understandable indulgences was the printing of two hundred copies of his *Notes on Virginia*, which was published anonymously for circulation among his friends.

He was particularly uneasy about those passages in the *Notes* concerning the emancipation of the slaves, and it was these sections on which he most earnestly solicited the reactions of his American friends. "I wish to put it [the *Notes*] into the hands of the young men at the college, as well on account of the political as physical parts," he wrote to Madison. And to Chastellux he proclaimed his faith in the students of his alma mater. "It is to them I look, to the rising generation, and not to the one now in power, for these great reformations."

Meanwhile Paris completely captivated him. John Adams, having arrived two years before full of puritan suspicion of licentious French ways, had finally succumbed to French charm, but with Jefferson there was no contest. He was already, as his enemies were to claim, a Frenchman at heart. His ability to keep the practical and theoretical aspects of things in separate compartments of his mind was perfectly French, as was his infatuation with reason, soon to become the goddess of the French Revolution. The great project of the French encyclopedia was going forward and Jefferson was its enthusiastic admirer. Imagine! All knowledge was to be collected and reduced to a system, bound in books, and placed on shelves, where it would be available to everyone.

If the art, architecture, music, and painting—the cultural

life of the French metropolis—delighted him, Jefferson was dismayed by the French social system, by the extremes of wealth and poverty and the barriers that existed between classes. He wrote a friend in Virginia, "Behold me, at length on the vaunted scene of Europe! . . . It is not necessary for your information that I should enter into details concerning it. But you are perhaps curious to know how this new scene has struck a savage of the mountains of America. . . . I find the general fate of humanity here most deplorable. The truth of Voltaire's observation offers itself perpetually, that every man here must be either the hammer or the anvil. . . . While the great mass of the people are thus suffering under physical and moral oppression," the wealthy few lived in dazzling opulence. Jefferson compared that situation to the "degree of happiness which is enjoyed in America by every class of people." He was especially disturbed at the number of unemployed. "I asked myself," he wrote Madison, "what could be the reason so many should be permitted to beg who are willing to work, in a country where there is a very considerable portion of uncultivated lands. . . . I am conscious that an equal division of property is impracticable. But the consequences of this enormous inequality producing so much misery to the bulk of mankind, legislators cannot invent too many devices for subdividing property, only taking care to let their subdivisions go hand in hand with the natural affections of the human mind."

The last phrase is ambiguous. One is not certain how "subdivisions" are to go "hand in hand with the affections of the human mind." Is this public opinion? Are the subdivisions of property simply to be such as the general public will approve of and support? One solution that Jefferson considered was "to exempt all from taxation below a certain point, & to tax the higher portions of property in geometrical progression as they rise. Whenever," Jefferson wrote, "there is in any country, uncultivated lands and unemployed poor, it is clear that the laws of property have been so far extended as to violate natural right. The earth is given as a common stock for man to labour & live on. If, for the encouragement of industry we allow it to be appropriated, we must take care that other employment be provided to those excluded from the appropriation. If we do not, the fundamental right to labour the earth returns to the unemployed. . . ." There was so much land and work still available in the United States that it was, in Jefferson's opinion, "too soon yet" to adopt such a policy. "But it is not too soon to provide by every possible means that as few as possible shall be without a little portion of land. The small landholders are the most precious part of a state."

Jefferson also discovered that in France "intrigues of love occupy the younger, & those of ambition the more elderly part of the great. Conjugal love, having no existence among them, domestic happiness, of which that is the basis, is utterly unknown. In lieu of this are substituted pursuits which nourish and invigorate all our bad passions, and which offer only moments of extasy amidst days and months of restlessness and torment." He wrote in a similar vein to Monroe. To visit France would make him "adore [his] own country. . . . My God, how little do my country men know what precious blessings they are in possession of, and which no other people on earth enjoy." To another friend he complained that a young American who visited Europe as part of his education would be hopelessly corrupted. He would be introduced "into a spirit for female intrigue, destructive of his own and others' happiness, or a passion for whores, destructive of his health, and, in both cases, learn to consider fidelity to the marriage bed as an ungentlemanly practice, and inconsistent with happiness."

The letter was classic Jefferson. One thinks of his strictures against George III. Jefferson was fascinated by the French and by French life. He plunged into it with the same kind of extravagant enthusiasm he warned the prospective American visitor against, and, of course, most ironically, his enemies declared to the end of his life that his philosophy and morals had been hopelessly corrupted by his stay in France. What Jefferson's criticisms of the French suggest most strongly is the ambiguity of his own feelings about that seductive atmosphere and his guilt over his own debts, which, as he put it, "for some time past [have] preyed on my spirits night and day."

Jefferson, Adams, and Franklin found that the business for which Congress had commissioned them, the negotiation of commercial treaties with the dominant European powers, was a slow and laborious undertaking. In common with his fellow ministers, Jefferson felt himself thwarted at every turn. (Adams spoke of negotiating for his life among a school of sharks as analogous to European diplomacy.) The triumvirate was soon dissolved, however. Franklin requested permission to return to the United States; John Adams was assigned as the first American minister to the Court of St. James's (where he felt very much more at home) and left for England to open the United States embassy with Abigail as his hostess. Jefferson became the minister to France.

While Jefferson pursued protracted and in the main fruitless efforts to develop trade between the United States and France, particularly in regard to the chief product of his native state—tobacco—he also was an assiduous tourist. He visited Versailles, of course, and as an insatiable student of architecture he examined the most famous buildings of the city.

In June, 1785, less than a year after Jefferson had arrived in France, Madison wrote on behalf of the Virginia assembly to inform him that the members wished to build a capitol in Richmond and had commissioned Jefferson to find a French architect to design the building. Jefferson of course had his own ideas about a proper design for the capitol. His predilection for the classical led him to seek out an architect with similar tastes, Charles Louis Clérisseau. It was Clérisseau whose book *Monuments de Nîmes* had introduced Jefferson to the Maison Carrée, a temple surviving from Roman times that Jefferson considered "the best morsel of antient architecture now remaining."

With Clérisseau becoming, in effect, his collaborator, Jefferson made minor modifications in the design of the Maison Carrée and sent it off posthaste to Virginia, to be followed by a plaster model. He wrote a friend, "I send by this conveiance designs for the Capitol. They are simple & sublime. More cannot be said. They are not the brat of a chimerical conception never before brought to light, but copied from the most perfect

Jefferson and architect Charles Louis Clérisseau (above right) chose the Maison Carrée at Nîmes (left) to be the model for Virginia's new state capitol. After seeing the nearly completed building (below, a view of Richmond by Benjamin Latrobe), Jefferson was pleased and commented: "Our new Capitol . . . will be worthy of being exhibited along side the most celebrated remains of antiquity."

186

model of antient architecture remaining on earth; one which has received the approbation of near 2,000 years and which is sufficiently remarkable to have been visited by all travelers." Since Jefferson's subsidiary aim was to improve the taste of his countrymen by using "every occasion when public buildings are to be erected of presenting to them models for their study and imitation," he had every reason to be pleased with the influence exerted by the Virginia capitol. It was the principal precursor of the classical revival in the new United States, much admired and widely copied.

At the same time it is characteristic of Jefferson (how readily one uses "characteristic" in speaking of him) that he was greatly attracted to a group of French architects who were eccentric to the point of freakishness in their notions; who were, in fact, the personification of that "brat of a chimerical conception never before brought to light" with which Jefferson had contrasted the chaste lines of the Nîmes temple. The architects, Étienne Louis Boullée and Claude Nicolas Ledoux, were devoted to dwellings shaped like triangles, spheres, cubes, and other geometric forms, and Jefferson, despite his infatuation with classical forms, was charmed by these extravagant imaginings. It could be said that three things fascinated Jefferson above all else: all things ancient, especially the classics; how things worked; and everything novel. France was thus a treasure-trove. He inspected and described new water pumps, new plows, new steam engines, and ancient monuments.

If his sojourn in France encouraged Jefferson's radical political philosophy, it also stimulated an interest less congenial to the modern mind: a kind of imperial temper which held as a central tenet that it was the destiny of the United States to extend its influence—or in other words to govern—the entire New World. If this seems an extravagant and presumptuous notion, it is important to remember that South and Central America (and Florida) were the possessions of corrupt and decadent monarchies, and Canada was governed by the British, whose tyranny the Americans had just overthrown. Jefferson and those Americans who thought as he did (and most shared the greater part of his vision) conceived of themselves not as conquerors but as liberators. After all, the Revolution had been fought not merely to free the colonists from the domination of Great Britain but to usher in a new historical era in which people in every part of the world would be encouraged to throw off their ancient chains. The reverse side of the great seal of the United States—*Novus Ordo Seclorum*—boldly proclaimed the beginning of "a new age," and a Congregational minister speaking at a July 4 celebration in Concord, Massachusetts, ended his sermon by predicting "the emancipation of a world" as the consequence of the American Revolution. It was thus not unnatural for many Americans to believe that the extension of American hegemony to less fortunate peoples throughout the New World, and far beyond it, was an important and wholly beneficent part of that emancipation.

It was, in Jefferson's opinion, important to be ready to accept those countries that, in a manner of speaking, were ripe simply to fall into the hands of the United States. This was particularly true of Spain's colonies. "Our confederacy," Jefferson wrote, "must be viewed as the nest from which all America, North and South, is to be peopled." The countries claimed by Spain "cannot be in better hands," meaning less competent or weaker hands, he noted, adding, "My fear is that they are too feeble to hold them till our population can be sufficiently advanced to gain it from them piece by piece. The navigation of the Mississippi we must have. This is all we are as yet ready to receive." Jefferson's reflections eventually became a major element in American foreign policy, from Florida to Cuba and the Philippines, not because Jefferson bespoke them but because they conformed perfectly to America's notion of its mission in the world.

Early in 1786 Adams sent an urgent request to Jefferson to join him in England. Adams needed the assistance of his fellow minister for three tasks: negotiation with the Barbary pirates, who were devastating American shipping in the Mediterranean; negotiation of a commercial treaty with Portugal; and efforts to get Britain to agree to a treaty that would give some modest trading privileges to American merchants. The first and last turned out to be abortive, although the treaty with Portugal was completed. Adams and Jefferson nonetheless enjoyed each other's company, and Jefferson plunged into an orgy of book buying, purchasing in addition a thermometer, solar microscope, globe, protractor, and telescope.

While the diplomatic pot bubbled away, Adams and Jefferson decided to indulge themselves in a tour of some of the famous British estates and gardens. They began with the estate of the duke of Devonshire, then on to Hampton Court, the Pelham mansion—Esher Place—Claremont, and Stowe, the estate of the marquis of Buckingham, where thirty-three gardeners labored on the grounds, and a temple to friendship was complemented by a temple to Venus. Marlborough's great estate at Blenheim employed two hundred people and boasted a herd of two thousand deer. As Jefferson wrote to John Page, "The gardening in that country is the article in which it surpasses all the earth. I mean their pleasure gardening. This, indeed, went far beyond my ideas. . . . The city of London, tho' handsomer than Paris, is not so handsome as Philadelphia." Viewing the luxurious habits of the English, Jefferson feared that his countrymen were becoming contaminated and longed for "a missionary . . . who would make frugality the basis of his religious system, and go thro the land preaching it up as the only road to salvation. . . ." Starting perhaps with Jefferson himself?

Despite his admiration of English gardens and the pleasure of the Adamses' company, Jefferson's brief visit confirmed him in his hostility toward the British. "That nation hates us, their ministers hate us, and their king more than all other men," he wrote Page. "I think their hostility towards us is much more deeply rooted at present than during the war." He was glad to return to Paris, immoral as that city might be.

Back in that enchanted spot Jefferson exchanged letters with Abigail Adams on the relative merits and demerits of the French and English. Abigail indeed proposed that they exchange Patsy Jefferson for one of her anticipated grandsons, adding, "I am for strengthening federal union." To Abigail's moderate preference of England, Jefferson replied: "Here we have singing, dauncing, laugh & merriment. No assassinations, no treasons, rebellions nor other dark deeds. When our king goes out, they fall down and kiss the earth where he has trodden; and then they go to kissing one another. And this is the truest wisdom. They have as much happiness in one year as an Englishman in ten."

11. The Head and the Heart

The intellectual life of the French city was intoxicating. With Lafayette as his patron, Jefferson had entrée to the great salons. He became a friend of the famous duc de La Rochefoucauld and of the marquis de Condorcet, whose belief in the perfectibility of the human mind was much to Jefferson's taste, and renewed his friendship with the marquis de Chastellux.

Jefferson also found himself, for the first time in his life, in the midst of a society that, if not dominated by fashionable and intelligent women, abounded in them. Like Franklin before him he soon acquired a delightful coterie of such ladies, and they brought out a quality latent in Jefferson, a particular delicacy and responsiveness quite feminine in its essence. His relations with women had been, for the most part, awkward and almost embarrassingly dependent if not, as in the case of Jack Walker's wife, Betsey, simply excruciating. The admiration of well-born French ladies, with their flattering attentiveness, knowledge, manifold arts and graces in pleasing and managing men, charmed Jefferson.

But it was an English lady, rather than a French one, who became a central figure in Jefferson's life. In August, 1786, young John Trumbull, the Connecticut painter who had been sponsored and encouraged by Abigail Adams, came to Paris at Jefferson's invitation. He brought with him two of the historical paintings for which he was to become famous, "Death of Montgomery at Quebec" and "Battle of Bunker Hill." Jefferson gave him advice on another large work—which portrayed the signing of the Declaration of Independence—and since he posed for his own portrait in that rendition, he not surprisingly or inappropriately emerged as the most striking figure in the ensemble. Among the circle of French women whose friendship Jefferson cultivated were three or four who were painters, and Jefferson eagerly solicited instruction from them in judging the merit of paintings, an area that he clearly (and properly) felt was beyond him.

It was through Trumbull that Jefferson met Maria Louisa Catherine Cecilia Hadfield Cosway, a painter of some reputation in England and the wife of Richard Cosway, a popular miniaturist. In addition to being talented, Maria Cosway was beautiful, with delicate features, large blue eyes, and enchanting blonde curls. Her husband was a small, foppish dandy, described by one critic as "a preposterous little Dresden china manikin." He was known to treat his wife badly, and a friend who believed she had married for her husband's money rather than love declared that "she always despised him." In addition to his fashionable miniature portraits he painted pornographic snuffboxes that brought extravagant prices. Apparently what initial happiness there may have been in the marriage ended when his wife realized that he had been having numerous affairs with other women and with men as well.

Maria Cosway came to Paris in the summer of 1786 with her husband, who had been commissioned to paint the portrait of the duchess of Orléans and her children in miniature. When Jefferson met her through Trumbull, who had known the Cosways in England, he was forty-three and she twenty-seven. What followed was a rapturous romance. Jefferson fell promptly and madly in love with Maria. They were like two young lovers in the ecstasy of their first encounter. The day they met both canceled plans for the afternoon and evening so that they might spend the suddenly precious time together. As Jefferson put it, "Lying messengers were to be despatched into every quarter of the city, with apologies. . . ." "If the day had been as long as a Lapland

Jefferson made numerous lasting friendships among the *philosophes* in Paris's intellectual circle (below, guests arrive at an eighteenth-century salon). The marquis de Condorcet (above) was Jefferson's age and the most like him in temperament. A brilliant mathematician, Condorcet believed in human perfectability and the primary role of scientists in the future of society.

summer day," Jefferson later wrote Maria, he would "still have contrived means . . . to have filled it. . . . When I came home at night and looked back to the morning, it seemed to have been a month gone."

For six weeks they were constantly together, exploring all the delights that Paris holds for two people in love. In retrospect, Jefferson recalled their ventures: "How beautiful was every object! the Port de Neuilly, the hills along the Seine, the rainbows of the machine of Marly, the terras of St. Germains, the chateaux, the gardens, the statues of Marly, the pavilion of Lucienne. Recollect too Madrid, Bagatelle, the King's garden, the Dessert." Time seemed to stand still when they were together and then rush by as fast as the heart's pulsing blood. In Jefferson's image, "The wheels of time moved on with a rapidity of which those of our carriage gave but a faint idea, and yet in the evening, when one took a retrospect of the day, what a mass of happiness had we travelled over!"

On one of their walks together Jefferson tried to jump over a fence, tripped and fell, and broke or dislocated his right wrist. Apparently they continued to meet after the accident, but Richard Cosway had finished his portrait and insisted on returning to England. Jefferson was devastated by the news. As he wrote of himself in the second person: "Remember the last night. You knew your friends were to leave Paris to-day. This was enough to throw you into agonies. All night you tossed us from one side of the bed to the other. No sleep, no rest. The poor crippled wrist too, never left one moment in the same position, now up, now down, now here, now there. . . ."

Jefferson went to say good-by to his beloved and then turned homeward "more dead than alive," in his own words. At home he began to compose, with his left hand, a strange, revealing epistle to Maria that he entitled "My Head and My Heart." The dialogue began with an account of the parting, and then the Head spoke: "Well, friend, you seem to be in a pretty trim.

"HEART: I am indeed the most wretched of all earthly beings. Overwhelmed with grief, every fibre of my frame distended beyond it's natural powers to bear, I would willingly meet whatever catastrophe should leave me no more to feel or to fear."

To which the Head replied: "These are the eternal consequences of your warmth and precipitation. This is one of the
scrapes into which you are ever leading us." But the Heart cries
out once more, "I am rent into fragments by the force of my
grief! If you have any balm, pour it into my wounds. . . . Spare
me this awful moment!"

When the Head reminds the Heart of their initial meeting
with Maria at the market and the Heart's immediate infatuation,
the Heart responds with a rhapsody on the joys of the meeting.
To which the Head replies sternly: "Thou art the most incorrigi-
ble of all the beings that ever sinned! . . . I often told you during
it's course that you were imprudently engaging your affections
under circumstances that must cost you a great deal of pain.
. . ." The Head goes on to list an inventory of Maria's charms,
"such as music, modesty, beauty," saying that these will only
"increase the pang of separation."

Then the Heart recalls that the Cosways said they would
return the next year so that it need not suffer the agony of final
separation.

"HEAD: . . . Upon the whole it is improbable. . . . Perhaps
you flatter yourself they may come to America?

"HEART: God only knows what is to happen. I see nothing
impossible in that supposition." The Heart then indulges itself
in another rhapsody about riding with Maria in the hills around
Monticello. Above all, Jefferson wishes to spare his friends, the
Cosways, grief such as his Heart has known, for he is "deeply
practised in the school of affliction, the human heart knows no
joy which I have not lost, no sorrow of which I have not drank!
Fortune can present no grief of unknown form to me!"

The Head then goes on to admonish the Heart for its recklessness. It should weigh and calculate the cost of its impetuousness and turn from its dependence on others, which makes it so
vulnerable—if one "loses a child, a parent or a partner," one
"must mourn the loss as if it was our own"—to the purer and
safer joys of scholarship. "Those," the Head says, "which depend on ourselves, are the only pleasures a wise man will count

on: for nothing is ours which another may deprive us of.''

The reflections on the safety of intellectual pleasures and the danger of all human attachments—"It is a fearful thing to love what death can touch" was another such cry—are some of the most revealing passages in all Jefferson's writings. Indeed, these are among the very few passages of personal reflection Jefferson allowed himself, and they tell us as clearly as anything can the terrible anguish of those losses in his own life that drove him further and further into a realm of the mind where the sorrows of the world have difficulty penetrating. One senses that Jefferson was always involved in this kind of emotional calculus. How much love could he afford to give—and to whom—lest he have to bear once more the devastating sorrow of losing someone he was profoundly attached to and dependent on.

So, to the advice to withdraw to a world of books and ideas, Jefferson's Heart replies, "In a life where we are perpetually exposed to want and accident, yours is a wonderful proposition, to insulate ourselves, to retire from all aid, and to wrap ourselves in the mantle of self-sufficiency! For assuredly nobody will care for him who cares for nobody." And then the Heart goes on to its most eloquent phrases in praise of the emotional (and moral) life, coming at last to the conclusive argument: "If our country, when pressed with wrongs at the point of the bayonet," the Heart asks the Head, "had been governed by it's heads instead of it's hearts, where should we have been now? hanging on a gallows as high as Haman's. You began to calculate and to compare wealth and numbers: we threw up a few pulsations of our warmest blood: we supplied enthusiasm against wealth and numbers: we put our existence to the hazard, when the hazard seemed against us, and we saved our country. . . . In short, my friend, as far as my recollection serves me, I do not know that I ever did a good thing on your suggestion, or a dirty one without it. I do for ever then disclaim your interference in my province. Fill paper as you please with triangles and squares: try how many ways you can hang and combine them together. . . . But leave me to decide when and where friendships are to be contracted."

And then, reminding himself and Maria that this uncommonly long sermon was, after all, a love letter, Jefferson added, "If your letters are as long as the bible, they will appear short to me. Only let them be brim full of affection. I shall read them with the dispositions with which Arlequin in les deux billets spelt the words 'je t'aime' and wished that the whole alphabet had entered into their composition."

The image of himself as a "natural man" ruled by his emotions was clearly one that appealed strongly to him. On a trip to Düsseldorf he saw a painting of Sarah delivering Hagar to Abraham, which, he wrote Maria Cosway, he thought "delicious. I would have agreed to have been Abraham though the consequence would have been that I should have been dead five or six thousand years. . . . I am but a son of nature, loving what I see and feel, without being able to give a reason, nor caring much whether there be one."

The dialogue of the Head and the Heart is certainly one of the most charming love letters that any great figure has written to the object of his infatuation. Profoundly revealing of Jefferson, it draws back, as it were, briefly and tantalizingly, the veil that always concealed his inner emotional life, a fleeting, vivid moment of self-revelation. The warmth of love overcame all his defenses, thawed the frozen spaces, made him certainly as irresistible to Maria as to us who read his tract on love. And it has disconcerted historians. Some have even declared the dialogue to be heavily weighted in favor of reason, though it is difficult to imagine through what reasonable lenses they read. Almost without exception they have hastened to assure us that Jefferson's affair with Maria Cosway was just a harmless little flirtation with no sexual overtones, entirely platonic. Perhaps the thought of the author of the Declaration of Independence, the future President of the United States, and the advocate of reason wandering around Paris in a daze of love with another man's wife was simply too much for them to handle. One thing seems certain, however. Jefferson did realize two classic fantasies. He met in Paris a beautiful young musician and artist, fell madly in love, and had that world center of Eros in which to savor his

VUE DE L'EXTÉRIEUR DE
LA HALLE AU BLED.

Introduced at a Paris grain market (above) in 1786,
Thomas Jefferson and Maria Cosway, an artist who
shared his interest in music, fell in love. Although
they remained friends for years, their affair ended
after a few months when Maria returned to England
with her husband (left, a portrait by Richard Cosway
of himself and his wife).

love. Fantasy Two: as a middle-aged man who thought himself invulnerable to or beyond the reach of romantic love, he became enamoured of a beautiful young artist and had a passionate affair with her.

But some interesting questions remain to be answered. If Jefferson did not advertise his romance, he carefully preserved all the memorabilia of it. Why did this secretive man, who destroyed the letters that had passed between him and his adored Martha, keep the correspondence relating to his affair with another man's wife, the correspondence that has proved such an embarrassment to the bulk of his biographers? Several points suggest themselves. Maria Cosway was a thoroughly "safe" love. She was married to another man, unhappily, to be sure, but with no thought of leaving him and apparently with no thought on Jefferson's part of ever suggesting such a course. Much as they may have been infatuated with each other, since they both understood that their relationship was a transient one and therefore cast it in the classic mold (one thinks of Washington's different but similar love for Sally Fairfax), a love destined to end, they were free to play out all the pains and pleasures of that romantic style.

Jefferson, for example, could not become love-dependent, the affair being prescribed and contained by the particular social context in which it took place. And human nature being what it is, this fact doubtless added to its delights. All the problems of the real world with which Jefferson was never much at home, among them such mundane matters as marrying, fathering children, growing old, having spats and misunderstandings, being grouchy in the morning—none of these entered into this idyllic love. Thus, much as Jefferson may have suffered at having to give up the charming Maria, it was a limited, manageable, entirely foreseen suffering that, happily, could be converted into literature, and the pain thereby considerably alleviated. So Jefferson's familiar impulse to eradicate all the evidence of acute suffering did not appear here. Moreover, the dialogue is quite a stunning work, a minor classic, and Jefferson knew it to be so —he carefully made a copy, something lovers in their impetuousness seldom do. Perhaps he had his biographers in mind: something for them to chew on (he could hardly have guessed at their ingenuity in explaining it away). And beyond this, one would like to think that he was quite humanly proud of his conquest and that it had roused him to life in a unique and, ultimately for him, very satisfying way. From a totally enthralling romance, it became a treasured and delightful memory.

The dialogue between the Head and the Heart was not the last word, of course. Jefferson and Maria continued to write passionate love letters to each other. The intervals between his letters, Maria wrote, were "the punishment of Tantalus." Of one of his long letters she wrote, "My heart is . . . full or ready to burst. . . . Your letter could employ me for some time, an hour to Consider every word, to every sentence I could write a volume. . . . Everything is tranquil, quiet and gloomy, there are no Bells ringing. . . . [Your letters] will never be long enough." When Jefferson's right hand was well enough to write with, he noted, "When sins are dear to us we are but too prone to slide into them again. The act of repentance itself is often sweetened with the thought that it clears our account for a repetition of the same sin."

Jefferson looked forward to the Cosways' making another trip to Paris in the spring, but when Maria wrote that her husband had delayed the projected visit, Jefferson whiled away the time by taking a tour through southern France and the Italian Alps. At Nîmes he saw for the first time the Maison Carrée, which he had so admired in paintings and engravings. To one of the French ladies whose companionship he enjoyed he wrote: "Here I am, Madam, gazing whole hours at the Maison quarrée, like a lover at his mistress." If he could not gaze upon his mistress, the Maison Carrée was clearly the next best thing. "The stocking weavers and silk spinners around it consider me a hypochondriac Englishman," he noted, "about to write with a pistol the last chapter of his history. This is the second time I have been in love since I left Paris. The first was with a Diana at the Château de Laye-Epinaye in Beaujolois, a delicious morsel of sculpture. . . . While in Paris, I was violently smitten with the

The main purpose of Jefferson's trip to the south of France (right, the Pont du Gard at Nimes; below, Marseilles) was to see Roman antiquities. However, he also had a prearranged meeting at Nimes with a Brazilian revolutionary hoping to secure $26 million in American aid. Jefferson made no commitment, but he wrote to Madison that Brazil was "too near us, to make its movements altogether indifferent to our interests, or to our curiosity."

Hôtel de Salm, and used to go to the Tuileries almost daily, to look at it. . . . I am immersed in antiquities from morning to night. For me, the city of Rome is actually existing in all the splendor of its empire."

But even with the joy of gazing, uninterrupted, at his favorite building, the trip was flat and dreary without Maria. Like all lovers he kept seeing things that he longed to share with her. "Why were you not with me?" he wrote when he returned to Paris. "So many enchanting scenes which only wanted your pencil to consecrate them to fame. . . . Come then, my dear Madam, and we will breakfast every day a l'Angloise, hie away to the Desert, dine under the bowers of Marly, and forget that we are ever to part again."

Finally, when her husband flatly refused to go to Paris, Maria Cosway went alone. To this part of their romance, Jefferson was discreet enough to destroy all allusions. Perhaps he felt that as long as her husband was in the offing, some ambiguity clung to the relationship—the American diplomat had an English artist friend of whose wife he was especially fond. Without her husband both Maria and Jefferson were more vulnerable to damaging gossip. Thus her return in August, 1787, was shrouded in secrecy. She stayed with a friend, the Princess Lubomirski, and announced to anyone interested that she was in Paris to visit galleries and museums. But her husband was furious at her absence and at her failure to write, and she and Jefferson were together only as often as they dared. It is also clear that Maria felt growing uneasiness about her husband's indignation at her absence and also about the state of her soul, since she was a devout Catholic. That she and Jefferson were often alone at his home is indicated by a postscript to one of her letters, dated December 1, 1787, "I hope Mr. Short [Jefferson's secretary] will not be out as is usual when I have the pleasure to come to you."

There is ample evidence that Maria Cosway was highly emotional and very changeable in her moods, and Jefferson seems to have found them increasingly difficult to handle. In addition, Maria became the dependent one in the relationship.

Her letters to Jefferson from England, often chiding him for
long delays in writing, took on an almost pleading tone. Con-
trasting her own situation with Jefferson's she showed that she
was jealous of him, surrounded as he was by attractive and
admiring women. So it was not Jefferson who suffered that emo-
tion of loss so familiar to him, but rather the charming and
volatile Maria. It is small wonder that between religious guilt,
fear of pregnancy, which was almost an obsession with her, and
anxiety about her husband's reaction she was often unhappy and
distraught when they were together, and the undiluted joy of
their first encounter was tarnished by her preoccupation with
problems that had no solution. Yet it is plain enough that their
love persisted, and even on the eve of his departure Jefferson
urged Maria and her friend Angelica Church to sail for America
with him. When she wrote of going to Italy instead, he replied:
"The one or the other of us goes the wrong way, for the way will
ever be wrong which leads us farther apart." To which she
responded, "Pray write, pray write, & dont go to America without coming to England."

Jefferson spent Maria's last evening with her and was to
have had breakfast with her the next morning. But she fled,
leaving a note behind: "I cannot breakfast with you tomorrow;
to bid you adieu once is sufficiently painful, for I leave you with
very melancholy ideas. You have given my dear Sir all your
commissions to Mr. Trumbull, and I have the reflection that I
cannot be useful to you; who have rendered me so many civili-
ties." As they continued to correspond, an increasing note of
desperation appears in her letters to Jefferson. "You are happy
you can follow so Much your inclinations," she wrote. "I wish
I could do the same. I do all I can, but with little success." She
urged Jefferson to come to London, promising "to Make Myself
and my Society according to your own wishes. At home we may
do it better." But the delight and pain were over for Jefferson,
and gradually and tactfully he disengaged himself from Maria.
She went on as surely to tragedy and disaster as Jefferson did to
greater fame and power as President of the United States and
founder of the party of democracy. Eventually she left her hus-

206

band and after various misadventures established a convent school for girls in Lodi, Italy. Her husband went mad and died a delusive, talking of his discussions with Dante and Praxiteles.

When Jefferson heard, in January, 1785, of the death of his daughter Lucy Elizabeth from whooping cough, he became determined that his second daughter, Polly, should be sent to join him in Paris. Although the child was devoted to her aunt, Elizabeth Eppes, with whom she lived, Jefferson began a campaign that culminated in the Eppeses' sending Polly to France in the care of Sally Hemings, one of John Wayles's black children whom his wife had inherited upon her father's death. Sally Hemings was a striking-looking light-skinned mulatto, known at Monticello as Dashing Sally. She was fourteen years old when she and her reluctant charge arrived in Paris. Evidently Sally, young as she was, was a determined and strong-willed girl. The captain of the ship on which Sally and Polly traveled to England had given it as his opinion, Abigail Adams wrote to Jefferson, that she "will be of so little Service that he had better carry her back with him. But of this you will be a judge. She seems fond of the child and appears good natured." Abigail herself described Sally as "quite a child." It seems evident that Sally Hemings gave little indication of having what might be called a slave mentality. She knew herself to be three-fourths white, and she understood plainly enough that despite her good looks and intelligence she was doomed to a life of hopeless ambiguity. Abigail, who knew as soon as she looked at Sally Hemings what if not who she was, realized also that this striking child with her frank, bold ways could pose a real threat to her friend Jefferson. Whatever else she might be, Sally was not going to become a quiet, self-effacing servant in the Jefferson household.

Abigail took Polly Jefferson immediately to her heart, writing her father that the young girl's "temper, her disposition, her sensibility are all formed to delight. I never felt so attached to a child in my Life on so short an acquaintance." Jefferson was waiting for Maria Cosway's solo visit to Paris, and, not daring to go himself to fetch his daughter, he sent his slave, Petit. Abigail was indignant with him and wrote that Polly herself had declared that "as she had left all her Friends in virginia to come over the ocean to see you, she did think you would have taken the pains to come here for her. . . ."

Jefferson had last seen Polly when she was five, almost four years earlier. The child did not recognize him or her sister, Patsy. Sally Hemings was reunited with her brother James, Jefferson's personal valet. Most of what we know of the subsequent relationship between Jefferson and Sally Hemings comes from their son Madison Hemings, who in 1873, as an old man, wrote an account for the *Pike County Republican,* a rural Ohio newspaper. Virtually all Jefferson's biographers have dismissed Madison Hemings's memoir as a fabrication. None of them writing prior to Fawn Brodie in *Thomas Jefferson, An Intimate History* have been willing to accept the possibility that Sally Hemings was indeed Jefferson's mistress and the mother of a number of children by him. Fawn Brodie has adduced considerable evidence, in addition to Hemings's letter, supporting his claim to be Jefferson's son. A substantial portion of this evidence is psychological in nature and thus subject, in the minds of most conventional historians, to serious question. But much of Brodie's attention is concentrated on *disproving* the arguments that other biographers have produced to *disprove* Madison Hemings's account (such as statements that Jefferson was not at Monticello when Sally Hemings's pregnancies began). If nothing existed beyond Madison Hemings's own reminiscence, and this could not positively be proved false, that document is of itself—in the intimate knowledge that it displays of the details of Jefferson's private life, details that could have been conveyed only by Sally Hemings herself to her son—wholly convincing. The set of conjectures that one would have to accept in order to disavow Hemings's letter confidently is so extensive that one's whole sense of the nature of truth and life rebels against it.

Madison Hemings was Sally's third son, born at Monticello in 1805. In his *Pike County Republican* article he wrote: My mother's "stay [in Paris] was about eighteen months. But during that time my mother became Mr. Jefferson's concubine, and when he was called back home she was *enciente* by him. He desired to

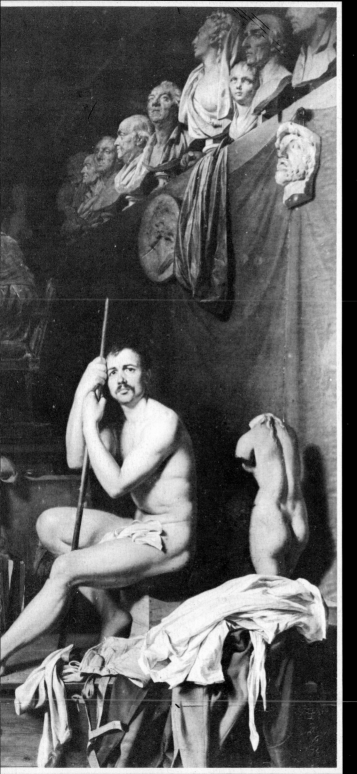

Jefferson commissioned famous French sculptor Jean Antoine Houdon to prepare a statue of George Washington (above) for Virginia's state capitol. The painting at left of Houdon at work in his studio shows busts of Franklin, Washington, and Jefferson in the background.

bring my mother back to Virginia with him but she demurred. She was just beginning to understand the French language well, and in France she was free, while if she returned to Virginia she would be re-enslaved. So she refused to return with him. To induce her to do so he promised her extraordinary privileges, and made a solemn pledge that her children should be free at the age of twenty-one years. In consequence of his promises, on which she implicitly relied, she returned with him to Virginia. Soon after their arrival, she gave birth to a child, of whom Thomas Jefferson was the father."

It will, in any event, be the assumption of this work that Sally Hemings did indeed become Jefferson's mistress, that the relationship ended in love if it did not begin in it, and that Sally Hemings was a notably self-reliant, independent woman who gave Jefferson all the love, attention, and tenderness that the most amiable of wives could give a husband. Jefferson reputedly had promised Martha on her deathbed not to marry again. There is no indication that he was ever tempted. Indeed, as we have suggested, the passionate affair with Maria Cosway may have been what it was for Jefferson largely because there was no possibility that marriage could have come of it. To marry again would have been to expose himself to that terrible experience of loss which he might, literally, not have been able to survive.

So Sally Hemings was in one sense the perfect mate. She belonged to Jefferson in two ways: she was his lover and his property. She was intelligent, handsome, perhaps beautiful, full of spirit and fire, undoubtedly "ardent"—a rewarding companion in bed—and above all unthreatening. If their relationship was, by the nature of it, ambiguous, she was not. Psychologists tell us there is a bondage complex in many men which involves a heightened sexual pleasure that is the consequence of masculine dominance expressed in the binding or confining of the sexual partner. Certainly the apparently almost universal indulgence of white masters with black slave women must have been related to this "bondage," which in turn is related to fantasies of rape; every relation of a white man with a black woman had this covert quality of rape, of taking something forbidden. Jefferson himself was unlikely to have been unaffected by it to some degree. What was secretive in Jefferson's nature must have responded to this most secret of relationships.

Finally, for a man bitterly opposed to slavery, the taking of a slave woman as a mistress was both a kind of expiation for his guilt and a self-crucifying act. In so doing, Jefferson placed the issue of race at the center of his life: at the point of sex and the siring of children. If Maria Cosway had stimulated his sexual desires without perhaps always fulfilling them and thus stirred him into new life, these desires moved readily and almost inevitably toward this exciting new female presence in the household.

12. Secretary of State

Although Jefferson's love affair with Maria Cosway often drew his mind far from the problems of his homeland, he chafed for news, depending on the faithful Madison to keep him informed of the problems and hazards facing the new nation. There was trouble in Massachusetts, where late in the summer of 1786 angry farmers, indignant at efforts to collect debts and taxes by foreclosing their farms, took up arms in a spirit reminiscent of the resistance to Great Britain and closed the law courts. Led by Captain Daniel Shays, they raised the specter of rebellion. The Reverend James Madison wrote that the uprising gave indications of "the Beginnings of a civil War there," which "appear to some as Proofs of ye Instability & Misery inseparable from a Republican Govt. But to others, who I trust judge better, they appear only as ye Symptoms of a strong & healthy Constitution, which, after discharging a few peccant Humours, will be restored to new Vigour."

Jefferson took the latter view. He had, in his *Notes on Virginia,* stated as a fact that "from the conclusion of this war we shall be going down hill"—that is to say, getting further and further away from the principles of the Revolution. Shays's Rebellion, so called, sounded to Jefferson like the fruit of the fulfillment of his prophecy, a desperate resistance against the growth of a society of privilege in which the ordinary man was the victim, increasingly, of exploitation by those who controlled the wealth and who in consequence wielded the power. "I hold it that a little rebellion now and then is a good thing," Jefferson wrote the other James Madison, "& as necessary in the political world as storms in the physical. Unsuccessful rebellions indeed generally establish the incroachments on the rights of the people which have produced them. An observation of this truth should render honest republican governors so mild in their punishment of rebellions, as not to discourage them too much. It is a medicine necessary for the sound health of government."

The sentences are among the most famous Jefferson wrote. Although like Holy Scripture they have been quoted in support of often opposing political philosophies, it seems safe to say that they have been most typically an obstacle to the champions of the status quo, indeed to all those Americans who have wished to preserve a privileged position and to whom the notion of revolution—except for a denatured American Revolution—is anathema. While historians and politicians have often stumbled over what here seems to be an incitement to political violence, we can perhaps get a better perspective today on the passage (and several like it) than at other times in our history because we are presently far more conscious of the tendency of all revolutionary movements to become rigid and reactionary. If power and privilege (and usually wealth as well) come to be concentrated in the hands of the leaders of a revolution, those leaders typically display an inclination to become conservative, that is, to be ready to put down any uprisings that threaten *their* power.

But even more dangerous to the liberties of the people is the fact that the further in time one moves from a revolution, the more attenuated the principles of the revolution become and the greater the opportunities for the unscrupulous and acquisitive to exploit those groups in society least able to protect themselves. These powerless groups constitute Jefferson's "people." Those controlling power, Jefferson seems to be saying, cannot be counted on to understand the needs of the powerless or to redress their grievances. They must have those needs presented to them in such a fashion that they cannot ignore or misunderstand them; this is best accomplished by "a little rebellion now and then," which forces the possessors of power to redistribute it or to become more sensitive and responsive in their uses of it. Those at the bottom—the mass of the people—must constantly remind those at the top—the managers of power—of the ultimate source of that power which they often wield so heedlessly.

"The people," Jefferson wrote to Edward Carrington in a similar vein, "are the only censors of their governors: and even their errors will tend to keep these to the true principles of their institution. To punish these errors too severely would be to suppress the only safeguard of the public liberty." He had observed enough in Europe to be convinced that "if once the people become inattentive to the public affairs, you & I, & Congress & Assemblies, judges & governors shall all become wolves," with "governments preying on the people and the rich on the poor."

To Ezra Stiles, president of Yale, whom he had met on his trip to New Haven, he wrote that Shays's Rebellion was "proof that the people have liberty enough, and I would not wish them less than they have. If the happiness of the mass of the people can be secured at the expence of a little tempest now & then, or even of a little blood, it will be a precious purchase." The notion of the tree of liberty being watered by the blood of martyrs, this bloody-mindedness of Jefferson's rhetoric, was most disconcerting to his critics. The American Revolution in the initial phases of its resistance to the authority of Parliament had been conspicuous for lack of blood. The patriots had spilled cascades of rhetoric but no blood prior to Lexington and Concord. They had put their faith in the British constitution and the laws until it was clear beyond cavil that those great systems were powerless to save them. So why the blood? Jefferson had never spilled any —his own or others'—in defense of liberty, or even seen any spilled.

Another bit of news from America that disturbed Jefferson was the reports of extravagance in personal habits and in government. People were, he understood, being corrupted by schemes to make quick fortunes. "From these accounts," he wrote a friend, "I look back to the time of war as a time of happiness and enjoyment, when amidst the privation of many things not essential to happiness, we could not run in debt, because nobody would trust us; when we practiced by necessity the maxim of buying nothing but what we had money in our pockets to pay for; a maxim which, of all others, lays the broadest foundation for happiness." Jefferson might speak as one who knew. He was deeply and perpetually in debt himself, and his efforts to meet the demands of his most persistent creditors were a constant strain. In the midst of such reflections on political philosophy, he could change pace to write a long letter to William Drayton of South Carolina on the various types of rice grown in different parts of the world and on other agricultural matters.

By early August, 1787, the first rumblings of the French Revolution could be heard. The French parliament was resisting the king's request for new taxes. The king summoned its members to Versailles, but they remained recalcitrant; Jefferson gave it as his opinion that "a spirit is advancing towards a revolution in their constitution."

While Jefferson carried out his diplomatic duties and his romance with Maria, delegates from the American states had met in Philadelphia in May, 1787, to try to repair the shortcomings that, time had made all too evident, were woven into the fabric of the Articles of Confederation. In France Jefferson followed developments as best he could. When the new United States Constitution was finally completed in September and a copy came to his hand from John Adams's son-in-law, William Smith, in London, Jefferson was especially disturbed by the absence of a clause limiting the number of terms a President could serve. He blamed the omission on the fear of instability aroused by Shays's Rebellion. Once again he could not forbear to point out that American leaders had overreacted to that event. "Can history produce an instance of rebellion so honourably conducted?" he asked William Smith. It was "founded in ignorance, not wickedness. God forbid we should ever be 20 years without such a rebellion. . . . What country can preserve

Jefferson remained in France while the Constitutional Convention met from May to September, 1787 (right, Washington presiding at a meeting). He expounded his views to James Madison (above) in letters and complained about the delegates' oath of secrecy: "I am sorry they began their deliberrations by so abominable a precedent as that of tying up the tongues of their members."

its liberties if their rulers are not warned from time to time that their people preserve the spirit of resistance? Let them take arms. The remedy is to set them right as to facts, pardon & pacify them. What signifies a few lives lost in a century or two? The tree of liberty must be refreshed from time to time with the blood of patriots & tyrants. It is its natural manure."

After pondering over the Constitution for some time, Jefferson wrote a letter to Francis Hopkinson, who had addressed him as a federalist. "I am not a federalist," he replied, "because I never submitted the whole system of my opinions to the creed of any party of men whatever in religion, in philosophy, in politics, or in anything else, where I was capable of thinking for myself. Such an addiction is the last degradation of a free and moral agent. If I could not go to heaven but with a party, I would not go there at all." But if he was not a federalist, he was "much farther from . . . the anti-federalist. I approved, from the first moment, of the great mass of what is in the new Constitution. . . ." His two major reservations were the "perpetual re-eligibility of the President" and the absence of a bill of rights.

It was ironic that Jefferson, obsessed by the problems of constitution making, should have been elsewhere when the two constitutions most important to him were fashioned. When the Virginia constitution was being drafted he was doing one of his brief stints in Congress, writing the document that, more than any constitution he could have framed, insured his fame. When the Constitution of the United States was being drafted in the summer of 1787, he was carrying on his diplomatic duties in a rather desultory way and courting Maria Cosway. Now he watched, fascinated, the opening phases of the great drama of the French Revolution. He was privy to its every movement and fluctuation through his friendship with Lafayette, himself deeply involved. Throughout June the members of the Third Estate, the body of the legislature representing the people in general (as opposed to the First Estate, representing the nobles, and the Second, representing the clergy), tried to take control of the finances of the kingdom and thereby assert themselves as the ultimate power in France. When they were locked out of their meeting hall by the king, they adjourned to a nearby tennis court and constituted themselves the National Assembly, vowing not to part until a constitution had been drafted and accepted by the other orders.

The enraged king through his master of ceremonies ordered the assembly to disband, but when that gentleman conveyed the message, a member of the assembly named Mirabeau, a defector from the order of nobles, called out, "Go tell those who sent you that we are here by the will of the people and that we shall not leave except at the point of the bayonet." As surely as any words heralded the onset of a revolution those of Mirabeau did. When the more reactionary nobles persuaded the king to dismiss the popular minister of finance, the Paris mob stormed the Bastille, the symbol of the arbitrary power of the king, and freed the prisoners held there.

Just as with the beginning of the American Revolution in the Stamp Act riots and demonstrations, the assault on the Bastille had happened suddenly and unpredictably. What started as a simple move for parliamentary reform triggered the mass discontent of the proletariat of Paris and flared at once into a full-scale revolution. For an advocate of revolutions and a little periodic bloodshed, it was a sobering experience. Jefferson continued to support the French Revolution long after many Americans had been revolted by its cruelties and bloodshed, but he did not speak soon again of the salutary effect of occasional bloodletting. He tried, indeed, to persuade those leaders of the assembly whom he knew to compromise with the king and his party in order to bring about some measure of constraint, but the more radical leaders saw an opportunity to use popular fury to achieve their ends. Jefferson blamed the queen's influence over the king for his intractability—"I have ever believed," he wrote later, "that had there been no queen, there would have been no revolution"—thereby demonstrating that he had a very imperfect grasp of this particular revolution.

In any event, the French Revolution was soon rushing along on its bloody and tumultuous course. Jefferson was persuaded by Lafayette to receive a group of moderates at his house to

In the spring of 1788 Jefferson journeyed north and visited Düsseldorf, Cologne, and Mannheim and toured the wine region at Hochheim. In Strasbourg he made several purchases at Amand Koenig's bookshop (above) and later wrote: "Koenig has the best shop of classical books I ever saw."

discuss strategy. This was a serious breach of diplomatic etiquette, but it passed without creating an incident, perhaps because Jefferson's weight was plainly on the side of moderation. He was convinced that "the King, the mass of the substantial people of the whole country, the army, and the influential part of the clergy, form a firm phalanx which must prevail."

For some time Jefferson had been anxious to return to the United States for an extended leave from his diplomatic duties, and Congress finally granted him permission to take a leave of absence. The word arrived in August, 1789, some three months after the inauguration of the government under the new Constitution, with Washington as President. Jefferson made preparations for his departure immediately. Although he intended to return to France, he had a vast collection of things to take with him to Virginia—eighty-six packing cases in all, including fifteen cases of books, in addition to mirrors, paintings, statuary, wines, tables, beds, forty-four chairs and sofas, and a host of other items.

Before he left he wrote Madison another famous letter, prompted by the upheaval of the French Revolution. On September 6, surrounded by crates and boxes, his household in all the disorder attendant upon packing, he sat down to indulge himself in some philosophical reflections. The question that perplexed him, he wrote Madison, was "whether one generation of men has a right to bind another. . . ." It was his opinion that it did not. "I set out on this ground, which I suppose to be self evident, *'that the earth belongs in usufruct to the living':* that the dead have neither powers nor rights over it. The portion occupied by any individual ceases to be his when he himself ceases to be, and reverts to the society." If then his heirs are allowed to retain it, it is at the pleasure, so to speak, of the society, and not a natural right of the heirs themselves to inherit it or of the deceased to entail it to them. Otherwise a man could, during his own lifetime, use up the fruit of his lands for several generations to come, "and then the lands would belong to the dead, and not to the living. . . ."

As with the individual, so with society in general. If one

could imagine a single generation all born on the same day, whose members would all "go off the stage at a fixed moment," then the principle would become clear. All would relinquish all their rights in land to the succeeding generation. From this conclusion Jefferson argued that a nation had no right to incur debts that could not be paid off within a generation, thirty-four years by his calculation. Later he added a kind of footnote in which he calculated that thirty-four years was too long. Nineteen was the proper number. "On similar ground," he continued, "it may be proved that no society can make a perpetual constitu-tion, or even a perpetual law. The earth belongs always to the living generation; they may manage it, then, and what proceeds from it, as they please. . . . Every constitution, then, and every law, naturally expires at the end of nineteen years."

Jefferson ended his letter with an admonition to Madison to reflect upon the principles he had adumbrated. "At first blush," he wrote, "it may be laughed at, as the dream of a theorist; but examination will prove it to be solid and salutary." Eccentric as the notion seems to us today, it was not entirely new. The radical and much denounced Pennsylvania constitution of 1776 had provided that a "Council of Censors" be appointed to review all laws in order to judge "whether the Constitution has been pre-served inviolate in every part; and whether the legislative and executive branches of government have performed their duty as guardians of the people." Although the notion there was to prevent abuse of the constitution, its provisions rose from the same concern that lay behind Jefferson's proposal: that those who held power would use it for their own interests to the cost of the "generality"—the mass of ordinary citizens.

Viewed in another way, it followed logically from Jeffer-son's rather cavalier statements at the time of Shays's Rebellion, when he recommended periodic insurrections to keep the rulers up to the mark. Having in the interim witnessed the conse-quences of bloodletting, Jefferson decided that some more or-derly process was desirable. Those who felt that their rights were being infringed and concocted a little rebellion to call attention to the fact, might, in consequence, all be shot. There-

Jefferson was initially sympathetic to the French Revolution and reported events to John Jay, secretary of foreign affairs. After the Tennis Court Oath of June 27, 1789, pictured here by Jacques Louis David, he wrote to Jay and prophesied incorrectly: "I shall not have matter interesting enough to trouble you with as often as I have done lately."

fore, assuming that power invariably corrupted and rulers invariably exploited the people whose rights and well-being they were charged with protecting, the only recourse seemed to Jefferson to be to tear everything up and start all over again every nineteen years.

If Jefferson meant simply to give dramatic emphasis to the point that all governments move, at varying speeds but inevitably, toward rigidity and oppression, his letter perhaps served its purpose. Certainly it has been quoted by revolutionaries the world over ever since Jefferson articulated it. If, on the other hand, he was serious, which is hard to believe, he must have been disappointed in the effect it produced—for the most part bafflement and incredulity. Like so many things that Jefferson said, his "earth belongs to the living" remains ultimately inscrutable, the kind of Delphic utterance that he was content to lay on a startled world without condescending to explain himself further and without considering that his latest prescription was quite inconsistent with a number of previous ones. But the persistence with which Jefferson's formulations have buzzed around in our heads reveals their fecundity. If they were merely eccentric—though eccentric they surely are—they would have long since been forgotten. In any event the letter to Madison of September 6, 1789, was a kind of valedictory to France, his second home. If the French would only adopt his scheme they might be spared a cataclysm such as that which they were presently suffering, and, it might be assumed, they would soon be suffering again when the reforms that they hoped might result from the present imbroglio had hardened into repressive and inhumane institutions.

Jefferson's enemies claimed that his five years abroad had completely alienated him from the temper of the American people, filled him with free-thinking deistic heresies, and quite addled his brain. Certainly the years in France were among the happiest years of his life if not the most productive. All the civilized delights of that most civilized of countries were savored by him. His tastes were refined, his enthusiasms indulged. The attentions of renowned philosophers and entrancing women drew him back from the brink of that chasm of despair into which he had so often stared. Most of all his giddy romance with Maria Cosway, touched though it was with overtones of sadness, gave him a new life, in part by arousing him from his morbid obsession with his wife's death and in part simply by sending the blood coursing more vigorously through his veins. The Heart, in practical fact, did triumph over the Head, and the triumph was not a temporary one. The place that Maria had created in that organ was quickly occupied by "Dashing Sally" Hemings, whose bewitchingness we can only surmise by the rapidity with which her relationship with her master developed and by its duration.

Thomas Jefferson returned to America a very different man from the one who had left it five years earlier. And he came back to a very different country. Washington was President, and Jefferson's friend, John Adams, Vice President, which was enough to dispose him favorably toward the new government. Alexander Hamilton, who had been an aide to Washington during much of the war and was perhaps closer to that august presence than anyone else, was secretary of the treasury, and he would use that office to strengthen both the financial position of the United States, which desperately needed strengthening, and the business and commercial interests of the country at the same time. At Richmond the new capitol was a-building, and Jefferson was sure it would be "worthy of being exhibited along side the most celebrated remains of antiquity." The assembly also gathered to do honor to Virginia's native son, doubtless glad to make amends for the unhappy memories of his wartime governorship and its subsequent investigation into his performance in that role. The original manuscript of Jefferson's answer to the assembly's effusive greeting, full of rephrasings, erasures, and emendations, is a kind of map of his own mixed feelings, and it reveals better than a volume of exegesis how keenly he still felt his humiliation almost ten years later.

When Jefferson arrived at the home of his brother-in-law, Francis Eppes, he found a message from Washington requesting him to become secretary of state in his new Cabinet. Jefferson, who had looked forward to returning to France after putting his affairs into some kind of order and enjoying a few months of solitude at Monticello, agonized over the proffered post, certainly one of the two most important positions in the government—the other being the office of secretary of the treasury. He wrote to Washington that he would prefer not to accept the secretaryship, and the principal reason he cited is revealing. There was, he noted, "the possibility that this may end disagreeably for me." He might be subjected to "the criticisms and censures of a public, just indeed in their intentions, but sometimes misinformed and misled." It was a characteristic objection from a man who professed to have a deep faith in the wisdom of the people yet so often shrank from their judgments as shallow and superficial. It is impossible to say how closely Jefferson's reluctance to become secretary of state was related to his desire to return to France. Doubtless Jefferson himself was not certain.

From the Eppes plantation Jefferson and his entourage traveled on to Monticello. There the great homecoming scene was enacted. The slaves had been assembled from Jefferson's various plantations two days before Christmas for the return of the master. At the base of the hill they greeted Jefferson and his daughters like the loyal subjects of a beloved potentate, as indeed Jefferson was. Cheering and hallooing, they unhitched the carriage and pulled it up the hill. "Such a scene," Martha wrote, "I never witnessed in my life. . . . When the door of the carriage was opened they received him in their arms and bore him to the house, crowding round and kissing his hands and feet—some blubbering and crying—others laughing. It seemed impossible to satisfy their anxiety to touch and kiss the very earth which bore him." A stranger drama was hardly to be imagined, or one that spoke more poignantly of the ambiguities at the heart of the relationship between masters and slaves in the American South. To be so demonstrably loved, indeed adored, is a heady experience, enough to make one forget, for the moment, the complicated evils of slavery. There was Sally Hemings, carrying his child, to remind Jefferson of the darker side of this homecoming.

At Monticello plans were made for the marriage of Patsy,

or Martha, to young Thomas Mann Randolph, her second cousin. Martha was seventeen, her husband-to-be four years older. They had met in Paris and had felt a strong mutual attraction. Jefferson thoroughly approved of the marriage, writing that "the talents, temper, family & fortune of the young gentleman are all I could have desired." One might even suspect that Jefferson was the amiable stage manager of the romance. Martha was, indeed, so sensitive to her father's desires that his endorsement of young Randolph might well have been enough to insure his daughter's cheerful acquiescence. It is, of course, a notoriously risky matter for a father to meddle in a daughter's affairs of the heart. Thomas Mann Randolph was, at least on the surface, an agreeable, pliant young man. Given Jefferson's determination to dominate his daughters' lives, Randolph was perhaps an ideal mate for Martha. The very fact that he was willing to have his wife devote a major part of her energies to her father's happiness and well-being prevented what otherwise might have been constant friction produced by two loyalties. Jefferson's enthusiasm for Martha's marriage was certainly not unrelated to the role of Sally Hemings in his life. He doubtless felt the weight of Martha's silent disapproval and was glad to have her out of the house, especially in view of the birth of Sally Hemings's son not long after the return to Monticello.

In the midst of the plans for Martha's wedding, Jefferson received another letter from Washington countering his objections and strongly urging him to join the Cabinet as secretary of state. This time Jefferson found it impossible to refuse, and after Martha's wedding he set out for New York, the temporary seat of the new government. There, in the middle of March, 1790, he took up his duties. The Pennsylvania democrat William Maclay met him soon after his arrival and gave us one of the great pen portraits of the Virginian: "Jefferson is a slender man; has rather the air of stiffness in his manner; his clothes seem too small for him; he sits in a lounging manner, on one hip commonly, and with one of his shoulders elevated much above the other; his face has a sunny aspect; his whole figure has a loose, shackling air. He has a rambling vacant look, and nothing of that

The reluctant first secretary of state arrived in New York in March, 1790 (seen here, New York's Federal Hall, first United States Capitol). Jefferson's initial clash with Secretary of the Treasury Alexander Hamilton (above, in a painting by John Trumbull) ended when he agreed to Hamilton's plan for the assumption of state debts in return for his concession that the new national capital be located in the South.

firm, collected deportment which I expected would dignify the presence of a secretary or minister. I looked for gravity, but a laxity of manner seemed shed about him. He spoke almost without ceasing. But even his discourse partook of his personal demeanor. It was loose and rambling, and yet he scattered information wherever he went, and some even brilliant sentiments sparkled from him. The information which he gave us respecting foreign ministers, etc., was all high-spiced. He had been long enough abroad to catch the tone of European folly."

Besides Jefferson and Hamilton, Washington's Cabinet was filled out by Henry Knox, the able general of artillery, serving as secretary of war, and Edmund Randolph, Jefferson's old friend, seasoned by a term as governor of Virginia, as attorney general.

It is not necessary to go into great detail here concerning Jefferson's tenure as secretary of state. In its general outlines it is as well known as any episode in our early history. It centered on his growing rivalry with Alexander Hamilton both for Washington's ear and in a sense for the shaping of the nation's destiny. The rivalry between the two men—Hamilton and Jefferson —seems, in retrospect, almost too pat a summary of the basic theses and antagonisms in American history. Jefferson, the Virginia aristocrat and slaveholder, emerged as the champion of democracy, the apostle of a predominantly agricultural society resting solidly on the small farmer—a nation of farmers. He was deeply suspicious of banks, financiers, commercial ventures, and all manipulators of money, and of immigrants, who with their alien values might weaken republican principles. While he supported the Constitution wholeheartedly, he interpreted it very differently from his adversary, particularly in the matter of the powers of the President. Jefferson believed that the chief executive should be held within the narrowest limits. He feared all movements toward the centralization and consolidation of power in the federal government; he wished to see the most substantial power vested in the states, with the national government exercising only those powers—such as foreign policy— that no individual state was competent to exercise. He envisioned a modest federal government, in the strict sense of the word "federal," thrifty and abstemious, with no standing army in peacetime to tempt it to overawe the populace and burden it with taxes.

Beyond these general principles relating to the nature of society, and the specific reservations, one might say, about the powers of the presidency and the federal government itself, Jefferson was most apprehensive about the progressive betrayal of the principles of the American Revolution as the nation moved further and further away from the event, further both in time and spirit—as money making, luxury, and self-indulgence erased those civic virtues on which all true republics rest.

Hamilton was the antithesis to Jefferson's thesis. Born in the humblest of circumstances in the West Indies, he had risen to power and importance through his remarkable energy and intelligence, aided by an advantageous marriage. Small and dapper, he had elbowed his way into the top echelons of a New York aristocracy as ancient and well-established in its own way as that of Virginia. As one of Washington's ablest staff officers he had come to exercise a considerable influence over the general during the course of the war, and then, in an absurd contretemps over precedence in going down the stairs of Washington's headquarters, he had broken with his chief and demanded an active-duty assignment with the army. At Yorktown he had performed with dash and bravery and soon after repaired the breach with Washington. He had recently played a leading role in the federal convention that drafted the new Constitution, speaking invariably on the conservative side of issues. A skillful debater and close reasoner, he was above all a man of action who plunged into politics with undisguised gusto. Indeed, when one considers the two men who now engaged each other in a titanic struggle, one can rather easily imagine a celestial casting office, where the Supreme Playwright-Director, with his marvelous sense of earthly drama, was writing the script and designating the roles they were to play. Both men were to suffer from the public revelation of their private sex lives. Hamilton, a notorious womanizer, finally caught in the toils of a female blackmailer, published an account of the sordid affair in order to clear his name of the imputation, spread by Jefferson's supporter, Monroe, a future President of the United States, that he had been accepting bribes for political favors. He thus sacrificed his private reputation for his public one. Jefferson's relationship with Sally Hemings likewise became a matter of public knowledge or public accusation. But Jefferson never replied to the charges.

Hamilton's vision of the future of the country was of a great, busy, bustling hive of commercial activity, of banks and factories, of a strong national government using its powers to stimulate business activity and protect infant industry with tariffs and subsidies; of swarms of immigrants to man the factories and fill up the vacant acres to the west; and of an efficient if modest army and navy. It was not so much that Hamilton was antidemocratic or opposed to republican government—though it must be said that he had an authoritarian streak in him—it was just that Jefferson's attachment to the rural life seemed to Hamilton old-fashioned romanticism, and his suspicion of banks and business as outmoded as a belief in witches. Hamilton's style was complete engagement in war or politics; Jefferson's was disengagement. Where Jefferson always wanted out, Hamilton always wanted in. Where Hamilton was direct, often brutally so, Jefferson was indirect. So there they were, alpha and omega, thesis and antithesis, making up, somehow, America. It might be enough, if anything were, to strike a historian dumb. But historians will go on mulling over this famous contest as long as any presumptuous enough to claim the title are around.

One thing the two men shared—that magic quality known, for want of a better word, as charisma, the power to draw others to them as a magnet draws filings, and bind them with ties of unquestioning loyalty. This quality, of the most essential importance, is in some ways the most difficult for the historian to handle. It is a quality that must be experienced directly in order to be understood. Why are people almost instantly captivated and bound to this individual and not to that one? What is the nature of the strange emanations that we experience in the presence of certain people? The problem is complicated by the fact that these emanations are often reciprocal with the power that the charismatic figure wields, so that we have a formula something like this: charisma is a personal, spiritual, moral (or whatever) force multiplied by the office held. What Jefferson and Hamilton shared, then, was the power to attract followers who felt sufficiently in the shadow of one or the other to create, for all practical purposes, two separate and distinct political parties. These were to a substantial degree the lengthened shadows of the respective men, or to put it another way, they were parties that the two men personified to an astonishing degree.

The arbiter of this contest was the President of the United States. Only a figure with *his* charisma could have encompassed and dominated their charismas and kept the whole enterprise from running off the tracks. So Washington was the third and essential member of this company. It was he, after all, who had summoned them. (Jefferson had written him: "My chief comfort will be to work under your eye, my only shelter the authority of your name, and the wisdom of measures to be dictated by you and implicitly executed by me.") After the two Cabinet members had locked horns Washington wrote Jefferson, "I believe the views of both of you to be pure and well-meant. . . . I have a great, a sincere esteem and regard for you both, and ardently wish that some line could be marked out by which both [of] you could walk."

If Washington was already, in a sense, Hamilton's "father" by virtue of their wartime relationship, Jefferson was plainly ready to claim Washington as *his* lost father. So, to cast the drama in quasi-Freudian terms, the two gifted "sons" contended for the approval and love, that is, "policy," of their "father" (as Jefferson later wrote, "Hamilton and myself were daily pitted in the cabinet like two cocks"). Jefferson in time shrank from the contest and more than once expressed his wish to abandon the struggle for the contemplative delights of Monticello. But Washington would not let him go. So he remained to become, almost in spite of himself, the founder of a party that claimed to be based on his principles of government.

Rival newspapers exacerbated the Hamilton-Jefferson clash. In this pro-Hamilton cartoon, Washington, driving the federal chariot, leads troops against French cannibals (Jeffersonian rabble) as Jefferson desperately tries to stop the wheels of government.

Stop de wheels of

de gouvernement

rish all its enemies.

though slow, is sure.

Presented to the New York
State Historical Society.
By Geo B. Reed. Montpelier
Vermont.

Having said all this we can pass over the details of the conflict. They are recounted in a hundred texts. One unhappy corollary was that as Jefferson became more and more closely identified with a position critical of the Washington administration, his friendship with John Adams began to cool. Adams was accused of having aristocratic and monarchical sympathies, in large part because of his emphasis on a strong President and his desire to surround the office with many of the formalities associated in the public mind with monarchy. When Jefferson, by implication, accused Adams of a preference for monarchy, Adams replied coolly, "I know not what your idea is of the best form of government. You and I have never had a serious conversation together, that I can recollect, concerning the nature of government," and to his wife he wrote, "I am really astonished at the blind spirit of party which has seized on the soul of this Jefferson. There is not a Jacobin in France more devoted to faction." Hamilton referred to Jefferson and Madison as having *"a womanish attachment to France and a womanish resentment against Great Britain."*

Jefferson sponsored a newspaper, edited by the poet Philip Freneau, which delighted in sniping at the administration. Even Washington was not immune from its assaults. The nuclei of what came to be called, rather confusingly for later generations, the Republican party—the party of which Jefferson was the leader (as opposed to the Federalist party, which it might be argued was the ancestor of the Republican party that we know today)—were the democratic societies that sprang up in many places as centers of opposition to Washington's administration. The principal common denominator of the clubs, or "societies" as they were often called, was an adherence to the cause of the French Revolution and a settled hostility toward Great Britain. The members of the democratic societies saw in the growing rapprochement with Great Britain what they thought was a betrayal of the Revolution. In their view the commercial and manufacturing interests of the country were actively encouraging the augmentation of the powers of government, confident that they could direct it to their own purposes. These societies looked to

Jefferson as their model and mentor.

Despite Washington's assurances, Jefferson felt himself constantly losing ground to Hamilton. In his hatred of the British and admiration of the French he was in opposition to the general policy of Washington's administration. Things came to a particularly demoralizing head in the affair of Citizen Genêt in 1793. Genêt appeared in America as an emissary of the French republic. The pro-French democratic societies took him to their hearts immediately, and he was lionized by all those who were opposed to Washington's administration. Emboldened by this adulation, Genêt became imperious and arrogant, demanding to be allowed to address Congress and threatening to appeal to the American people over the head of Washington, who was cool but correct in his dealings with the Frenchman. The whole episode was intensely embarrassing to Jefferson and, along with what he felt to be the erosion of his own influence in the Cabinet, helped to strengthen his determination to resign his office. When Jefferson wrote to Madison of his desire to resign at the end of Washington's first term and Madison urged him to remain, Jefferson replied, "The motion of my blood no longer keeps time with the tumult of the world. It leads me to seek for happiness in the lap and love of my family, in the society of my neighbors and my books, in the wholesome occupations of my farm and my affairs, in an interest or affection in every bud that opens, in every breath that blows around me." He described himself as "cut off from my family & friends, my affairs abandoned to chaos and derangement, in short, giving everything I love, in exchange for everything I hate."

After driving unhappily in tandem with Hamilton for almost four years, Jefferson resigned his office at the end of 1793, despite Washington's efforts to persuade him to remain, and set out for Monticello. Again he was abandoning the field, in a manner of speaking, to a more tenacious opponent. But he had persevered for four years and that, as it turned out, was enough.

13. Vice President

When Jefferson left Philadelphia in January, 1794, for Monticello, he re-enacted his earlier returns to that haven. There he was loved and pampered by everyone, the slaves, his daughters when they were there, and Sally Hemings. In the three years between Jefferson's retirement as secretary of state and his return to office as Vice President under John Adams, Martha and her husband were away much of the time and Jefferson immersed himself in the life of his plantation. It was his first considerable spell at Monticello since shortly after his wife's death in 1782. He was in a real sense sharing it with a young bride in all but name. Sally had just turned twenty-one. She was the mother of his son, Tom. She was handsome, vivacious, independent. His romance with Maria Cosway had demonstrated his capacity for love, which brought out the most humane and playful qualities in him; it is not hard to imagine that a great part of the delight he took in being back at Monticello was related to an infatuation with his young mistress. But whatever joys Jefferson may have found in Sally were tainted by the perpetual need for secrecy, by the subterfuges and stratagems, by the ultimate and corrosive falsity of the situation itself. Nevertheless, to Washington's request that he take a post as special envoy to Spain, he wrote, "No circumstances, my dear sir, will ever tempt me to engage in anything public." And in a letter to Madison he declared that he would not give up the life he was then enjoying "for the empire of the universe."

To a letter from Maria Cosway he replied, "I am become
. . . a real farmer, measuring fields, following my ploughs, help-
ing the haymakers. . . . How better this, than to be shut up in
the four walls of an office, the sun ever excluded . . . the morning
opening with the fable repeated of the Augean stable, a new load
of labours in place of the old. . . . From such a life, good Lord,
deliver me!"

But all was certainly not peace and tranquillity at Monticello. Despite his attentions, his farms remained unproductive,
his cherished fruit trees died in the thin soil, his nail manufac-
tory could not compete with cheap imported nails from England, and his debts continued to pile up year by year. His son-in-
law Thomas Mann Randolph gave signs of serious emotional
instability, riding madly about the country and giving vent to
towering rages. After the Randolphs had left Monticello for
their own estate, the children returned to live for a time with
Jefferson, apparently so that they would be away from their
father. Sally Hemings gave birth to two daughters in this period,
Harriet and Edy, who evidently died at birth or shortly
thereafter, and it soon became evident to Jefferson that his pas-
toral idyll was an illusion. He later wrote revealingly to Polly,
now called Maria, "From 1793 to 1797 I remained closely at
home, saw none but those who came there, and at length became very sensible of the ill effect it had upon my own mind, and
of it's direct and irresistible tendency to render me unfit for
society, and uneasy when necessarily engaged in it. I felt enough
of the effect of withdrawing from the world then, to see that it
led to an antisocial and misanthropic state of mind, which
severely punishes him who gives in to it: and it will be a lesson
I never shall forget as to myself."

The major project that he had set for himself—the remodeling of Monticello based on ideas he had acquired in France—
he did not undertake for many months. First there were bricks
to be made by the slaves—Jefferson wrote George Wythe, "We
are now living in a brick kiln"—and boxes and crates brought
from Paris and later from Philadelphia lay around the house

242

waiting to be moved. His basic plan was to give the house the appearance of a single-story structure from the front, with extended wings. Since it would in fact contain three stories, the windows of the second-floor bedrooms must be at floor level so that from the outside they appeared to be the top segment of long French windows. The bedrooms of the third, or attic, floor were to be lighted by skylights, and a dome was to be added on the back of the house (actually the house had no back or front in the conventional sense; so that the most famous views of it are of the dome side, which is in fact the rear). It was as if Jefferson, by a vast effort of the will, were attempting to rebuild his own life. Even the concealment of the architecture corresponded to the secrets of his heart. Historian Fawn Brodie interpreted the remodeling as a symbol of Jefferson's determination to re-enter political life and throw off the deep depression that she believed had begun the previous year. Without challenging her view, it is worth recalling that there was already a long history of Monticello as therapy. The therapeutic (or obsessive) aspect of the remodeling is suggested by the fact that Jefferson, as always deeply in debt, had to mortgage his slaves to raise the necessary funds. It is also likely that he sometimes felt desperately trapped by his relationship with Sally Hemings, and the presence of her and her children at Monticello in the long run made impossible the tranquillity he had hoped to enjoy there. In any event, despite the constructive work on the house, or perhaps because of it—certainly it produced further confusion and disorder—Jefferson's health became so bad that he began to think his death was near. He wrote to a friend, "My health has suddenly broken down, with symptoms which give me to believe I shall not have much to encounter of the *tedium vitae.*"

His gloom was augmented by his conviction that the country was drifting on a disastrous course, led by "timid men who prefer the calm of despotism to the boisterous sea of liberty." In the matter of Washington's successor, Adams as Vice President felt himself, and was considered by many others, to be the heir apparent. Yet Madison, dismayed at the prospect that Adams would perpetuate the pro-British character of the Wash ington administration and prove an enemy to France, worked assiduously to procure the presidency for Jefferson, who remained at Monticello, above the battle. Since under the system then prevailing the candidate with the largest number of electoral votes became President and the runner-up Vice President, Adams was elected by the margin of three votes, 71 to 68, and Jefferson became Vice President under a man whose political principles he firmly opposed. Like Adams before him and most Vice Presidents since, Jefferson found his office "a cipher," a nothing, and he divided his time equally between the seat of the federal government and Monticello. Even though he was at odds with Adams on most issues, he resented the President's failure to consult him. "It gives me great regret to be passing my time so uselessly when it could have been so importantly employed at home," he wrote Martha.

In the early months of Adams's administration, the Hamiltonian wing of the Federalist party did its best to push Adams in the direction of war with France. Little as Adams sympathized with the French Directory, largely under the control of the astute Talleyrand, he was determined to avoid outright war if possible, if only because it was sure to strengthen the hand of the enemies in his own party. He therefore dispatched three American envoys to negotiate with the Directory. Once in France, the envoys—Charles C. Pinckney, John Marshall, and Elbridge Gerry—were told that the United States would have to pay a substantial bribe for peace. When word of this insult to the United States reached America, it gave rise to a war hysteria that spread throughout the country and led directly to the Alien Act and soon after the Sedition Act. The Alien Act gave the government the authority to arrest or deport all aliens regarded as dangerous (American paranoia saw French agents under every bed); and the Sedition Act stipulated that any attacks on officers of the government or on governmental policies were libels under federal law. The Jeffersonian Republicans proved equally paranoid. They believed that the whole story of the bribe attempt (the XYZ Affair, so called because the letters were substituted for the names of Talleyrand's agents) was simply a Fed-

TO
MAZZEI

Sardinia

Dutch

american
Spoliations

The breach between John Adams (above, a 1790's drawing) and Jefferson began during Washington's first term. In the detail at left from a venomous 1800 cartoon, the American eagle prevents Jefferson from burning the Constitution on an "Alter to Gallic Despotism." The phrase "To Mazzei" refers to an intemperate Antifederalist letter from Jefferson to his Italian friend Philip Mazzei.

eralist plot to provide a pretense for passing the Alien and Sedition Acts and using them in turn to destroy the nascent Republican party.

Jefferson, in an intense state of agitation, left his chair as presiding officer of the Senate and headed home for Monticello while the Sedition Bill was still being debated. When his friend John Taylor raised the question of whether the secession of Virginia and North Carolina might be the only possible recourse, Jefferson dismissed the notion, writing, "If on a temporary superiority of the one party, the other is to resort to a scission of the Union, no federal government can ever exist. If to rid ourselves of the present rule of Massachusetts and Connecticut, we break the Union, will the evil stop there?" If only the champions of freedom and democracy had "a little patience" they would see "the reign of witches pass over, their spells dissolved, and the people recovering their true sight."

But as more and more Jeffersonian editors and publicists were harassed and prosecuted, Jefferson's feelings began to change. Initially demoralized by the XYZ Affair and the strong anti-French feeling that it generated, Jefferson gradually recovered his resolution. With that resurgence of courage came the conviction that the Federalists were the avowed enemies of the Constitution determined to forestall free debate and political dissent. He thus proceeded to draft a set of resolutions to be introduced by a sympathetic state legislature describing the rights of the states as paramount over the federal government. If the national legislature passed statutes that in the opinion of particular states were unconstitutional, those states had the right to declare them null and void and, as a last resort, to secede from the Union. Since in the highly charged atmosphere created by the cold war with France such a doctrine must have seemed to many Americans to be little short of treason, Jefferson undertook his enterprise in the profoundest secrecy. The kingpin of Jefferson's thesis was that "whensoever the general government assumes undelegated powers, its acts are unauthoritative, void, and of no force," and further that each party "has an equal right to judge for itself, as well of infractions as of the mode and measure of address." The main body of the resolutions was composed of a specific attack on the Alien and Sedition Acts.

The resolve did not stop there, however; it went on to state in uncompromising terms the doctrine of the sovereignty of the states over Congress, Congress being not a party to the agreement—that is, the Constitution—"but merely the creature of the compact, and subject as to its assumptions of power to the final judgment of those by whom, and for whose use itself and its powers were all created and modified." If the tendency that Jefferson had observed in the federal government to claim powers not granted it under the Constitution were not checked, he warned, it would "necessarily drive these States into revolution and blood." The final resolution called for what was in effect a revolutionary committee of correspondence to concert a common plan of action.

These were doctrines fraught with mischief that were to haunt Jefferson's own presidency and await resolution by a long and bloody civil war. They can perhaps be taken not as a closely reasoned document worthy of Jefferson at his best, but as a measure of his desperation, his heartfelt conviction that the country was in the direst extremity. The fact that Jefferson was Vice President of the United States when he wrote his resolutions, that they were composed in conspiratorial secrecy and were manifestly intended to overturn the existing administration of his former friend, John Adams, is a measure of the degree to which partisan politics had fastened on the minds of a great majority of Americans. When one reads the resolutions, Jefferson's comments at the time of Shays's Rebellion come inevitably to mind. Was he ready to water the tree of liberty with the blood of patriots and tyrants scarcely fifteen years after the end of the great revolution that had secured American independence?

The word "blood" appears again. Fifteen years would be four years ahead of schedule, but history could not follow schedules, especially when freedom was imperiled. When it was suggested that if he would frame his resolutions they would be introduced in the Kentucky legislature, Jefferson agreed on the condition that his authorship would never be divulged. As pre-

FIFTH CONGRESS OF THE UNITED STATES:

At the Second Session.

Begun and held at the city of *Philadelphia*, in the state of PENNSYLVANIA, on *Monday*, the thirteenth of *November*, one thousand seven hundred and ninety-seven.

An ACT in addition to the act, entitled : An Act for the punishment of certain crimes against the United States.

BE it enacted by the Senate and House of Representatives of the United States of America, in Congress assembled. That if any persons shall unlawfully combine or conspire together, with intent to oppose any measure or measures of the government of the United States, which are or shall be directed by proper authority, or to impede the operation of any law of the United States, or to intimidate or prevent any person, holding a place or office in under the government of the United States from undertaking, performing or executing his trust or duty; and if any person or persons, with intent as aforesaid, shall, counsel, advise or attempt to procure any insurrection, riot, unlawful assembly, or combination, whether such conspiracy, threatning, counsel advice, or attempt shall have the proposed effect or not, he or they shall be deemed guilty of a high misdemeanor, and on conviction, before any court of the United States having jurisdiction thereof, shall be punished by a fine not exceeding five thousand dollars, and by imprisonment during a term not less than six months nor exceeding five years; and further, at the discretion of the court may be holden to find sureties for his good behaviour in such sum, and for such time, as the said court may direct.

Sect. 2. And be it further enacted, That if any person shall write, print, utter or publish, or shall cause or procure to be written, printed, uttered or published, or shall knowingly and willingly assist or aid in writing, printing, uttering or publishing any false, scandalous and malicious writing or writings against the government of the United States, or either House of the Congress of the United States, or the President of the United States, with intent to defame the said government, or either House of the said Congress, or the said President, or to bring them, or either of them, into contempt or disrepute; or to excite against them, or either or any of them, the hatred of the good people of the United States, or to stir up sedition within the United States, or to excite any unlawful combinations therein, for opposing or resisting any law of the United States, or any act of the President of the United States, done in pursuance of any such law, of the powers in him vested by the constitution of the United States, or to resist, oppose, or defeat any such law or act; or to aid, encourage or abet any hostile designs of any foreign nation against the United States, their people or government, then such person, being thereof convicted before any court of the United States having jurisdiction thereof, shall be punished by a fine not exceeding two thousand dollars, and by imprisonment not exceeding two years.

Sect. 3. And be it further enacted and declared, That if any person shall be prosecuted under this act, for the writing or publishing any libel aforesaid, it shall be lawful for the defendant, upon the trial of the cause, to give in evidence in his defence, the truth of the matter contained in the publication charged as a libel. And the jury who shall try the cause, shall have a right to determine the law and the fact, under the direction of the court, as in other cases.

Sect. 4. And be it further enacted, That this act shall continue to be in force until the third day of March, one thousand eight hundred and one, and no longer: Provided, that the expiration of the act shall not prevent or defeat a prosecution and punishment of any offence against the law, during the time it shall be in force.

Jonathan Dayton Sp———

Theodore Sedgwick ———

Approved July 14, 1798

John Adams
President of the United States.

Tensions in the Fifth Congress peaked when Congressmen Matthew Lyon and Roger Griswold brawled on the floor of the House (right). Nine months later Federalists pushed through Congress the Alien and Sedition Acts (above, the Sedition Act). Vice President Jefferson secretly submitted his objections (far right) to the Kentucky legislature, where the acts were declared "altogether void."

Resolved that [alien] friends are under the jurisdiction and protection of the laws of the state wherein they are that no power over them has been delegated to the US. nor prohibited to the individual states distinct from their power over citizens: and it being true as a general principle, and one of the amendments to the constitution having also declared, that 'the powers not delegated to the US. by the constitution nor prohibited by it to the States, are reserved to the states respectively, or to the people' the act of the Congress of the US. passed on the ___ day of July, 1798. intituled 'an Act concerning aliens' which assumes powers over alien friends not delegated by the constitution is not law, but is altogether void & of no force

Resolved that in addition to the general principle as well as the express declaration, that powers not delegated are reserved, another and more special provision, inserted in the constitution from abundant caution, has declared that 'the migration or importation of such persons as any of the states now existing shall think proper to admit, shall not be prohibited by the Congress prior to the year 1808' that the [common]wealth does admit the migration of [alien] friends described as the subject of the said act concerning aliens; that a provision against prohibiting their migration, is a provision against all acts equivalent thereto, would be nugatory; ...rated is equivalent ...n, and is therefor ...constitution, an

...approved by the ...y sundry of ...constitution ...power 'to lay & ...ray the debts & ...al welfare of ...which shall be necess ...prop. for... ecution the powers ...ested by the constitution in the government of the US. ...in any department... officer thereof' goes to the des ...ction of all the li... prescribed to their power by ...constitution; that... ods meant by that instrument be subord... the execution of limited power

sented to and passed by that body, Jefferson's draft was considerably softened by John Breckinridge of Kentucky. In the meantime Madison had been working on similar resolutions, which were introduced in and passed by the Virginia assembly. These too were more moderate than Jefferson's, and he was plainly annoyed at Madison's temperate position. These so-called Virginia and Kentucky Resolutions, issued in 1798, declared the Alien and Sedition Acts unconstitutional and provided a base for all later states' rights movements.

It is not sufficient simply to dismiss the Virginia and Kentucky Resolutions as the consequence of an overwrought imagination—an ailment by no means confined to Jefferson—though they were certainly that. Jefferson, for one thing, wrote as though no Supreme Court existed. At the very least one would think that he would have proposed waiting until the court had had an opportunity to rule on a matter of such importance. Although the court had yet to decide a great constitutional issue in which it declared an important piece of legislation unconstitutional, it had already given signs of moving firmly in that direction. So one must say that the resolutions were the product of an immediate crisis—the Alien and Sedition Acts—and of what presumably was a long-standing predilection for revolution as a matter of principle. Jefferson nowhere connects his rather thinly veiled call for a revolutionary uprising with his earlier support of periodic revolutions and his letter to Madison declaring that all laws and constitutions should be rewritten every nineteen years, but the connection is too obvious to avoid. There is an intemperance and an open invitation to violence in Jefferson's resolutions as he originally phrased them that is not easy for biographers to explain. In addition to allowing insufficient time for the courts to pass on the constitutionality of the acts (it might be said in defense of Jefferson that the federal courts were serving as the instrument for enforcing the Alien and Sedition Acts and thus were not likely to be perceived as a remedy against them), Jefferson rejected the notion of applying to Congress for repeal of the obnoxious acts, the course adopted by the Kentucky legislature. Breckinridge wrote a friend that he hoped his modifications of Jefferson's original resolutions "will silence all calumnies, with respect to our disposition towards disorganization or disunion. I think the ground we have taken cannot be shaken; that no just exception can be made to the firm but decent language in which we have expressed ourselves. I assure you with confidence, we have but one object, & that is, to preserve the constitution inviolate, & that by constitutional efforts."

Most of the states north of the Mason-Dixon line specifically rejected the resolutions. The other southern states failed to endorse them. That rebuff marked a turning point in Jefferson's thinking. Though he had apparently been ready to foment a revolution and dismantle the new union in order to be rid of the hated Alien and Sedition Acts, it now appeared that he had no revolutionaries to flock to his banner. His first recourse, revolution, having failed, he proceeded to his second—politics. Madison and Monroe, who had worked hard to soften his adamantine stand on nullification and secession, now worked with him to prepare the ground for his election as President in the forthcoming election. Jefferson's anxieties about a war with France were also alleviated by Adams's rejection of the Hamiltonian war hawks and his efforts to achieve some kind of understanding with the French foreign minister, Talleyrand. With the threat of war over, at least for the moment, and the Federalist party split into bitterly antagonistic Hamilton and Adams factions, Republican hopes for success in the coming presidential election rose. Jefferson would unquestionably be the Republican candidate.

14. President

As the elections of 1800 approached, political rancor changed gradually into a genuine anxiety about the ability of the country to survive them. Hamilton, who had tried to undermine Adams by attacking him publicly and maneuvering to get General Charles Cotesworth Pinckney elected in Adams's place, would himself be outmaneuvered in his home state by Republican Aaron Burr, who, it was assumed, would become Vice President in the new administration as a reward for steering New York into the Jefferson column. While Adams tried, in vain as it turned out, to extricate himself from the collapse of his party, Hamilton foresaw the possible election of Burr and the "reform [of] the government *à la Buonaparte.* He is as unprincipled and dangerous a man as any country can boast—as true a Cataline as ever met in midnight conclave." Jefferson himself considered that the government under Adams's administration and with Hamilton's manipulation had become a "Monarchic Masque." If republican principles could not be restored, Jefferson wrote, "we shall be unable to realize the prospects held out to the people, and we must fall back into monarchism. . . ."

Christopher Gadsden, the South Carolina leader, observing the rancor and bitterness that existed between the parties and factions, wrote, " 'tis impossible the union can much longer exist . . . our government must prove *an abortion* or smothered in its earliest infancy, will afford to anti-republicans and future historians the strongest example ever heard of, of the instability and very short duration of such kind of government." Revolution and bloodshed were openly discussed; the mood of the country was one of irreconcilability. When the electoral votes were tallied in December Jefferson and Burr each had 73 votes. Jefferson immediately took the line that Burr would accept what the voters had obviously intended—that he, Jefferson, would be President and Burr Vice President. But Burr, whose intrigues had carried New York for the Republicans, was intoxicated by the prospect of being President by accident and began to work to that effect. In the case of a tie the Constitution required that the election be decided in the House of Representatives. This left fertile ground for chicanery, since the House was full of Federalists who had no use for Jefferson and were tempted therefore to conspire with Burr to steal the presidency from the Virginian. Another widely circulated rumor was that the Federalists intended to pass a bill providing that the presidency should go to the Chief Justice of the Supreme Court or to John Marshall, secretary of state.

As weeks went by with no solution in sight and the wildest rumors flying, John Quincy Adams wrote to his brother, Thomas Boylston Adams, "It is impossible for me to avoid the supposition that the ultimate necessary consequence, if not the *ultimate object of both the extreme parties which divide us* [the Hamiltonians and the Jeffersonians, presumably] *will be a dissolution of the Union and a civil war."* Thus when the House of Representatives met in February to decide the issue, there had been two months of doubt and anxiety about the outcome of the election and the fate of the country.

For five days the balloting was deadlocked, with eight states for Jefferson, six for Burr, and two—Maryland and Vermont—undecided. It was said that the people of Philadelphia, outraged at the prospect of Jefferson being cheated of the presidency, "had seized upon the public arms." In this interim Jefferson and his lieutenants apparently had decided that if the Federalists connived with Burr's Republican supporters in the House to rob Jefferson of the presidency or tried to have John Marshall suc-

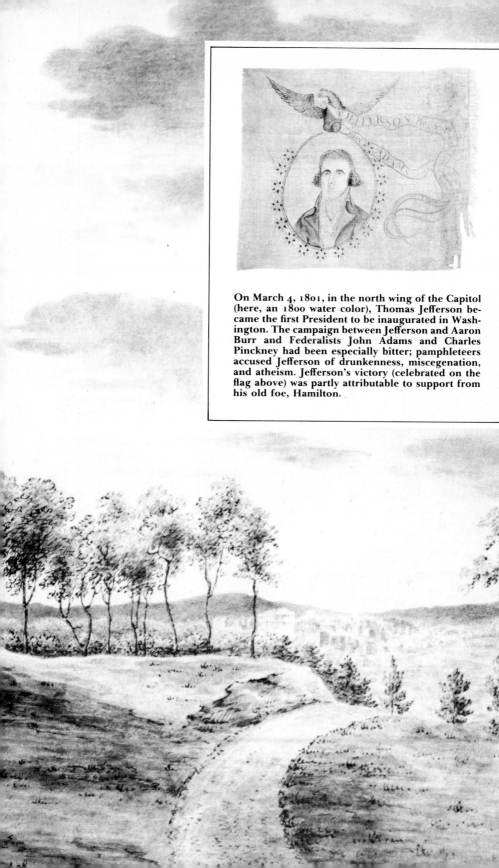

On March 4, 1801, in the north wing of the Capitol (here, an 1800 water color), Thomas Jefferson became the first President to be inaugurated in Washington. The campaign between Jefferson and Aaron Burr and Federalists John Adams and Charles Pinckney had been especially bitter; pamphleteers accused Jefferson of drunkenness, miscegenation, and atheism. Jefferson's victory (celebrated on the flag above) was partly attributable to support from his old foe, Hamilton.

ceed to the office, the Jeffersonians would have recourse to an armed uprising. This, at least, is the implication of Jefferson's letter to Monroe written on February 15. "We thought it best," he wrote, "to declare openly and firmly, one & all, that the day such an act [to devolve the government on Marshall] passed, the middle States would arm, & that no such usurpation, even for a single day, should be submitted to. This first shook them; and they were completely alarmed at the resource for which we declared, to wit, *a convention to re-organize the government, & to amend it.* The very word convention gives them the horrors, . . . in the present democratical spirit of America. . . ." The letter makes clear that unless Jefferson and his followers were bluffing, and there is no reason to believe that they were, a revolution was in the making.

Finally, with public indignation mounting after a week of deadlock, James Bayard, a Delaware Federalist, convinced that further delay would mean the destruction of the Constitution and armed conflict, changed his vote from Burr to Jefferson, thus splitting the Delaware delegation evenly and subtracting Delaware from the Burr column. Maryland finally came out for Jefferson, and the Virginian became thereby the third President of the United States. Civil war had been averted by the narrowest of margins.

Historians have made much of the bloodless "revolution" of 1800. Jefferson himself gave it that name and wrote, "The Revolution of 1800 was as real a revolution in the principles of our government as that of 1776 was in its form; not effected by the sword, as that, but by the rational and peaceable instrument of reform, the suffrage of the people." That was, of course, stating it a good bit too simply. Adams, who had repudiated the right-wing Federalists of his own party, lost by a few votes involving a good deal of political chicanery. It is difficult to argue that his re-election would have resulted in any of the dire consequences that the Jeffersonians predicted, any more than Jefferson's election confirmed the fears of the hard-core Federalists. It is less certain that given Jefferson's revolutionary tendencies, he and his adherents might not, in fact, have undertaken open opposition to an administration that they were convinced was turning—or perhaps had turned—into a "Monarchic Masque," especially if the Federalists had succeeded in replacing Adams with Marshall. That was never, however, more than a rumor— a rumor in whose name Jefferson was able to bring additional pressure to bear on the Federalists to make him President.

So, in the last analysis, Jefferson's real intentions must remain obscure. What does seem clear is that he was ready to talk repeatedly of revolution and bloodshed if, in his opinion, revolution was necessary to preserve the liberties of the people. Unless we are to write him down as "a mere theorist"—as a number of his contemporaries did—we must count him as favoring not simply "reforms in the manner of government" or "peaceable revolution," but revolution as bloody as necessary to preserve what he understood to be the original principles of the Revolution.

To the present-day observer, the nature of the revolution that Jefferson claimed had been effected by his election is not quite clear. If it was simply the transfer of power from one party to another, well and good, that was revolution enough; but if it was supposed to represent a wholly new distribution of power, that point is far more difficult to argue. It did result in the repeal of the Alien and Sedition Acts, but in a period when war hysteria had subsided and the French Revolution in the form of Napoleon Bonaparte could claim few American adherents, that proved not to be a permanent achievement. Under the influence of subsequent wars, hot or cold, Americans were to accept, often enthusiastically, infringements of their First Amendment rights (and other rights as well) hardly to be distinguished in character from the original Alien and Sedition Acts.

The thinly veiled call for a revolution expressed in Jefferson's draft of the Kentucky Resolutions gives us a clue to the extent that the leader of the Republican party had himself become alienated from the party in power. So, in a sense, the question is perhaps less what the Federalists would have done to rivet the chains of bondage on the country than what the Jeffersonians might have done under the conviction that chains were about to be fastened on them. In the extremes of each party mutual suspicion had grown to such a point that political conflicts could well have escalated into armed clashes. Beyond such speculations lies the fact that the Jeffersonians proved by the length of their tenure—some twenty-four years, from 1801 to the end of Monroe's second term—that they reflected the mood and temper of the American people far better than their rapidly fading rivals.

In the last days of his administration Adams, bitter at his rejection by the voters and gloomy about the future of the nation under his former friend, now infatuated with democratic illusions, tried to erect in the courts a barrier against democratic excesses by appointing a number of federal judges in the dying days of his administration—the midnight judges as they came to be called, because many names were submitted to Congress in the final hours before Adams's successor took office. The most notable of Adams's judicial appointments was John Marshall, formerly secretary of state and a staunch Virginia Federalist, who was to become a thorn in Jefferson's side. Marshall himself had dark forebodings at the overthrow of federalism. On the day of Jefferson's inauguration he wrote, "Today the new political year commences. The new order of things begins. . . . There are some appearances which surprize me. I wish however more than I hope that the public prosperity & happiness may sustain no diminution under democratic guidance. The democrats are divided into speculative theorists & absolute terrorists. With the latter I am not disposed to class Mr Jefferson. If he arranges himself with them it is not difficult to foresee that much calamity is in store for our country—if he does not they will soon become his enemies & calumniators."

The Capitol building was still unfinished on March 4, 1801, when Jefferson rose to give his inaugural address in the chamber occupied by the Senate. The members of both houses were present. Aaron Burr, as Vice President, presided, and John Marshall was seated on the dais, at Jefferson's left, to administer the oath of office. Jefferson read his address in an almost inaudible voice. The recent elections, he told his audience, might well be misunderstood by those "unused to think freely and to speak and to write what they think." But the election having now been decided "by the voice of the nation . . . all will, of course, arrange themselves under the will of the law and unite in common efforts for the common good. All, too, will bear in mind this sacred principle, that though the will of the majority is in all cases to prevail, that will, to be rightful, must be reasonable; that the minority possess their equal rights, which equal laws must protect, and to violate which would be oppression. . . . Let us restore to social intercourse that harmony and affection without which liberty and even life itself are but dreary things."

Jefferson then alluded to the passions excited by the French Revolution and their effect on Americans. "But every difference of opinion," he declared, "is not a difference of principle. We have called by different names brethren of the same principle. We are all Republicans—we are all Federalists. If there be any among us who would wish to dissolve this Union or to change its republican form, let them stand undisturbed as monuments of the safety with which error of opinion may be tolerated where reason is left free to combat it.

"But," he asked, "would the honest patriot, in the full tide of successful experiment, abandon a government which has so far kept us free and firm, on the theoretic and visionary fear that this government, the world's best hope, may by possibility want energy to preserve itself? I trust not. I believe this, on the contrary, the strongest government on earth. . . .

"Let us then with courage and confidence pursue our own Federal and Republican principles, our attachment to our Union and representative government." America was far removed from the "exterminating havoc" of European politics, with enough room for "our descendants to the hundredth and thousandth generation," with everything needed "to make us a happy and prosperous people." The only other requirement was a "wise and frugal government which shall restrain men from injuring one another, which shall leave them otherwise free to regulate their own pursuits of industry and improvement, and shall not take from the mouth of labor the bread it has earned. This is the sum of good government, and this is necessary to close the circle of our felicities."

Here once more we encounter Jefferson as a superb stylist. The inaugural address is full of memorable phrases. But, as we have said before, for style to seize men's imaginations it must appear in conjunction with historical forces that raise it above the level of mere rhetoric or eloquence and make it reverberate in memory. The address at once took its place beside the Declaration of Independence, Washington's Farewell Address, and later Lincoln's Gettysburg Address as one of the three or four testaments of American history that served, in some essential way, to define us as a people. It became one of those "mystic chords of memory," its words as carefully and artfully crafted as though they had been carved in stone.

The beginning of his administration was the best. Jefferson moved into the still unfinished White House, bringing with him his garden implements and carpentry tools, his beloved maps and books, his plants and his mockingbird, which ate from his lips. The East Room became as untidy as his sanctum sanctorum at Monticello. In the political realm, the new President soon found himself embroiled in a series of unpleasant wrangles, many of them having to do with patronage. Who was to get what public office in the President's appointing? More specifically, which Federalists were to be turned out of office and replaced by Republicans? And equally perplexing, which Republicans were to get the vacated offices? Jefferson did not forgive Burr for what he believed to be the New Yorker's machinations against him in the recent election, and he pursued him with a vindictiveness that he not infrequently displayed toward his enemies.

In addition James Callender, a muckraking Republican editor whom Jefferson had subsidized and who had been relentless in his attacks on Washington and Adams, became furious with Jefferson for having failed to remit his fine in a case growing out of Callender's persecution under the Sedition Act. Callender turned on Jefferson and revealed that the President had been his patron, and then he finally "broke" the story of Sally Hemings as Jefferson's mistress and the mother of children by him. "It is well known," Callender wrote, "that the man, *whom it delighteth the people to honor,* keeps and for many years has kept, as his concubine, one of his slaves. Her name is SALLY. The name of her eldest son is Tom. His features are said to bear a striking though sable resemblance to those of the president himself. The boy is ten or twelve years of age. . . . By this wench Sally, our president has had several children. There is not an individual in the neighbourhood of Charlottesville who does not believe the story, and not a few who know it. . . ."

The more rabid Federalist editors seized upon the story with glee. Others approached it cautiously. Many Americans waited for a denial from Jefferson, but none came; several Virginia editors with Federalist leanings made independent "investigations" on their own and reported that so far as they could ascertain the facts were substantially as Callender had stated them. Satiric poems and songs were composed, and a literary journal of strongly Federalist persuasion published a song to be sung to the tune of "Yankee Doodle":

> Of all the damsels on the green,
> On mountain, or in valley,
> A lass so luscious ne'er was seen
> As Monticellian Sally.
>
> Yankee Doodle, who's the noodle?
> What wife were half so handy?
> To breed a flock of slaves for stock,
> A blackamoor's the dandy. . . .
>
> When press'd by load of state affairs,
> I seek to sport and dally,
> The sweetest solace of my cares
> Is in the lap of Sally. . . .
>
> What though she by the glands secretes;
> Must I stand shil-I shall-I?
> Tuck'd up between a pair of sheets
> There's no perfume like Sally.

The editor of the Lynchburg *Virginia Gazette* declared that he discovered "nothing but proofs of [the] authenticity" of the charges against Jefferson. John Adams, who had met Sally in London, believed the charges, writing to Abigail that the situation was "a natural and almost unavoidable consequence of that foul contagion in the human character—Negro slavery." The public discussion of his relationship with Sally Hemings was certainly one of the most lacerating experiences of Jefferson's life, although he gave no outward indication. Fawn Brodie pointed out that he took his daughters, Martha and Maria, back to Washington with him when he returned to the White House after the scandal had become general knowledge and that their presence was obviously intended to help quiet rumors of a family breach over Sally, as well as to help bolster the President's own battered morale.

To the Hemings matter was added the story of Jefferson's advances years earlier to his friend Jack Walker's wife, Betsey. When that episode was spread across the newspapers, Walker, in classic cavalier fashion, decided he must vindicate his honor by challenging Jefferson to a duel. Although Walker was persuaded to withdraw it, his challenge gave a touch of the bizarre to what was already a kind of Gothic horror story. We are reminded again of Jefferson's shrinking from public office and his obsession with privacy, not to say secrecy. He had placed himself at the head of his party, accepted the role of leader, and been crucified in consequence. Nonetheless his public tone was unflaggingly optimistic. After ten months in office, Jefferson wrote his friend the Italian Philip Mazzei: "You cannot imagine what progress republican principles have made here. Business is conducted calmly, and with unanimous consent in both Chambers. The Tories are generally either converted or silenced by rational evidence or by prudence. All the excess expenditures which were turning the ship of state toward monarchy are being rapidly abolished, and the fundamental principles of 1775, once more assert themselves vigorously. Briefly, there is every proof that people are enjoying life, although none have exclusive privileges. . . . Our country will be a haven for the oppressed

. . . and we have found a way of carrying on affairs without any need for an Act of Sedition. . . ."

At the height of his personal travail, with the press buzzing over the matters of Sally Hemings and Betsey Walker, Maria, his younger daughter, died. This time he was able to speak of his distress, but for several weeks he was almost incapacitated with grief. Gradually he picked up the routines and duties of his office again; he was now more than ever dependent on Martha and frequently solicited assurances from her that he was first in her love.

Thomas Paine, who had mixed in the French Revolution with an ardor that almost cost him his life, returned to the United States in 1802 at the height of the Sally Hemings scandal. Paine had made himself an object of opprobrium by his book *The Age of Reason,* a classic statement of the postulates of deism that was bitterly attacked by orthodox Christians as a model of impiety. Jefferson, who shared many of Paine's theological as well as political ideas, invited him to stay at the White House for several weeks, thereby confirming the conservatives' image of the President as one who encouraged and consorted with atheists and radicals.

In the meantime Jefferson was moving with adroitness and secrecy to consummate the greatest real estate deal in American history, including the purchase of Manhattan from the Indians —the Louisiana Purchase. As part of the settlement that concluded the Seven Years' War (called the French and Indian War in America), France had ceded the Louisiana Territory of some 828,000 square miles to Spain. It was returned to France in the Treaty of Madrid in 1801 in exchange for assistance against Portugal in the War of the Oranges. Jefferson was alarmed when he heard that the territory had reverted to France. Spain, in his view, was no threat to United States dominance on the continent, but an aggressive and expansionist France under Napoleon's leadership was a far more serious matter. The federal Constitution, which Jefferson had sworn to uphold and furthermore to interpret in the narrowest manner, had no provision for acquiring new territory, and this power, if it could be adduced

Unable to communicate with Jefferson after the startling offer to sell the entire Louisiana Territory (right), Ambassador Robert Livingston and James Monroe negotiated with François de Barbé-Marbois, French finance minister, and settled on a price of $15 million (above, Barbé-Marbois, Monroe, and Livingston; left, a copy of the purchase agreement). Jefferson first argued that an amendment was necessary to ratify the purchase but came to believe that "the less we say about constitutional difficulties the better."

RUPERT'S LAND

L O U I S I A N A

PACIFIC OCEAN

GULF OF MEXICO

A Map of Louisiana AND MEXICO.

Carte DE LA LOUISIANE ET DU MEXIQUE,

Dressée par P. Tardieu fils ainé.

Gravée par P.A.F. TARDIEU père.

PARIS 1820.

SCALES

Common French Leagues

English Miles

Spanish Leagues

from various articles in the document, clearly did not belong to the President.

As soon as word of the terms of the Treaty of Madrid reached him, Jefferson instructed his minister in Paris, Robert R. Livingston, to undertake negotiations designed to guarantee the rights of trade and navigation on the Mississippi to American citizens. Not satisfied with such a modest accommodation, Jefferson sent Monroe on a mission a year later with authority granted by Congress to purchase New Orleans and West Florida for $2,000,000. Monroe also had secret instructions from Jefferson to pay far more if necessary. The outbreak of war between France and Britain confronted Napoleon with the problem of defending the Louisiana Territory, or more specifically New Orleans, against British naval power. To sell to the United States what would doubtless be taken from him by the British suddenly seemed a good bargain to Napoleon. Thus when Livingston approached Talleyrand and renewed his offer for New Orleans and West Florida, Talleyrand offered the startled American the whole vast territory claimed by France. Congress had authorized $2,000,000. Jefferson had raised the ante to $10,000,000 simply for two relatively small areas. Livingston and Talleyrand agreed on $15,000,000, or approximately four cents an acre, for the entire territory of Louisiana.

The steps by which Jefferson came to authorize the purchase in splendid disregard of the powers granted him under the Constitution are hidden behind his characteristic reserve. We know that one of his obsessions was what might be called a westerly yearning. The vast westward reaches of the continent had tugged at him since childhood. He had been a pioneer in a real sense: Monticello was well west of the Tidewater plantations. In addition, Jefferson had a romantic infatuation with Indians and exploration. But what had this philosopher of democracy to do with limitless empires, thinly peopled with aborigines? Certainly there was nothing "reasonable" about those endless spaces. As the President had assured his fellow citizens in his inaugural address, the United States already claimed territory sufficient to accommodate their progeny for a hundred or even a thousand generations. It seems safe to say that once again the heart triumphed over the head. Certainly it was a splendid acquisition, an unparalleled bargain, and we can only be glad that Jefferson had the enterprise to bring it off. By the same token we can hardly avoid speculating on the rationalizations with which he assuaged his conscience.

Jefferson's imperial passion, which had prompted him to encourage George Rogers Clark's campaigns into the Northwest during the Revolution, led him to conceive a dazzling scheme to explore the whole interior of the United States as far west as the Pacific Ocean. Under the pretext of developing western trade routes, Jefferson won the approval of Congress for an expedition to follow the line of the Missouri River westward, and he immediately recruited his own secretary, Meriwether Lewis, and William Clark, younger brother of George Rogers, who had shown ability as an army officer. These two men were given instructions by Jefferson to take careful note of all the flora and fauna they encountered and of the customs and manner of life of the Indian tribes, to map the terrain, and to report on the climate and soil in the regions through which they passed.

Although Jefferson had planned the trip before the Louisiana Purchase, the explorers did not set off until after it had been consummated. In the process of making the purchase Jefferson and Madison rode roughshod over the rights of Spain, and in this they were abetted by Napoleon. Indeed, the Louisiana Purchase aside, the area of foreign policy was, increasingly, a disaster area. Although Jefferson had in James Madison an unusually able secretary of state, he mismanaged diplomatic relations with almost every European nation. He bullied and misused Spain, was by turns highhanded and supplicating to England, and proved no match for Napoleon and Talleyrand.

Although Jefferson loved fine clothes, costly wines, gourmet French food, and luxurious living in general and did not hesitate to go deeply into debt to enjoy them, as President he affected a dramatically informal air, receiving guests in odd old clothes and carpet slippers. When he entertained members of the diplomatic corps, he eschewed all the precise and elaborate

Before the Louisiana Purchase was consummated Congress, at Jefferson's urging, had appropriated $2,500 for a scientific expedition to the West. Led by William Clark (top) and Meriwether Lewis (left), it set out in May, 1804, and was acclaimed a complete success on its return to St. Louis in September, 1806. Above is a detail of their map of the Columbia River's Great Falls, and below is their return route, a chain of the Montana Rockies. Sheheke, a Mandan chief who returned with them, is at far right, along with a silver peace medal presented to a Nez Perce chief and drawings of two of their specimens, a mountain quail (top) and a woodpecker.

protocol that governed such occasions, thus infuriating the respective diplomats. They assumed, understandably, that he was deliberately insulting them. Such behavior reminds us that Jefferson was always the conscious actor, the artificer of the particular persona he chose to present—simple farmer, philosopher, artist, man of the people. In addition he had a basic contempt for politics and especially for that branch of international politics known as diplomacy, and he wished to dramatize his contempt for it and for its practitioners. "I have ever considered diplomacy as the pest of the peace of the world, as the workshop in which nearly all the wars of Europe are manufactured," he wrote a friend. This was Jefferson at his most doctrinaire. The Louisiana Purchase had been a diplomatic triumph in the best (or worst) tradition of European intrigue. As the philosopher of equality, Jefferson was determined, by the adoption of a particular style, to demonstrate republican simplicity in contrast to Federalist pomp and ceremony. As he put it, he wished to bury "levees, birthdays, royal parades, and the arrogation of precedence in society by certain self-stiled friends of order, but truly stiled friends of privileged orders." He thus adopted the practice of what came to be called "pell-mell"—no order or precedence, guests finding their own places at table. "In social circles," he declared, "all are equal, whether in, or out, of office, foreign or domestic; & the same equality exists among ladies as among gentlemen . . .'pell-mell' and 'next the door' form the basis of etiquette in the societies of this country." In all of which there was a substantial amount of cant.

15. Re-elected

In 1804 Jefferson was re-elected President by an overwhelming majority. He held the South and Middle States and won all the old Federalist strongholds of New England with the exception of Connecticut. Armed with a new confidence, he set out to diminish the power of the federal judiciary, that stronghold of Federalist principles. He was determined to undo, so far as possible, the last-minute appointments of John Adams and in the process to whittle away the powers of his greatest remaining rival, John Marshall. One is reminded of his titanic struggle with Alexander Hamilton when the two men were the poles of Washington's Cabinet. Hamilton had won that engagement, but Jefferson had ultimately triumphed and now had the pleasure of seeing his opponent the discredited leader of a divided and impotent party.

Like Hamilton and Jefferson, Marshall and Jefferson were well matched. Both Virginians, they had parted company years earlier. Marshall was as simple and austere in his manner of life and quality of mind as Jefferson was flamboyant and mercurial. While Jefferson was constantly dominated by his passions—his likes and dislikes, his possessive loves, and those animosities in which he so often indulged himself—Marshall, whose mind drove to the heart of issues, pursued a clear course, the strengthening of the Supreme Court, with notable single-mindedness.

The attack on the Court was prompted by Jefferson's conviction that it had raised itself above "the people," above the legislature and the President, and had made itself a kind of independent power beyond the control of the electorate, which, of course, was exactly what most of the framers of the Constitution had intended. Jefferson began his assault on the weakest link in the federal judiciary, a New Hampshire judge named John Pickering, a Federalist and a man notorious for the most violent and abusive behavior toward those who came before him. The instrument for cutting the federal courts down to size was, in Jefferson's plan, the process of impeachment. The House, under strong pressure from Jefferson, presented articles of impeachment against Pickering, and the Senate convicted him of "high crimes and misdemeanors" (although there was substantial evidence that Pickering was simply insane) and removed him from office. Jefferson's next target was Samuel Chase, a Federalist judge who had been outspoken in his denunciations, in some instances from the bench, of Jeffersonian principles. Chase was a splenetic and intemperate man, but the charge of "high crimes and misdemeanors" could not be sustained against him even in a predominantly Republican Congress very much under Jefferson's control. Chase was exonerated and Jefferson suffered a humiliating defeat.

Another enemy, in Jefferson's view, was Aaron Burr. The President had not forgiven Burr for trying, in Jefferson's opinion, to steal the presidency from him. He therefore set about to destroy Burr's base of power in New York by denying him federal patronage and parceling out the offices under the President's appointment to Burr's Republican rivals in New York, the Livingstons and Clintons. Burr then did Jefferson a great if unintended service by killing Hamilton in the famous duel at Weehawken on July 11, 1804, thus removing Hamilton from the scene and destroying his own career in the process.

After his single term as Vice President, Burr entered into a bizarre plan to seize Mexico from the Spanish and establish, at least by one interpretation, an empire of his own. His fellow conspirator was General James Wilkinson, a paid agent of Spain and Jefferson's appointee as governor of the Louisiana Territory. When it appeared that his involvement might be discovered, Wilkinson betrayed Burr to Jefferson. Jefferson ordered Burr arrested and taken to Richmond for trial as a traitor. Then proceeded one of the strangest episodes in our history. The President of the United States became, for all practical purposes, a prosecuting attorney, directing a relentless campaign to convict Burr through the district attorney for Virginia, George Hay, who had little stomach for the job. Rejecting all cautionary advice from friends who perceived that the case against Burr was a weak one, Jefferson exposed himself to the charge of simple vindictiveness by the determination with which he pursued his goal of destroying a man who, having once held the second highest office in the land, had already virtually destroyed himself by his own folly.

The only way to make sense of Jefferson's pursuit of Burr is to keep in mind that Marshall and the Supreme Court were Jefferson's ultimate targets. If Jefferson threw down the gauntlet to Marshall, the latter did not hesitate to pick it up. Marshall presided over the case himself, which pleased Jefferson, who believed that the Chief Justice's handling of the trial would so inflame partisan feeling as to give impetus to the movement to clip the wings of the Court. He wrote to the villainous Wilkinson, who had become his principal witness against Burr, "The scenes which have been acted at Richmond are such as have never before been exhibited in any country where all regard to public character has not yet been thrown off. . . . However, they will produce an amendment to the Constitution which, keeping the judges independent of the Executive, will not leave them so, of the nation."

Burr was found not guilty by a jury whose foreman was Jefferson's cousin and one-time friend and supporter, John Randolph of Roanoke. The President pressed for another indictment and again Burr was exonerated. Of all Jefferson's official acts as President, many impulsive and ill-conceived, his persecution of Burr is the strangest and the most discreditable. It shows us a man in the grip of an ungovernable hatred, a man too stubborn to turn back from the edge of disaster, too recalcitrant

FIAT JUSTITIA

REPORT

OF THE

TRIAL

OF THE

HON. SAMUEL CHASE,

ONE OF THE ASSOCIATE JUSTICES

OF THE

SUPREME COURT OF THE UNITED STATES,

BEFORE THE

HIGH COURT OF IMPEACHMENT,

COMPOSED OF THE

Senate of the United States,

FOR CHARGES EXHIBITED AGAINST HIM BY THE

HOUSE OF REPRESENTATIVES,

In the name of themselves, and of all the People of the United States,

FOR

HIGH CRIMES & MISDEMEANORS,

SUPPOSED TO HAVE BEEN BY HIM COMMITTED;

WITH THE NECESSARY

DOCUMENTS AND OFFICIAL PAPERS,

From his Impeachment to final Acquital.

TAKEN IN SHORT HAND,

BY CHARLES EVANS,

AND THE ARGUMENTS OF COUNSEL REVISED BY THEM

FROM HIS MANUSCRIPT.

BALTIMORE:

PRINTED FOR SAMUEL BUTLER AND GEORGE KEATINGE.

1805.

Jefferson's first term was marked by attacks on the federal judiciary, headed by Chief Justice John Marshall (above), and on Aaron Burr (left), whom he considered disloyal. The campaign climaxed with the impeachment trial of Samuel Chase (right, title page of the printed proceedings), presided over by Burr, recently returned from his duel with Hamilton. Most historians agree that if Chase had been convicted—the Senate acquitted him three days before Jefferson's second inaugural—Marshall would have been the next target.

to listen to the counsel of his closest advisers. But the picture is not, after all, inconsistent with other, less spectacular animosities—his hostility toward Patrick Henry, toward Lighthorse Harry Lee, toward Hamilton and Samuel Chase, toward John Marshall, and finally John Randolph. Inveteracy characterized most of these antagonisms, an unwillingness to acknowledge any good motive or quality in a man who had become an "enemy." The reverse (and far more attractive side) of Jefferson's hostility toward his enemies was his concern for and devotion to his friends, most notably perhaps John Page, for whom he sorely strained the bounds of propriety in trying to provide a sinecure when Page was ill and impoverished. Jefferson's behavior toward Burr was perilously close to the pathological. The disposition to demand absolute loyalty from his followers and associates was perhaps another manifestation of Jefferson's acute need for love and approval. We see in Jefferson's increasing demands on his supporters a familiar syndrome of the psychologically dependent: prove you love me by measuring up to these tests that I impose on you! And the tests grow more and more severe.

Jefferson had two more obsessions that were to cause him grief. One was that neither land forts nor an expensive army and navy were needed to secure the safety of the United States from attack by foreign powers. For forts and warships, "gunboats" could sometimes be substituted—large bargelike structures that had to be towed into position and were simply floating platforms for mortars and cannon. Jefferson's gunboats became objects of derision to a seafaring people. To the Federalists they were a classic example of Jefferson's impractical and "theoretical" disposition. To the great majority of the Republicans they were an embarrassment. But in the face of general opposition Jefferson persisted, building year after year more of the clumsy and inefficient "things"; one could not, for a certainty, call them ships.

Just as Jefferson wished to replace a conventional navy with his eccentric gunboats, he planned to replace a regular army with a militia force, and he attempted to try out his scheme in the new Louisiana Territory, to which he refused to give any substantial rights of self-government. He proposed to Congress a plan to settle a number of young men in the territory, giving each of them 160 acres of land in return for their agreement to serve in a militia force. The Senate received the bill but postponed action on it, and Jefferson was reported to have said, with tears in his eyes, "The people expect I should provide for their defense, but congress refuses me the means."

The other obsession that was to cause him (and the country) grief was his conviction that in the game of international power politics, the manipulation of commerce could force capitulation to the wishes of the United States where those wishes clashed with the policies and ambitions of other nations. Jefferson was a dedicated pacifist—although he did not hesitate to use the modest navy he had inherited from John Adams to beat the Tripolitan pirates into submission—and he was convinced that there must be some better way than war to decide differences between nations.

Since trade was the lifeblood of most modern nations, it followed that withholding commerce as a punishment for countries that had offended American dignity or disregarded its rights must inevitably exact compliance. This was a strange doctrine for a man who professed suspicion of commercial activities, distrusted banks, and praised self-sufficiency. It meant, in effect, coercing one's own citizens to coerce one's enemies. It meant a kind of war of attrition on the assumption that one could bear more hardship than one's opponent. Apparently such a policy was based on Jefferson's conviction that since the United States was overwhelmingly an agricultural country it could bear constraints on its trade better than such great commercial nations as Great Britain and France. There was also more than a suggestion that the part of the country most dependent on commerce, New England, was the stronghold of Federalist-monarchist principles, which to Jefferson were close to treason; that under such a policy of commercial constraints this section would be called upon for disproportionate sacrifices, or "punishment." While it was true that most New Englanders had repented and become good Republicans, a little suffering might

The North African state of Tripoli, indignant because Jefferson refused to pay its increased tribute demands, declared war on the United States in May, 1801. The war lasted four years (left, Navy hero Stephen Decatur in hand-to-hand combat; below, a squadron attacking Tripoli), and tribute demands did not cease. However, the peace treaty was favorable to the United States, whose young navy had gained valuable experience.

serve to remind them of their past sins and discourage future ones. We do not know, of course, how strongly such sentiments entered into Jefferson's almost fanatical devotion to his cherished plan for an embargo.

The most pressing public issue of Jefferson's second term was the harassment of American shipping by the belligerent powers of Europe—England and France—which were engaged in a bitter struggle in which England controlled the seas while Napoleon's armies dominated land warfare. The most serious threat to Britain's power on the seas was not the French fleet but the inclination of British sailors to desert. Madison estimated that five thousand British sailors had deserted to American merchant and naval vessels. England felt that it had to close this wound or bleed to death, and it therefore undertook to stop and search American vessels on the high seas and even in American waters and take off those seamen whose papers did not show them to be American citizens. It was a chancy and awkward business, who was British and who was American, and the British, arrogant by nature, not infrequently carried off bona fide Americans to the understandable rage of their shipmates, friends, and families. One tally showed that 781 Americans had been seized by British warships as deserters in a single year.

In addition to impressment, there was the complex question of what cargoes could be carried in what vessels to what ports of the belligerent powers. This problem seemed almost incapable of solution, since both France and Britain issued a series of orders in council declaring blockades of each other's coasts and asserting their right to seize contraband cargoes as they defined them. The first and most dangerous event involved a vessel of the United States Navy, the *Chesapeake*. The *Chesapeake* had just been commissioned and was on its shakedown cruise when it was intercepted by His Majesty's ship *Leopard*, whose captain demanded the right to come aboard and search for deserters. When the American commander, James Barron, refused, the British warship opened fire and reduced the American vessel to a battered hulk before its crew could get off a shot. With his ship dead in the water and a number of his crew dead or wounded, Barron struck his colors; a British boarding party then carried off a number of sailors declared to be deserters.

The reaction among Americans of all parties and sections was fury. Mobs pursued British sailors on shore leave; British ships were attacked at dock, and Jefferson was besieged with demands that he avenge the honor of the United States by declaring war against Great Britain. Jefferson temporized and delayed, believing that time would allow the war fever to subside. By a series of skillful maneuvers he held off the more militant elements in the country and tried to resolve the issue by diplomacy, sending Monroe to England to attempt to extract a treaty from the British ministry.

Meanwhile dissension mounted in his own party. Cries arose for a decisive policy that would protect American interests and American lives. One of Jefferson's most faithful supporters, Dr. George Logan, warned him: "Your errors in conducting the exterior [foreign] relations of our country oppress the minds of your best friends with the most anxious solicitude—you may yet retrieve your character and preserve the confidence of your fellow citizens. Call together your too long neglected Council [Cabinet], take the state of the Union into consideration, submit every subject with frankness to discussion, and, united with them, determine on such measures as may preserve the peace and honour of your country. Your own reputation imperiously demands that you should recede from pretensions and projects, which are demonstrably groundless and unjust." These were strong words, hinting to a President committed to democratic principles that he was running the country in an autocratic and highhanded manner.

Napoleon vastly complicated matters for Jefferson by his Berlin Decree of November 21, 1806, which stated that England was under blockade and that all trade with her or her colonies was interdicted. Britain responded on January 7, 1807, with her own Order in Council forbidding all neutral trade with France or any of her allies. Jefferson had, with his open contempt for the diplomatic corps, alienated those gentlemen with the exception of the French minister, Louis Marie Turreau, who, though he was friendly with Jefferson, was dismayed at his indecision. The President, he wrote, was in need of "that audacity which is indispensable in a place so eminent, whatever may be the form of government. The slightest event makes him lose his balance, and he does not even know how to disguise the impression he receives."

A growing gap appeared between Jefferson's theory and practice. In a letter to William Short he described the way his administration operated, or should operate. "Our government, altho', in theory, subject to be directed by the unadvised will of the President is, and from its origin has been, a very different thing in practice. . . . All matters of importance or difficulty are submitted to all the heads of departments comprising the cabinet; sometimes by the President's consulting them separately & successively as they happen to call on him; but in the gravest cases by calling them together, discussing the subject maturely, and finally taking the vote, on which the President counts himself but as one: so that in all important cases the Executive is, in fact, a Directory, which certainly the President might control, but of this there was never an example either in the first or the present administration. I have heard indeed that my predecessor sometimes decided things against his council by dashing & trampling his wig on the floor."

What is one to say to such a statement? We know enough of the workings of Jefferson's Cabinet to conclude that few Presidents have dominated Congress *and* the Cabinet as completely as Jefferson did and that he was often cavalier in consulting the Cabinet and resistant to its advice when he did. Was he hypocritical? Or was he, once again, simply displaying his remarkable gift for believing what he wished to believe, for rearranging reality to conform to theory?

On December 22, 1807, the Embargo, having been hurried through both houses of Congress, was signed by Jefferson, and the stormiest part of his administration began. It is hard to imagine a measure Jefferson could have adopted that would have done more to destroy the harmony which he prided himself on having created out of the disintegration of the Federalists and the elevation of democracy. In New England and New York commerce came to a virtual standstill. In Maine and Vermont smuggling on a grand scale developed along the Canadian border. Jefferson, furious, issued a proclamation declaring the Champlain region to be in a state of insurrection and invoking military authority to put down the insurgents. But defiance of the law became endemic. Smuggling grew so serious in New York that Jefferson decided to have the New York militia called out to close the border with Canada. To the governor of New York he wrote: "I think it so important an example to crush these audacious proceedings and to make the offenders feel the consequences of individuals daring to oppose a law by force, that no effort should be spared to compass this object."

At Newburyport, Massachusetts, an armed mob cowed the customs officers and enabled ships to sail. James Sullivan, the Republican governor of the state, aided and abetted the defiance of the law, and a British traveler in New York wrote of the effects of the embargo: "The port indeed was full of shipping, but they were dismantled and laid up; their decks were cleared, their hatches fastened down, and scarcely a sailor was to be found on board. Not a box, bale, cask, barrel, or package was to be seen upon the wharves. Many of the counting-houses were shut up, or advertised to be let; and the few solitary merchants, clerks, porters, and laborers that were to be seen were walking about with their hands in their pockets. The coffee-houses were almost empty; the streets, near the water-side, were almost deserted; the grass had begun to grow upon the wharves." Even the South felt the pinch as tobacco fell precipitously in price. But Jefferson was adamant. As his Cabinet members deserted him one by one—first Gallatin, then Robert Smith, secretary of the navy—convinced that he was sowing havoc in the country and destroying his party, Jefferson's migraine headaches, not surprisingly, returned with a vengeance.

In New England the doctrine of nullification that Jefferson had first spelled out in the Kentucky Resolutions was revived and used against his administration. There was open talk of New England and the Middle States splitting off from the South to form a separate political entity. But every defiance of the Embargo brought threats of repressive action from Jefferson. It did not seem to occur to him that a policy so offensive to so large a segment of the country could not possibly be maintained without, in the end, general insurrection and civil war. In the crisis Jefferson showed little regard for the constitutional limitations of his office. "This embargo law," he wrote to Gallatin, "is certainly the most embarrassing one we have ever had to execute. I did not expect a crop of so sudden & rank growth of fraud & open opposition by force could have grown up in the US." But, by the democratic principles he espoused, should not the President have accommodated himself to the sentiments of the people? The idea apparently did not occur to Jefferson. "I am satisfied with you," he continued, "that if orders & decrees are not repealed, and a continuance of the embargo is preferred to war (which sentiment is universal here), Congress must legalize all *means* which may be necessary to obtain its end." The passage is a remarkable one, hinting, as it does, at dictatorial powers to suppress dissent.

The "sentiment" in favor of the Embargo that Jefferson claimed as universal "here" (he was at Monticello when he wrote and thus he may have been technically correct) was far from universal elsewhere.

With the end of his administration in sight Jefferson, who had hand-picked his successor, James Madison, weathered the storm and withdrew gratefully to Monticello for the last time. "Never did a prisoner," he wrote a friend, "released from his chains feel such relief as I shall on shaking off the shackles of power. Nature intended me for the tranquil pursuits of science, by rendering them my supreme delight. But the enormities of the times in which I have lived, have forced me to take a part in resisting them, and to commit myself on the boisterous ocean of political passions." And then came a final sentence. "I thank God for the opportunity of retiring from them without censure, and carrying with me the most consoling proofs of public approbation." Few Presidents have left office in the face of the bitterness and recrimination that surrounded Jefferson as a consequence of his ill-fated Embargo.

What judgment is one to make of his presidency? On the personal side his period in office witnessed the surfacing of the Hemings and Walker scandals, the death of his younger daughter, Maria, and his own uncertain health: he was plagued by chronic diarrhea at the beginning of his administration and by his terrible migraine headaches at the end. When he left office he was so deeply in debt that he had to borrow a substantial sum of money simply to extricate himself from Washington. On the political side he had gone, one might say, from disaster to disaster. His foreign policy had been characterized by expediency and by an intransigence characteristic of so many of his actions. While the United States was essentially the helpless victim of the arrogant and aggressive policies of France and England, Jefferson's efforts to reach some kind of accommodation with the two belligerent powers came to nothing. His ultimate weapon, the Embargo, was a hopelessly unrealistic response to an admittedly awkward dilemma. It did not avoid a war, it simply postponed one, and it paid a very heavy price in domestic friction and discord. His gunboats were a fiasco; his efforts to replace the regular army with a national militia force, abortive. On the domestic scene, his attempt to undermine the authority of the federal courts and restrict the powers of the Supreme Court by amendment ended in defeat. His relentless pursuit of Aaron Burr likewise came to nothing. Thus by one set of standards his administration could be judged to be a series of setbacks, of contradictions, of ambiguities, of dubious decisions, pressed with a kind of fanatical zeal to final defeat. Yet that interpretation clearly was only part of the story and perhaps, in the last analysis, the less important part. His remarkable luck held. The Louisiana Territory fell into his hands like a ripe plum, and although he imposed on it a thoroughly undemocratic regime, the glory of that windfall profit compensated for any number of errors. In commissioning the Lewis and Clark Expedition he dramatized the West in a way that would forever identify his name and his administration with the westward movement.

Jefferson also put an end to the harassment of American

PIRACY.

...rn, Sink, and Deſtroy your

founded; and then Vote

...he voyage; that ...mpany with the ...ton, and on Tueſ- ...en in lat. 48 40 London, ſtanding the ſhip Poca- ...ut three leagues o'clock in the ...W. by. S. two ...hem on fire; at ...ame up with the ...officer, who or- ...which was ac- ...and boat's crew ...d the ſhip's pa- ...and crew of the ...e's ſhip, which ...s Hermione and ...bound to France ...turned from the ...ake out the bag- ...board the Com- ...ſhip to be bur- ...e appearers and ...ard the French

nicating ſupplies to the Britiſh Weſt In- dies, againſt which, it is in fact leveled. Rather, it is intended to compreſs Great Britain in all her relations in which it is thought ſhe is dependent upon us. Mr. Jefferſon thinks he can ſtarve that nation

---

British Barbarity and Piracy!!

The Federalists say that Mr. Christopher Gore ought to be supported as Governor—for *his attachment to Britain.*—If British influence is to effect the suffrages of a free people, let them read the following melancholy and outrageous conduct of British Piracy, and judge for themselves.

The " LEOPARD OUTSPOTTED" or Chesapeak Outrage outdone.

Jefferson's disastrous second-term foreign policy nearly ruined the nation's economy and bitterly divided the country (left, an 1809 cartoon showing Jefferson being robbed by George III and Napoleon; above, Federalist broadsides push for war with France, while Republicans decry British barbarities).

shipping by the Tripolitan pirates, proving that he could act with force and decisiveness when the occasion required. Indeed, although he was often charged with being weak and indecisive, his temper was rather the reverse. He delayed and equivocated when, for reasons of policy, he wished to avoid taking any action, but he did not hesitate to use all the powers of his office, and a few more besides, on numerous occasions.

Once he had set himself on a particular course, he pursued it without regard to the advice of his friends and supporters or to the consequences. He had, in short, little or no capacity to distance himself from problems and issues with which he was called upon to deal. Every issue tended to become a personal one; by the same token his lack of any deep and saving sense of humor was closely related to his lack of perspective on himself. It was not, then, hypocrisy that led him to describe to William Short the democratic and quite imaginary functioning of his Cabinet. He genuinely *believed* that the Cabinet functioned in that manner.

He was equally insensitive to charges that he had imposed an undemocratic regime on the Louisiana Territory, because he felt complete confidence in the integrity of his own actions. He could not imagine himself acting in bad faith, and thus he seemed at times to be acting exactly that way. There was, it must be said, a good deal of the self-righteous schoolmaster about Jefferson—always lecturing, usually brilliantly, to a rather obtuse world. And when the world, or the portion of it with which he was particularly concerned, failed to pay attention and learn its lesson properly, he could be very severe in his chastisements.

But we never finish with Jefferson. And having said one thing we must perpetually be adding another. He personalized the presidency in a way that neither of his predecessors could have imagined. He made himself, quite self-consciously, the symbol of democratic simplicity and unpretentiousness, even at the risk, as in his diplomatic pell-mell, of seeming to the more sophisticated to be indulging in absurd posturings. However such posturings may have offended the sophisticated, they delighted the ordinary folk, who were able, as we say today, to "identify" with this tall, informal, democratic aristocrat who put down foreigners with their fancy airs and stilted manners.

Again, Jefferson carried party management—the direction and manipulation of Congress most specifically—far beyond anything conceived by Washington or Adams. He also began the preoccupation with "presidential style"—the idea that each President has to "come across" as a particular, sharply and dramatically conceived individual—an idea that was to become so central to the American presidency.

Perhaps most important of all, he began his presidency with the fairest hopes. He brought a unity to the new nation that it had not known since the beginning of the Washington adminis- tration more than a decade earlier. He fixed and defined the tone and mode of democratic republicanism. His rhetoric and his "style" turned out to be far more important than his often clouded and doctrinaire policies, for he was, in essence, a medi- umistic, shamanistic figure. That quality in the final analysis gave him his remarkable hold on the imaginations and loyalties of Americans, not only his own contemporaries but successive generations, and it, finally, makes him still a central and compel- ling figure for all of us. If his administration grew increasingly disheveled, increasingly disorganized and capricious, it was not conspicuously different from many of the episodes of Jefferson's own life. He was a good beginner but a poor ender. His principal contribution to the American Revolution came at the beginning. When he encountered difficulties he became quickly dis- couraged or immovably stubborn. Abounding in charisma, he lacked stamina. His nerves were bad, his constitution uncertain, his grip on reality precarious; even his sanity was imperiled from time to time. He was devious, secretive, evasive—guarding, often desperately one suspects, the hidden agonies of his inner life—always thin-skinned, excruciatingly vulnerable. He was great because he embodied, as Washington had though vastly differently, an essential portion of the American consciousness.

Founders are just that—founders, establishers. In our founding fathers different principles were embodied. Washing- ton stood for unity, discipline, order, and self-control, a self-control so dramatic and unique that it withstood the temptations of power as that of no other figure in history had done. He was the central and essential figure in the American pantheon; he embodied the Union. Alexander Hamilton stood for the practical, commercial, money-making, progressive element in the American character. Basically nonideological, he was the consummate manager, the shrewd businessman, the friend of enterprise. John Marshall embodied the power of the law, the revolutionary principle of a government of laws not of men, of a higher power to which all earthly power must answer, in harmony with which all mundane law must vibrate. And Thomas Jefferson embodied the democratic principle—that all power resided ultimately in the people; that they were the masters, and the rulers simply their servants; that they had the last word, and that in them was some essential element of health and goodness which must always determine aright and needed no check or control.

He stood also for the endless westward yearning of a people and for their naive belief in the efficacy of education and reason and science, the three combining to produce eons of progressive enlightenment, wisdom, and happiness. Out of this unfathomably complicated man came the simplest of doctrines that became the treasured orthodoxies of the American faith. Enduring what he could not cure, he lived out the terrible ambiguity of his own life and bequeathed to history a romantically simplified image, the familiar picture of the beloved squire of Monticello, the farmer, the devoted husband and father, the champion of liberty and equality, the republican scholar. He was the master illusionist, the magician of democracy, perhaps above all the stylist, the writer of memorable phrases and paragraphs, of incantations so powerful they would never cease to reverberate in his country's collective memory; the artist-scientist called from his easel, the farmer called from his plow. And under it all the haunting symbol of an inescapable doubleness, the technically, legally "black" woman, kin to his wife, mother of his children, beloved, never to be denied but never to be acknowledged.

Perhaps we might say that if Jefferson was, by conventional judgment, a poor President, he was nonetheless a great one.

16. Back to Monticello

Jefferson went back to Monticello in a late, chilling March snow that must have reminded him of the snowy evening when he had brought his wife to the magic mountain for the first time years before. He returned to the last age, the last act, the sage of Monticello, enshrined on his mountaintop in the shrine of his own building and rebuilding. There, intermittently attended by his faithful daughter, part wife, part mother, and by Sally Hemings, he filled his days with his books, his plants and flowers, his projects for improvement of the plantation, his ingenious devices, his architectural drawings, his proposals for a new university on progressive and enlightened principles. He designed comfortable and convenient clothes—a pair of overalls to wear on his daily rides, some oddly pointed shoes reminiscent of a court jester's, his favored red waistcoats and corduroy jackets—and enjoyed all the memorabilia of a memorable life, paintings and etchings, pieces of fine silver, sculptured busts, chairs of improved design. He turned the house into a strange, disorderly universe of mastodon bones and Indian artifacts, pursuing every novelty and innovation as avidly as a lover pursues his mistress.

Monticello became the mecca of democracy. From various corners of the nation and the world a constant stream of pilgrims made the difficult and inconvenient journey to Charlottesville, up the long, arduous hill to the mountaintop. There they were received by the sage a bit vaguely or aloofly until they touched upon one of his many enthusiasms. Then the remarkably timeless face lighted up; the expression that had been masked and remote became charming and animated. That was what the pilgrims came for, the flash of brilliant eccentricity, the warm glow of banked fires blown into a brief blaze by an agreeable recollection or suggestive comment. The visitors, especially if they had caught Jefferson in one of his sunny and expansive moods, hurried away to write down their impressions of the great man. Gradually a whole literature of Jefferson at Monticello accumulated.

Two occurrences stand out in the seventeen years that Jefferson spent at Monticello between the time of his retirement and his death in 1826. The first was the healing of the breach between Jefferson and Adams. This was brought about through the efforts of Dr. Benjamin Rush, that appealing Philadelphia physician who was so strongly of the Jeffersonian persuasion in politics as well as in medicine. Rush had preserved his ancient friendship with John Adams, and he set about to reconcile the two old friends. The way had been paved by the visit of a young friend of Jefferson's, Edward Coles, to Adams in the summer of 1811. At the mention of Jefferson, Adams said, "I have always loved Jefferson and still love him." Coles reported Adams's statement to Jefferson, prompting him to write to Rush: "This is enough for me. I only needed this knowledge to revive towards him all the affections of the most cordial moments of our lives."

Adams opened the correspondence by sending Jefferson a book by his son, John Quincy Adams, and Jefferson replied, "A letter from you calls up recollections very dear to my mind. It carries me back to the times when, beset with difficulties and dangers, we were fellow laborers in the same cause, struggling for what is most valuable to man, his right of self-government. Laboring always at the same oar, with some wave ever ahead threatening to overwhelm us and yet passing harmless under our bark, we knew not how, we rode through the storm with heart and hand, and made a happy port."

How felicitous! Rush was properly pleased with himself for

having brought these two splendid planets into conjunction. "I rejoice in the correspondence . . . ," he wrote Adams. "I consider you and him as the North and South Poles of the American Revolution. Some talked, some wrote, and some fought to promote and establish it, but you and Mr. Jefferson *thought* for us all." It was a singularly apposite compliment. Between them, they had indeed "thought for us all." They had been the grand theoreticians, Adams the sober, systematic thinker, Jefferson the brilliant intuiter. In them were combined the yin and yang of American political theory. They composed another of those dramatic dualities that seem so characteristic of Jefferson's entire life: Jefferson and Hamilton, Jefferson and Marshall, Jefferson and Adams—Jefferson always one pole of those shifting polarities. This was immediately evident in their letters. Adams plunged in like a swimmer stimulated by the surf. He could not, he declared, "stand upon Epistolary Ettiquette"; he could not wait for an answer but must write two, three, four letters to Jefferson's one as the ideas, questions, queries came pouring out: "Never mind it, my dear Sir, if I write four letters to your one; your one is worth more than my four. . . . You and I ought not to die, before We have explained ourselves to each other." Cautious at first, they soon ventured into more roiled waters. Or Adams did. He plainly wished to explore the nature of their philosophical and political differences; he wished a debate. But Jefferson was more reserved, inclined as always to be evasive.

He did, to be sure, accuse Adams of being somewhat obscurantist. Adams had been quoted as saying that the main purpose of education was to pass on the inherited wisdom of the race. Jefferson felt almost personally affronted. "One of the questions you know on which our parties took different sides, was on the improvability of the human mind, in science, in ethics, in government, etc. Those who advocated reformation of institutions, pari passu, with the progress of science, maintained that no definite limits could be assigned to that progress. The enemies of reform, on the other hand, denied improvement, and advocated steady adherence to the principles, practices and institutions of our fathers, which they represented as the consumma-

Benjamin Rush, Philadelphia physician, political leader, and reformer (left, a portrait by Thomas Sully), worked for two years to effect a reconciliation between his good friends Thomas Jefferson and John Adams. He was finally successful in 1811, and from that time until their deaths on July 4, 1826, they carried on a lively correspondence (far left, Jefferson in 1821, painted by Sully; above, Adams in an 1825 portrait by Gilbert Stuart).

tion of wisdom, and akmé of excellence, beyond which the human mind could never advance." Although Adams, in the passage that offended Jefferson, had disclaimed "the wish to influence the freedom of enquiry," he had predicted that it would "produce nothing more worthy of transmission to posterity, than the principles, institutions, and systems of education recieved from their ancestors." Jefferson added, "I do not consider this as your deliberate opinion. You possess, yourself, too much science, not to see how much is still ahead of you, unexplained and unexplored." Jefferson could not have expressed more succinctly his own faith in reason, science, progress, and the improvement of the human mind. Adams replied, suggesting that such modern luminaries as Joseph Priestley, Richard Price, and Brand Hollis, whom Jefferson so admired, adhered to follies and superstitions as great as those they castigated from an earlier time. And then he noted: "Checks and Ballances, Jefferson, however you and your Party may have ridiculed them, are our only Security, for the progress of Mind, as well as the Security of Body. . . . Every Species of these Christians would persecute Deists, as soon as either Sect would persecute another, if it had unchecked and unballanced Power. Nay, the Deists would persecute Christians, and Atheists would persecute Deists, with as unrelenting Cruelty, as any Christians would persecute them or one another. Know thyself, human Nature!"

To Jefferson the debate came down to a basically simple proposition. There had been party and political differences since the beginning of time and these would always exist. Everyone took sides in these controversies "in favor of the many, or of the few, according to his constitution, and the circumstances in which he is placed. . . ." He considered that he and his Republicans had cast their lot with the many, and Adams with the few. Beyond that it was always a struggle between the defenders of the status quo, typically the few who profited unduly from it, and the many who wished for a better and more just society. Science above all held the greatest promise for the future. "Science," Jefferson wrote, has "liberated the ideas of those who read and reflect. . . . An insurrection has consequently begun, of science, talents and courage, against rank and birth, which have fallen into contempt."

Adams was convinced that aristocracies would keep reasserting themselves in history. The aristocracy of talents of which Jefferson spoke so enthusiastically would, in time, become a "hierarchical Despotism" as onerous as any that had appeared earlier. But, Adams wrote teasingly, "Our pure, virtuous, public spirited federative Republick will last for ever, govern the Globe and introduce the perfection of Man, his perfectability being already proved by Price Priestly, Condorcet Rousseau Diderot and Godwin." And again: "Human Nature, in no form of it, ever could bear Prosperity."

Jefferson replied: "My temperament is sanguine. I steer my bark with Hope in the head, leaving Fear astern." But Jefferson seemed to move toward Adams when he deplored the tendency of "our post-revolutionary youth" to behave as though they had acquired all knowledge "in their mothers' womb, and bring it into the world ready-made" with no need for books and teachers. "Every folly," he added, "must run it's round; and so, I suppose, must that of self-learning, and self sufficiency; of rejecting the knolege acquired in past ages, and starting on the new ground of intuition."

In his long retirement the dream of a university established on enlightened scientific principles obsessed Jefferson, and he inquired, "Have you ever turned your thoughts to the plan of such an institution?" To which Adams replied: "Education! Oh Education! The greatest Grief of my heart, and the greatest Affliction of my Life! To my mortification I must confess, that I have never closely thought, or very deliberately reflected upon the Subject, which never occurs to me now, without producing a deep Sigh, an heavy groan and sometimes Tears." All this because he had not had time to supervise the education of his own children as he would have wished, thus, "If I venture to give you any thoughts at all, they must be very crude." And later, ruminating on the subject, Adams wrote, "Education, which you brought into View . . . is a Subject so vast, and the Systems of Writers are so various and so contradictory: that human Life is too short to examine it; and a Man must die before he can learn to bring up his Children."

Jefferson, needless to say, was not daunted. He occupied many days and nights happily planning his ideal educational system, while through all the letters between him and Adams ran the persistent theme of the inherent wickedness of man (Adams) versus his perfectability (Jefferson). At one point Adams broke out, "I leave those profound Phylosophers whose Sagacity perceives the Perfectability of Humane Nature, and those illuminated Theologians who expect the Apocalyptic Reign, to enjoy their transporting hopes; provided always that they will not engage Us in Crusades and French Revolutions, nor burn Us for doubting. . . . Power always thinks it has a great Soul, and vast Views, beyond the Comprehension of the Weak; and that it is doing God Service, when it is violating all his Laws."

Adams: "I can only say at present, that it should seem that human Reason and human Conscience, though I believe there are such things, are not a Match for human Passions, human Imaginations and human Enthusiasms."

Finally, Adams's tireless probes at the armor of Jefferson's optimism discovered a chink and wrung from his friend a poignant and desperate question. "There are, I acknolege," Jefferson wrote, "even in the happiest life, some terrible convulsions. . . . I have often wondered for what good end the sensations of Grief could be intended. All our other passions, within proper bounds, have an useful object. . . . I wish the pathologists then would tell us what is the use of grief in the economy, and of what good it is the cause, proximate or remote." What use was grief? The grief that had pursued him from childhood, the terrible and recurring trauma of loss that time seemed never to heal in Jefferson's heart. Jefferson never asked a more keenly felt or revealing question. Adams promptly addressed himself to it: "Grief drives Men into habits of serious Reflection sharpens the Understanding and softens the Heart . . . to elevate them to a Superiority over all human Events; . . . in short to make them Stoiks and Christians." It had made Jefferson neither. His capacity and the occasions for suffering remained undiminished.

As the years passed, more and more of the correspondence was concerned with Jefferson's plans for what began taking shape as the University of Virginia. Jefferson planned to import the greatest scholars of Europe as teachers, and Adams protested. "Your University is a noble employment in your old Age," he wrote, "and your ardor for its success, does you honour, but I do not approve of your sending to Europe for Tutors, and Professors." They would bring with them too many Old World prejudices. More "active ingenuity, and independent minds" could be found in America.

There is no question that the correspondence was a tonic for the two old men. For Adams it was an opportunity to pour out a torrent of prickly observations on men and events. For Jefferson it was in the nature of a reconciliation, not just to Adams, but to the world. Thin-skinned as both men were, in "explaining themselves to each other" they brought their own lives and thoughts into a sharper focus and, while they repaired their friendship, gave dramatic highlight to their substantial philosophical and temperamental differences; so that their letters can be read as a kind of map of the consciousness of the American Revolutionary generation, encompassing a very considerable part of the mind of the age.

In the same way, it is marvelously appropriate that Jefferson's final accomplishment should have been an educational institution, the University of Virginia, and above all that he should have been the bricks-and-mortar architect of it all as well as the architect of its educational philosophy. The bricks-and-mortar part of the undertaking was perhaps the happiest achievement of his long life. Standing on "the lawn" of the University of Virginia, a precious kernel in a large and otherwise architecturally undistinguished modern university, one is entirely captivated by the harmonious and cloistered space, the perfect expression of an idea. More than the Richmond capitol, more even than Monticello, it speaks of its artificer's triumph over the tragedy and disorder of his own life—that in the end he could establish this enchanting vista. The dome of the central hall is really a dome, not merely, as at Monticello, an architec-

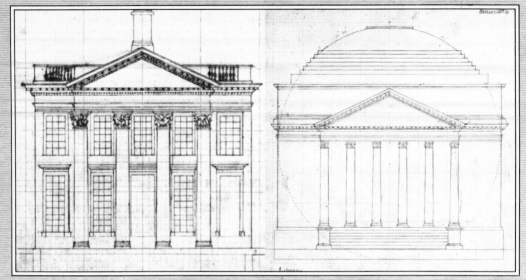

Thomas Jefferson's retirement was dominated by his planning for the University of
Virginia at Charlottesville, which opened its
doors in March, 1825 (below, an 1830's en-
graving). Jefferson visualized the university
as an academic village rather than one huge
building (left, his sketches for Pavilion III
and the Rotunda, which housed the library)
and said: "This institution will be based on
the ultimate freedom of the human mind."

tural adornment. The masters' houses, beautifully proportioned variations on the classical theme, are deft interjections in the long rows of student rooms, now fiercely competed for by a "natural aristocracy" of students, a substantial portion of them women. Artists impose, or once did, their own vision of order and harmony on a chaotic world. They create worlds in which we are invited to live. At the end the artist in Jefferson asserted itself in this powerful unified vision, so gracious, so inviting. This, one knows, is what education might have been, perhaps once was, and may be again. At the very least it is a charming illusion, a perfect work of art. Indeed, one might say that Jefferson built his answer to Adams. In that enchanted environment, in those beautifully contrived buildings, one can at last believe in the triumph of reason and science and the ultimate perfectability of man. Reality is banished in the gardens, the serpentine walls, the classic façades, which are as expressive as intelligent faces. It is Jefferson's final universe—a univers-ity—as perfect a work of art as any American has created.

To suggest that Jefferson in his old age found Monticello the ideal realm of happiness and peace that he so often acclaimed it would be cheering, but that inescapable doubleness —that grief whose purpose he could not comprehend—remained at the heart of his existence. It was not just Sally and her growing brood of children—*his* children. Thomas Mann Randolph, Martha's husband, always unstable, went quite mad and threatened Martha's life. Jefferson's nephews, the sons of his dead sister, murdered a slave for breaking a teacup that had belonged to their mother. A flood swept away the costly dam and waterworks that Jefferson had built on the river, a loss estimated at some $30,000. (A visitor to Monticello noted with astonishment that Jefferson, already deeply in debt, showed no emotion at the news.) Indeed, debts piled up nightmarishly until he was forced to sell his library to Congress to become the nucleus of *its* library—the Library of Congress. Having done so, he began at once to collect a new library, for, as he wrote Adams, "I cannot live without books."

In addition to such catastrophes, there was the complicated

day-to-day life at Monticello to contend with. Martha and her children were often, and finally permanently, at Monticello, in addition to Maria's children, the young Carrs, and the uninterrupted stream of visitors. Jefferson's three- and four-hour horseback rides were one means of escape, and when these were insufficient he withdrew to the remoteness and quiet of Poplar Forest.

The correspondence with Adams dwindled from a torrent to a trickle. Adams, his hand so palsied he could no longer write, dictated laboriously to a succession of patient granddaughters. Jefferson replied in his perfect script, as even and controlled as though turned out by some kind of newfangled writing machine. One suspects that sometime during the winter or spring of 1826, without complicity but with an acute sense of historical drama, they determined to survive until July 4, 1826, the day on which, fifty years earlier, the Declaration of Independence had been adopted by Congress. In any event, whether by acts of will or an act of that God about whom they had expressed varying degrees of skepticism, they did, in fact, both die on July 4. Adams's last words were, "Thomas Jefferson still survives." But Jefferson had died a few hours earlier.

Their concurrent deaths sealed their original pact—that they should not die until they had explained themselves to each other, and of course, not entirely coincidentally, to the world.

John Adams's grandson Charles Francis Adams, hearing of the death of the two ancient heroes of the republic, wrote in the diary that was almost a genetic inheritance for members of the Adams clan: "There is nothing more to be said. With all the volumes of Eulogies that have been published on these men, and the remarks that have been studied upon this coincidence, nothing has been produced so eloquent as the simple fact. There are occurrences sometimes in the course of Human affairs, too great for words. The mind is already so exalted that any attempt to shackle it by expression destroys the flight, and lets it down again to common place. The wonder, the awe, the feeling of undefinable grandeur which comes over one though they might earnestly seek an outlet in language, would vanish in

JEFFERSON LOTTERY.

Register No.

1979

Combination Nos.

3 15 31

MANAGERS.
John Brockenborough,
Philip Norb. Nicholas,
Richard Anderson.

This Ticket will entitle the holder thereof to such prize as may be drawn to its numbers in the JEFFERSON LOTTERY.

Richmond, April, 1826.

For the Managers,

STATE OF VIRGINIA.

Wm. Grattan, Printer.

The bronze bust of Jefferson at right was cast from a life mask made in October, 1825, by John Henri Isaac Browere. At that time Jefferson was in ill health, over $100,000 in debt, and worried about his family's future. His scheme to sell some of his land by lottery (above) did not work, but his plight prompted pledges of money from all over the country. Not enough was raised, and in 1831 Monticello and 525 surrounding acres were sold for $7,000.

the attempt. The greatest of all eloquence in the known world is the eloquence of *facts.*"

Jefferson was buried in the Monticello graveyard that he had laid out years earlier, the plot whose first occupant had been his brother-in-law and dearest friend, Dabney Carr. A simple granite shaft of his own design was erected over his grave. He had specified his epitaph:

Here was buried
Thomas Jefferson
Author of the Declaration of American Independence
of the Statute of Virginia for religious freedom
& Father of the University of Virginia

The extraordinary and enigmatic life was over. The protean appetites and unanswerable mysteries were safely underground. It remained only for biographers and historians to tidy things up, which they set about assiduously to do. Piety soon rose like a ground-mist to obscure the darkness and tragedy, to compose in its place a classic American success story, the familiar account of the brilliant young author of democracy's primary testament mellowing into the benign sage of Monticello, surrounded by adoring relatives and slaves, spoken of reverentially as "Mr. Jefferson," as he is today by the amiable ladies who steer slightly perplexed tourists around the beautiful and eccentric mansion, now—like his life—put in an immaculate order it most certainly never knew during its builder's lifetime.

Historians do not bestow greatness, nor can they withdraw it. Greatness accrues to an individual because he seizes upon some essential portion of the popular imagination. He need meet only a single requirement of his times, a requirement rising out of the deepest levels of the collective consciousness to insure his immortality. Thus Washington's greatness was, in large part, to be found in his rocklike enduringness; that of John Adams in his intelligent industry, of Hamilton in his financial genius, of Jefferson in his ability to articulate the noblest ideals of democracy. How it should ever have become implanted in our minds that the great man must also be an unflawed figure and that to acknowledge his humanness would be to diminish his greatness is a story too intricate to recount in detail here. But it clearly has had to do with our self-image, individual and collective. We could not bear ambiguity; we could not face the mixture of good and evil that inheres in the very substance of our daily lives, and we demonstrated our intolerance of ambiguity by our attitude toward our heroes, *unconsciously* suppressing everything about them that was less than immaculate, perfect, ideal. Once that had been accomplished, once we had sealed them up in their immaculateness, to refer to their human foibles and weaknesses became a form of treason that seemed to threaten good order and the stability of the state. The power of the myth proved far stronger than our avowed devotion to the truth.

Perhaps if we take, as we have done from time to time, a perspective on Jefferson other than the explicitly political, we may be better able to understand this paradoxical man and accept his substantial failings as well as his remarkable gifts. It is, after all, as an artist that we have seen Jefferson most sympathetically—a creative person as opposed to a practical one, an artist-architect, artist-writer, interrupted by a revolution, called by the "enormities" of the time to abandon his secluded life for the basically uncongenial world of practical politics. Jefferson's major personality traits fit most naturally into the pattern that modern researchers have identified as belonging to the exceptionally creative person, typically the artist—his obsessiveness, his morbidity, his excessive love-dependence, his secretiveness, his vanity and vulnerability, his incipient schizophrenia, his megalomania, his inability to sustain routine labors, his abject failure to manage his financial affairs, his self-indulgence, his primarily sensuous rather than rational apprehension of the world, even his terrible migraine headaches—all these qualities, while by no means confined to artists and exceptionally creative people, are characteristic, in this "clustering," of the type. By the same token, they are definitely antithetical to the character of the successful politician.

Monticello, today in good repair, had to be restored after years of neglect and mistreatment. First James Barclay purchased it to raise silkworms. The project failed, and in 1836 he sold it to Uriah Levy for $2,500. Levy did some repair and restoration and left Monticello to "the people of the United States" when he died in 1862. But his family broke the will, and for years the house served as a cow barn and rubbish heap. In 1881 Jefferson Levy, Uriah's nephew, began restoration. In 1923 he sold Monticello to the Thomas Jefferson Memorial Foundation for $500,000.

I suspect that Americans who would find it difficult to accept the real Jefferson in the guise of politician-statesman would have little difficulty with him as artist. We clearly allow artists a moral latitude that we deny—or attempt to deny—to our political leaders. A Van Gogh may go mad and cut off his ear or a Gauguin live with native women in Tahiti, a famous writer may shoot his mistress, without our thinking any the less of them, but politics—that is a different matter. There the American intolerance of ambiguity most clearly asserts itself. All this is not to say that we have cast Jefferson in the role of artist merely to make his eccentricities and shortcomings more palatable to the public, but rather that this is indeed the true Jefferson and that once we have grasped this fact much that was troublesome and obscure becomes understandable. Out of the shadows emerges a figure splendidly luminous, the articulator of democracy, the inexhaustible artificer, the artist as tragic hero.

Acknowledgments

The author gratefully acknowledges his debt to the established and extensive biographies of Thomas Jefferson which presently dominate that field of scholarship, particularly the vast and still unfinished work by Dumas Malone, the biography by Nathan Schachner, and interpretations by Fawn Brodie of Jefferson's relations with Maria Cosway and Sally Hemings.

The editors wish to thank the following institutions and individuals for their special cooperation in making available materials in their collections.

Library of Congress, Manuscripts Division— Dr. Paul G. Sifton

National Archives, Center for the Documentary Study of the American Revolution— George Chalou

University of Virginia Library, Manuscripts Department—Edmund Berkeley, Jr., and Gregory Johnson

University of Virginia Library, Rare Books Department—Cynthia Sinnott

Virginia State Library, Photo Library—Katherine M. Smith

Wheaton College, Art Department—Professor Thomas J. McCormick

Among the many useful devices Jefferson invented for his household was this revolving music stand, which is believed to have been made at Monticello about 1810.

Picture Credits

2 New-York Historical Society 4 Thomas Jefferson Memorial Foundation 10 top McGregor Library, University of Virginia 10–11 *Start of the Hunt* (detail), National Gallery of Art, gift of Edgar William and Bernice Chrysler Garbisch, 1953 18 top Assay Office, Birmingham, England 18–19 Colonial Williamsburg Foundation 19 top Earl Gregg Swem Library, College of William and Mary 26 Columbia University Law School Library 27 Colonial Williamsburg Foundation 32–33 left photo by Thomas L. Williams right Thomas Coram Foundation for Children, London 38 top left Giraudon top right New York Public Library bottom Culver Pictures 39 top left *The English Works of Sir Henry Spelman*, 1727, New York Public Library top right New York Public Library bottom Library of Congress 46–47 top left New York Public Library bottom left Massachusetts Historical Society right photo by Joseph Farber 56 bottom photographed from *The Domestic Life of Thomas Jefferson*, Sarah K. Randolph, Frederick Ungar Publishing Co., Inc., 1958; orginal document in the Virginia State Library 56–57 Valentine Museum, Richmond, Virginia 64 Colonial Williamsburg Foundation 65 top Rare Book Division, New York Public Library bottom *The Pictorial Field-Book of the Revolution*, B. Lossing, Volume II, 1860 70 Rare Book Division, Library of Congress 71 top Virginia Historical Society bottom Library of Congress 76–77 Free Library of Philadelphia 77 top New-York Historical Society 84 Board of Regents, Gunston Hall Plantation 85 Virginia State Library 90 top National Archives bottom photographed by Hirst Milhollen. From *The Story of the Declaration of Independence*, bicentennial editon, by Dumas Malone, Milton Kaplan, and Hirst Milhollen. Copyright © 1954, 1975 by Oxford University Press, Inc. Reprinted by permission 91 Independence National Historical Park 99, 100–101 *The Declaration of Independence, July 4, 1776* (details), Yale University Art Gallery 110 Manuscript Division, Library of Congress 111 Historical Society of Pennsylvania 118 Princeton University Library 119 American Philosophical Society 122–23 left Rare Book Division, Library of Congress center *The Compleat Tutor for the Harpsichord or Spinnet*, Rare Book Division, Library of Congress right Manuscript Division, Library of Congress 128 Indiana Historical Bureau 129 Executive Mansion, Richmond 136–37 Anne S. K. Brown Military Collection 137 top left photographed from *The Papers of Thomas Jefferson*, Volume 6, Julian P. Boyd, editor, copyright 1952 by Princeton University Press; original document in the records of the U.S. General Accounting Office, National Archives top right Emmet Collection, New York Public Library 144 left McGregor Library, University of Virginia 144–45 Prints Division, New York Public Library 152 Massachusetts Historical Society 153 Colonial Williamsburg Foundation 160 top McGregor Library, University of Virginia bottom Prints Division, New York Public Library 161 Massachusetts Historical Society 168–69 *Columbian Magazine*, February, 1789 169 top Virginia State Library 174 William L. Clements Library 174–75 New Jersey Historical Society 178–79 Pierpont Morgan Library, New York 179 bottom Diplomatic Reception Rooms, Department of State 184 top left *Antiquités de la France*, Charles-Louis Clérisseau top right Musée Carnavalet, photo Bulloz 184–85 detail of water color in the papers of Benjamin Henry Latrobe, Maryland Historical Society 185 top Musée Carnavalet, photo Bulloz 192–93 Giraudon 193 top Bibliothèque Nationale 198 Prints Division, New York Public Library 199 Bibliothèque Nationale 202–3 Mariners Museum, Newport News, Virginia 203 top Louvre, photo Giraudon 208–9 left Musée de Cherbourg, photo Archives Photographiques right Virginia State Capitol, photo Virginia State Library 216–17 left New-York Historical Society right Free Library of Philadelphia 220–21 Cabinet des Estampes, Musées de la Ville de Strasbourg 224–25 Louvre 230–31 Metropolitan Museum of Art, Edward W. C. Arnold Collection 231 top portrait by John Trumbull, Yale University Art Gallery 236–37 New-York Historical Society 244–45 left American Antiquarian Society right Metropolitan Museum of Art, gift of William H. Huntington, 1883 248–49 left National Archives center New-York Historical Society right Manuscript Division, Library of Congress 254–55 Library of Congress 255 top Smithsonian Institution 264 top Office of the Architect of the Capitol, Washington, D.C. bottom National Archives 265 Geography and Map Division, Library of Congress 268 top and bottom left portrait by Charles Willson Peale, Independence National Historical Park top right American Philosophical Society 268–69 U.S. Pacific Railroad Survey Reports, Volume XII, Book 1, 1855 269 left American Philosophical Society top right American Philosophical Society bottom right American Museum of Natural History, New York 274 courtesy of Kennedy Galleries, Inc., New York 275 left United States Supreme Court 278 top Henry E. Huntington Library 278–79 Rhode Island Historical Society 286 bottom Prints Division, New York Public Library 286–87 American Antiquarian Society 287 bottom Rare Book Division, Library of Congress 294–95 left American Philosophical Society center Pennsylvania Hospital, Philadelphia right National Collection of Fine Arts, Smithsonian Institution 300 top both: Jefferson Papers, University of Virginia Library 300–301 Library of Congress 304 Thomas Jefferson Memorial Foundation 305 New York State Historical Association, Cooperstown 308–9 Virginia State Travel Service 312 Thomas Jefferson Memorial Foundation

Index

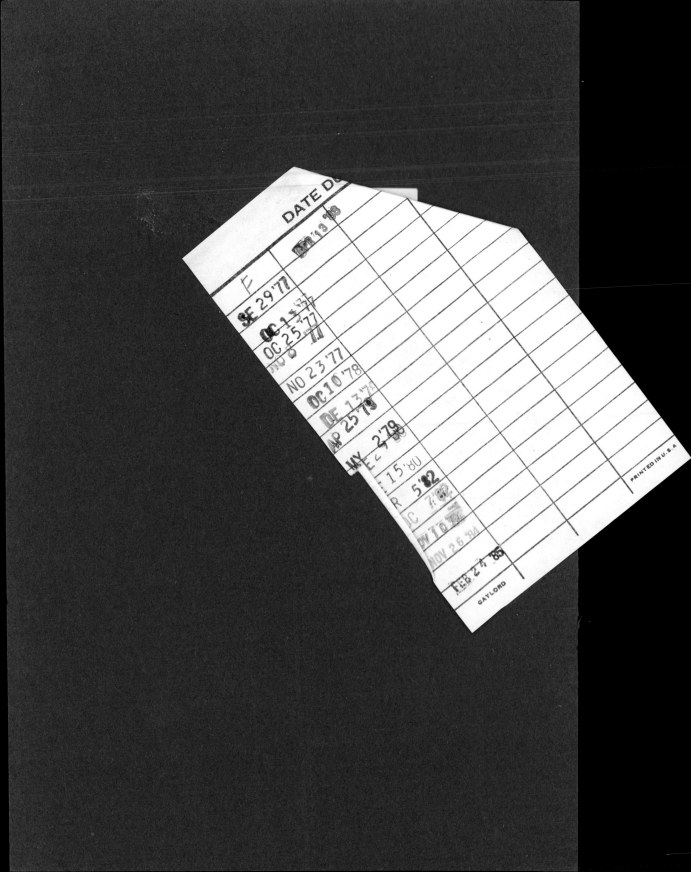